Global Economic Governance and the Development Practices of the Multilateral Development Banks

As pillars of the post-1945 international economic system, the Regional and Sub-Regional Development Banks (RDBs) have long been considered mini-World Banks, reiterating the policy approach of the largest official multilateral development lender in the world. The main objective of the collection is to identify what role the RDBs play in global economic governance and why.

This edited collection draws together cutting-edge original research on these understudied institutions. In the burgeoning sub-field of global economic governance as well as the broader study of international organisations (IOs), too often the focus remains on the World Bank and the International Monetary Fund (IMF). Second-order IOs, such as the RDBs, receive much less attention despite their longevity and regional importance. This volume corrects this oversight by bringing together research on the RDBs that interrogates the role and impact of these organisations in global economic governance.

The book investigates: the African Development Bank (AfDB); the Asian Development Bank (ADB); the Inter-American Development Bank (IDB); the European Bank for Reconstruction and Development (EBRD); and select sub-regional development banks in comparison to the World Bank. It will be of great interest to students and scholars of IPE, IR and Development Studies.

Susan Park is an Associate Professor in International Relations at the University of Sydney. Susan has been a Visiting Scholar at George Washington University, the London School of Economics, the American University and the Centennial Center for Political Science and Public Affairs in Washington, DC.

Jonathan R. Strand is an Associate Professor of Political Science at the University of Nevada, Las Vegas. Previously he taught at Niagara University, New York and held a research position at the United Nations University's Institute of Advanced Studies, Japan.

RIPE Series in Global Political Economy
Series Editors: Jacqueline Best (University of Ottawa, Canada), Ian Bruff (Manchester University, UK), Paul Langley (Durham University, UK) and Anna Leander (Copenhagen Business School, Denmark)

Formerly edited by Leonard Seabrooke (Copenhagen Business School, Denmark), Randall Germain (Carleton University, Canada), Rorden Wilkinson (University of Manchester, UK), Otto Holman (University of Amsterdam), Marianne Marchand (Universidad de las Américas-Puebla), Henk Overbeek (Free University, Amsterdam) and Marianne Franklin (Goldsmiths, University of London, UK)

The RIPE series editorial board are:

Mathias Albert (Bielefeld University, Germany), Mark Beeson (University of Birmingham, UK), A. Claire Cutler (University of Victoria, Canada), Marianne Franklin (Goldsmiths, University of London, UK), Randall Germain (Carleton University, Canada) Stephen Gill (York University, Canada), Jeffrey Hart (Indiana University, USA), Eric Helleiner (Trent University, Canada), Otto Holman (University of Amsterdam, the Netherlands), Marianne H. Marchand (Universidad de las Américas-Puebla, Mexico), Craig N. Murphy (Wellesley College, USA), Robert O'Brien (McMaster University, Canada), Henk Overbeek (Vrije Universiteit, the Netherlands), Anthony Payne (University of Sheffield, UK), V. Spike Peterson (University of Arizona, USA) and Rorden Wilkinson (University of Manchester, UK).

This series, published in association with the Review of International Political Economy, provides a forum for current and interdisciplinary debates in international political economy. The series aims to advance understanding of the key issues in the global political economy, and to present innovative analyses of emerging topics. The titles in the series focus on three broad themes:

- the structures, processes and actors of contemporary global transformations
- the changing forms taken by governance, at scales from the local and everyday to the global and systemic
- the inseparability of economic from political, social and cultural questions, including resistance, dissent and social movements.

The RIPE Series in Global Political Economy aims to address the needs of students and teachers. Titles include:

Transnational Classes and International Relations
Kees van der Pijl

Globalization and Governance
Edited by Aseem Prakash and Jeffrey A. Hart

Nation-States and Money
The past, present and future of national currencies
Edited by Emily Gilbert and Eric Helleiner

Gender and Global Restructuring:
Sightings, sites and resistances
Edited by Marianne H. Marchand and Anne Sisson Runyan

The Global Political Economy of Intellectual Property Rights
The new enclosures?
Christopher May

Global Political Economy
Contemporary theories
Edited by Ronen Palan

Ideologies of Globalization
Contending visions of a new world order
Mark Rupert

The Clash within Civilisations
Coming to terms with cultural conflicts
Dieter Senghaas

Capitalist Restructuring, Globalisation and the Third Way
Lessons from the Swedish Model
J. Magnus Ryner

Transnational Capitalism and the Struggle over European Integration
Bastiaan van Apeldoorn

World Financial Orders
An historical international political economy
Paul Langley

Global Unions?
Theory and strategies of organized labour in the global political economy
Edited by Jeffrey Harrod and Robert O'Brien

Political Economy of a Plural World
Critical reflections on power, morals and civilizations
Robert Cox with Michael Schechter

The Changing Politics of Finance in Korea and Thailand
From deregulation to debacle
Xiaoke Zhang

Anti-Immigrantism in Western Democracies
Statecraft, desire and the politics of exclusion
Roxanne Lynn Doty

The Political Economy of European Employment
European integration and the transnationalization of the (un)employment question
Edited by Henk Overbeek

A Critical Rewriting of Global Political Economy
Integrating reproductive, productive and virtual economies
V. Spike Peterson

International Trade and Developing Countries
Bargaining coalitions in the GATT & WTO
Amrita Narlikar

Rethinking Global Political Economy
Emerging issues, unfolding odysseys
Edited by Mary Ann Tétreault, Robert A. Denemark, Kenneth P. Thomas and Kurt Burch

Global Institutions and Development
Framing the world?
Edited by Morten Bøås and Desmond McNeill

Contesting Globalization
Space and place in the world economy
André C. Drainville

The Southern Cone Model
The political economy of regional capitalist development in Latin America
Nicola Phillips

The Idea of Global Civil Society
Politics and ethics of a globalizing era
Edited by Randall D. Germain and Michael Kenny

Global Institutions, Marginalization, and Development
Craig N. Murphy

Governing Financial Globalization
International political economy and multi-level governance
Edited by Andrew Baker, David Hudson and Richard Woodward

Critical theories, international relations and 'the anti-globalisation movement'
The Politics of Global Resistance
Edited by Catherine Eschle and Bice Maiguashca

Resisting Intellectual Property
Debora J. Halbert

Globalization, Governmentality, and Global Politics
Regulation for the rest of us?
Ronnie D. Lipschutz, with James K. Rowe

Neoliberal Hegemony
A global critique
Edited by Dieter Plehwe, Bernhard Walpen and Gisela Neunhöffer

Images of Gramsci
Connections and contentions in political theory and international relations
Edited by Andreas Bieler and Adam David Morton

Global Standards of Market Civilization
Edited by Brett Bowden and Leonard Seabrooke

Beyond Globalization
Capitalism, territoriality and the
international relations of modernity
Hannes Lacher

Global Public Policy
Business and the countervailing
powers of civil society
Edited by Karsten Ronit

**The Transnational Politics of
Corporate Governance Regulation**
*Edited by Henk Overbeek, Bastiaan
van Apeldoorn and Andreas Nölke*

**Critical Perspectives on
Global Governance**
Rights and regulation in
governing regimes
Jean Grugel and Nicola Piper

**National Currencies
and Globalization**
Endangered specie?
Paul Bowles

**Conflicts in Environmental
Regulation and the
Internationalization of the State**
Contested terrains
*Ulrich Brand, Christoph Görg,
Joachim Hirsch and
Markus Wissen*

Beyond States and Markets
The challenges of
social reproduction
*Edited by Isabella Bakker and
Rachel Silvey*

**Governing International
Labour Migration**
Current issues,
challenges and dilemmas
*Edited by Christina Gabriel and
Hélène Pellerin*

The Industrial Vagina
The political economy of the global
sex trade
Sheila Jeffreys

**The Child in International
Political Economy**
A place at the table
Alison M.S. Watson

Capital as Power
A study of order and creorder
*Jonathan Nitzan and
Shimshon Bichler*

**Global Citizenship and the Legacy
of Empire**
Marketing development
April Biccum

**The Global Political Economy of
Intellectual Property Rights,
Second Edition**
The new enclosures
Christopher May

**Corporate Power and Ownership in
Contemporary Capitalism**
The politics of resistance
and domination
Susanne Soederberg

Savage Economics
Wealth, poverty and the temporal
walls of capitalism
*David L. Blaney and
Naeem Inayatullah*

Cultural Political Economy
Edited by Jacqueline Best and Matthew Paterson

Development, Sexual Rights and Global Governance
Resisting global power
Amy Lind

Cosmopolitanism and Global Financial Reform
A pragmatic approach to the Tobin Tax
James Brassett

Gender and Global Restructuring
Second Edition
Sightings, sites and resistances
Edited by Marianne H. Marchand and Anne Sisson Runyan

Variegated Neoliberalism
EU varieties of capitalism and international political economy
Huw Macartney

The Politics of European Competition Regulation
A critical political economy perspective
Hubert Buch-Hansen and Angela Wigger

The Political Economy of Global Remittances
Gender and governmentality
Rahel Kunz

A Critical History of the Economy
On the birth of the national and international economies
Ryan Walter

The International Political Economy of Transition
Neoliberal hegemony and Eastern Central Europe's transformation
Stuart Shields

The Global Political Economy of Trade Protectionism and Liberalization
Trade reform and economic adjustment in textiles and clothing
Tony Heron

Transnational Financial Associations and the Governance of Global Finance
Assembling wealth and power
Heather McKeen-Edwards and Tony Porter

The Capitalist Mode of Power
Critical engagements with the power theory of value
Edited by Tim Di Muzio

The Making of Modern Finance
Liberal governance and the gold standard
Samuel Knafo

The State of Copyright
The complex relationships of cultural creation in a globalized world
Debora J. Halbert

Transnational Financial Regulation after the Crisis
Edited by Tony Porter

The Political Economy of Global Capitalism and Crisis
Bill Dunn

Global Capitalism
Selected essays
Hugo Radice

Debtfare States and the Poverty Industry
Money, discipline and the surplus population
Susanne Soederberg

Currency Challenge
The Euro, the Dollar and the global financial
Miguel Otero-Iglesias

Fringe Finance
Crossing and contesting the borders of global capital
Rob Aitken

Asymmetric Crisis in Europe and Possible Futures
Critical political economy and post-Keynesian perspectives
Edited by Johannes Jäger and Elisabeth Springler

Hybrid Rule and State Formation
Public–private power in the 21st century
Edited by Shelley L. Hurt and Ronnie D. Lipschutz

Global Economic Governance and the Development Practices of the Multilateral Development Banks
Edited by Susan Park and Jonathan R. Strand

Global Economic Governance and the Development Practices of the Multilateral Development Banks

Edited by
Susan Park and Jonathan R. Strand

LONDON AND NEW YORK

First published 2016
by Routledge
2 Park Square, Milton Park, Abingdon, Oxon OX14 4RN

and by Routledge
711 Third Avenue, New York, NY 10017

Routledge is an imprint of the Taylor & Francis Group, an informa business

© 2016 selection and editorial material, Susan Park and Jonathan R. Strand; individual chapters, the contributors

The right of Susan Park and Jonathan R. Strand to be identified as authors of the editorial material, and of the individual authors as authors of their contributions, has been asserted by them in accordance with sections 77 and 78 of the Copyright, Designs and Patents Act 1988.

All rights reserved. No part of this book may be reprinted or reproduced or utilised in any form or by any electronic, mechanical, or other means, now known or hereafter invented, including photocopying and recording, or in any information storage or retrieval system, without permission in writing from the publishers.

Trademark notice: Product or corporate names may be trademarks or registered trademarks, and are used only for identification and explanation without intent to infringe.

British Library Cataloguing in Publication Data
A catalogue record for this book is available from the British Library

Library of Congress Cataloging in Publication Data
A catalog record for this book has been requested

ISBN: 978-1-138-82712-7 (hbk)
ISBN: 978-1-315-73693-8 (ebk)

Typeset in Times New Roman
by Taylor & Francis Books

Printed and bound in Great Britain by
TJ International Ltd, Padstow, Cornwall

Susan dedicates this book to Matt, Will and Chris.
Jonathan dedicates this book to Helen.

Contents

List of illustrations	xv
List of contributors	xvii
Preface	xix
Acknowledgements	xx
Acronyms	xxi

PART 1
Explaining the policies of the MDBs   1

1 Global economic governance and the development practices of the multilateral development banks   3
SUSAN PARK AND JONATHAN R. STRAND

2 The Asian Development Bank: Joining the fight against corruption?   21
YASUMASA KOMORI

3 The Inter-American Development Bank: Poverty alleviation and the millennium development goals   39
KENNETH J. RETZL

4 Civil society and policy reforms in the Asian Development Bank   60
ANDERS UHLIN

5 The African Development Bank: From follower to broker and partner   80
KAREN A. MINGST

6 Ambivalent engagement: Human rights and the multilateral development banks   99
DANIEL B. BRAATEN

xiv *Contents*

PART 2
The role of the MDBs in the international political economy 119

7 Implications of accommodating rising powers for the regional development banks 121
JONATHAN R. STRAND AND MICHAEL W. TREVATHAN

8 The "hassle factor" of MDB lending and borrower demand in Latin America 143
CHRIS HUMPHREY

9 The European Bank for Reconstruction and Development as organic intellectual of neoliberal common sense in post-communist transition 167
STUART SHIELDS

10 Sub-regional development banks: Development as usual? 187
TINA M. ZAPPILE

11 The RDBs in the twenty-first century 212
JONATHAN R. STRAND AND SUSAN PARK

Index 224

List of illustrations

Figures

7.1	Voting share changes in AfDB, 2004–2013	129
7.2	Voting share changes in the ADB, 2004–2013	131
7.3	Voting share changes in the IADB, 2004–2013	132
8.1	Outstanding public debt by source in Latin America	143
8.2	MDB shareholder voting power, 2012	145

Tables

3.1	IADB projects	47
3.2	Five-year average of total IADB projects by sector	50
3.3	Five-year average of IADB project amounts by sector	52
3.4	Average loans by sector under IADB presidents	55
4.1	Comparison between key civil society demands and final AM	65
4.2	Comparison between key civil society demands in review of ADB information disclosure policy 2003–2005 and ADB PCP 2005	71
4.3	Comparison between key civil society demands in the review of ADB's safeguard policies 2005–2009 and ADB Safeguard Policy Statement 2009	74
6.1	MDB Safeguard Policies 2015	108
7.1	Change in World Bank (IBRD) voting shares, 2004–2014	125
7.2	Change in AfDB voting shares, 2004–2013	130
7.3	Change in ADB voting shares, 2004–2013	131
7.4	Change in IADB voting shares, 2004–2013	132
7.5	American support for BRICS projects, 2004–2011 (percentage)	136
8.1	Loan approval procedures and times	147
8.2	Comparison of two safeguards	155
10.1	Portfolio analysis of SRDBs	192
10.2	Governance structure and membership of SRDBs	196
10.3	Presence of accountability mechanisms in SRDBs	200
10.4	Inclusion of civil society and environmental interests in SRDBs	202

10.5	SRDB commitment to transparency	204
10.6	Evidence of performance or project evaluation	206

Box

3.1	The Millennium Development Goals	43

List of contributors

Daniel B. Braaten is an Assistant Professor of Political Science at Texas Lutheran University and his research focuses on US foreign policy, human rights, and international organisations. He has previously published works in the *Review of International Studies, Journal of Peace Research* and *Journal of Human Rights*.

Chris Humphrey is a guest lecturer and researcher at the Department of Political Science, University of Zurich, focusing on how global economic and political changes are reshaping development cooperation. He completed his PhD at the London School of Economics, and works as a consultant for development institutions including the World Bank, Inter-American Development Bank, African Development Bank, Overseas Development Institute and Global Green Growth Institute.

Yasumasa Komori is an Associate Professor of International Relations at Michigan State University's James Madison College. His publications include 'In Search of Regional Governance in East Asia: Processes and Outcomes' in the *Asian Journal of Political Science*.

Karen A. Mingst is the Lockwood Chair in the Patterson School of Diplomacy and International Commerce and Professor of Political Science at the University of Kentucky. She has published a book *Politics and the African Development Bank*. She is co-author with M. P. Karns of *International Organizations: The Politics and Processes of Global Governance*. She has published numerous other books and articles.

Susan Park is an Associate Professor in International Relations at the University of Sydney. She researches how state and non-state actors shape the Multilateral Development Banks. She has published in *Pacific Review, Global Environmental Politics* and *Third World Quarterly*. Her book *The World Bank Group and Environmentalists* was published in 2010.

Kenneth J. Retzl is a doctoral candidate at the University of Nevada, Las Vegas. His research interests include social development and the study of good governance principles in international organizations.

xviii *List of contributors*

Stuart Shields teaches International Political Economy at the University of Manchester. His book *The International Political Economy of Transition* was shortlisted for the 2013 BISA IPEG book prize. He is co-editor of *Critical International Political Economy: Dialogue, Debate, Dissensus* and recent articles have been published in *Critical Sociology, Third World Quarterly* and the *Journal of International Relations and Development.*

Jonathan R. Strand is an Associate Professor in the Department of Political Science at the University of Nevada, Las Vegas. His research has appeared in *Foreign Policy Analysis, World Development, World Economy* and *International Relations of the Asia Pacific*. His book *The Regional Development Banks: Lending with a Regional Flavor* will be published by Routledge.

Michael W. Trevathan is a PhD student in the Department of Political Science at the University of Nevada, Las Vegas and is an instructor at the University of West Florida. His research interests include international political economy, global economic governance, and the economic and security implications of great power transitions.

Anders Uhlin is a Professor of Political Science at Lund University. Recent publications include *Legitimacy Beyond the State: Re-examining the Democratic Credentials of Transnational Actors* (co-edited with Eva Erman) and articles in journals such as *Journal of Civil Society, Democratization, Global Governance* and *Third World Quarterly.*

Tina M. Zappile is an Assistant Professor of Political Science at Stockton University in Galloway, New Jersey. Her research focuses on 'space' for developing countries and civil society in the intersection of trade, development, and international organizations. She has written on the World Bank, the African Growth and Opportunity Act (AGOA) and voting patterns in multilateral development banks.

Preface

The origin of this book was Susan's research journey from exclusively studying the World Bank to having her eyes opened to the world of the Regional Development Banks (RDBs). As a student, Susan was, like so many others, familiar with the heated debates regarding the role of the World Bank in developing countries. As a scholar, she continued to examine the role of the Bank as a leading development player, engaging with others over the ability of this international organisation to truly change. Once she finished scrutinising the World Bank's capacity for change, she realised that very few people were looking at the RDBs. One of those scholars was Jonathan R. Strand. At our first meeting we discussed the possibility of bringing together as many people working on the RDBs as possible in order to create a critical mass of knowledge on these severely understudied institutions. The result was an ISA-funded 'Catalytic Workshop', held in Toronto in 2014, where we gathered most of the contributors to this volume and people such as Morten Bøås. Based on the excellent research presented, we took our idea for a volume to Routledge, which enthusiastically supported the project. We feel that this collection portrays how and why these institutions behave as they do. We hope this volume provides a roadmap for other scholars to continue to unpack the regional banks in the international political economy.

Susan and Jonathan,
Sydney and Las Vegas April 2015

Acknowledgements

The editors would like to thank all the people involved in the creation of this edited collection. People interviewed by the contributors, discussants at our workshop – especially Morten Bøås and his encouragement – the International Studies Association (ISA) workshop team, editors at Routledge and our four anonymous reviewers, this volume would not have been possible without you. We are especially thankful for the financial support of ISA and the College of Liberal Arts at UNLV and the outstanding research assistance provided by Roman Lewis.

Acronyms

ADB	Asian Development Bank
ADF	Asian Development Fund
AFCT	Africa China Growing Together
AfDB	African Development Bank
AfDF	African Development Fund
AGF	African Guarantee Fund for Small and Medium-sized Enterprises
AIIB	Asian Infrastructure Investment Bank
ANGOC	Asian NGO Coalition
AM	Accountability Mechanism
ASEAN	Association of Southeast Asian Nations
BASIC	Brazil, India, China, South Africa
BIC	The Bank Information Center
BOAD	West African Development Bank
BRIC	Brazil, Russia, India and China
BRICS	Brazil, Russia, India, China and South Africa
BRICSAM	BRICS plus Mexico and members of ASEAN
BSTDB	Black Sea Trade and Development Bank
CABEI	Central American Bank for Economic Integration
CAF	Andean Development Corporation
CASDB or BDEAC	Central African States Development Bank
CDB	Caribbean Development Bank
CESI	Committee on Environmental and Social Impact
CIVETS	Colombia, Indonesia, Vietnam, Egypt, Turkey and South Africa
COMESA	Eastern and Southern African Trade and Development Bank
CPI	Transparency International's Corruption Perceptions Index
CPS	Country Partnership Strategies
CRA	Contingent Reserve Arrangement of the NDB
CRP	Compliance Review Panel
CSO	Civil Society Organization

DAC	OECD Development Assistance Committee
DAI	Disclosure and Access to Information
DBSA	Development Bank of Southern Africa
DIME	Development Impact Evaluation Initiative
DMC	Developing Member Countries
EADB	East African Development Bank
EBRD	European Bank for Reconstruction and Development
ECE	Eastern and Central Europe
ECLAC	Economic Commission for Latin America and the Caribbean
EDB	Eurasian Development Bank
ELF	Emergency Liquidity Facility
FONPLATA	Financial Fund for the Development of the River Plate Basin
FPP	Forest People's Program
GACAP II	Second Governance and Anticorruption Action Plan
GCI	General Capital Increases
IADB	Inter-American Development Bank
IATI	International Aid Transparency Initiative
IBRD	International Bank for Reconstruction and Development
ICSF	Institutional Capacity Strengthening Thematic Fund
IDA	International Development Association
IDG	International Development Goals
IF	Inspection Function
IFC	International Financial Corporation
IFI	International Financial Institution
IFAD	International Fund for Agricultural Development
IGO	Intergovernmental Organisation
IMF	International Monetary Fund
IO	International Organisation
IRM	Independent Review Mechanism
IsDB	Islamic Development Bank
MDB	Multilateral Development Bank
MDG	Millennium Development Goal
MENA	Middle East/North Africa
MFI	Multilateral Financial Institution
MIGA	Multilateral Investment Guarantee Agency
MINT	Mexico, Indonesia, Nigeria, and Turkey
NDB	New Development Bank
NEPAD	New Partnership for Africa's Development
NGO	Non-Governmental Organisation
NIB	Nordic Investment Bank
NIEO	New International Economic Order
OAI	ADB Office of Anticorruption and Integrity

OAS	Organization of American States
ODA	Official Development Assistance
OECD	Organisation for Economic Co-operation and Development
OPEC Fund	OPEC Fund for International Development
PCP	Public Communication Policy
PDAC	Public Disclosure Advisory Committee
PIDB	Pacific Islands Development Bank
PRC	People's Republic of China
PRC RCPRF	PRC Regional Cooperation and Poverty Reduction Fund
PRSP	Poverty Reduction Strategy Paper
RDB	Regional Development Bank
SAP	Structural Adjustment Program
SDB	Sovereign Development Bank
SPF	Special Project Facilitator
SRDB	Sub-Regional Development Bank
UEE	Ex-Post Evaluation Unit
UN	United Nations
UNDP	United Nations Development Programme
WB	World Bank
WBIP	World Bank Independent Inspection Panel
WID	Women in Development

Part 1
Explaining the policies of the MDBs

1 Global economic governance and the development practices of the multilateral development banks

Susan Park and Jonathan R. Strand

Where do the regional development banks (RDBs) fit within the contentious debate over the power and impact of international financial institutions (IFIs), often discussed under the rubric of the Washington Consensus? Curiously, it is not a question frequently asked. Yet it should be. The International Monetary Fund (IMF) and the World Bank are frequently invoked as either friends or foes of developing countries. These institutions exist to provide financing for economic growth and development – providing loans, technical assistance, grants and guarantees to developing countries with limited access to private capital markets and experiencing significant balance of payments problems. Yet since the 1980s these 'sister' institutions have been attacked for their prescriptive (Washington Consensus) policies, harsh conditionalities and questionable success (Mosely, Harrigan and Toye 1991; Peet 2003; George and Sabelli 1994).[1] Scholars debate whether much has changed since lending modifications were introduced in the 1990s, contributing to the discussion over whether this constitutes a post-Washington Consensus (Kuczynski and Williamson 2003; Onis and Senses 2005). Some argue that the Bretton Woods institutions today exemplify 'provisional governance' such that the Fund and the Bank are now aware of the possibility of failure even as they prescribe their standard policy recommendations (Best 2014).

Since the global financial crisis of 2008, scholarly and policy attention has remained overwhelmingly on how to fix the global financial architecture, comprised of the IMF, the World Bank, the G20, and the reconstituted Financial Stability Board (see, for example, RIPE 2012, Special Edition). Given that most of the oxygen for analyzing global economic governance continues to be spent on these universal IOs, the regional development banks remain overlooked. It is surprising just how little has been written on the African Development Bank (AfDB), the Asian Development Bank (ADB), the Inter-American Development Bank (IADB), and the European Bank for Reconstruction and Development (EBRD). There even exists an entire overlooked sub-category of 'sub-regional' multilateral development banks such as the Caribbean Development Bank (CDB). These banks are neglected despite sharing the same policy space as the IMF and World Bank, both of which continue to be the subject of hotly contested debates over their power and impact. There is little scholarly analysis of RDBs despite their longevity and regional importance and irrespective of the fact that all the RDBs were modeled on the World Bank; share many of the same member states on their boards; have similar or the same policies; and often engage in co-financing with the World Bank.

Two possible assumptions explaining their relative neglect spring to mind: first, that because they resemble the World Bank there is little to say – what stands for the World Bank must be applicable to the 'other' MDBs. Second, that because these are regional banks concerned with regional development issues and with predominantly regional members, they need not concern scholars of global economic governance. This volume aims to dispel both of these notions by bringing together work on RDBs that interrogates the role and impact of these banks in the international political economy. The book grapples with an important empirical puzzle regarding their role in global economic governance to shed light on the matter of whether RDBs should be subject to the same criticism as the World Bank. It seeks to unpack why attacks on the 'other' MDBs are muted and few, exploring for example whether RDBs are subject to less criticism because their regional member states have greater ownership and therefore protect the reputation of 'their' bank from criticism or whether it is because they operate in a fundamentally different manner.

RDBs in global economic governance: different to the World Bank?

In examining the RDBs in global economic governance we challenge the idea that what stands for the World Bank stands for RDBs. From the very beginning of RDBs the literature aimed to establish what made these institutions unique (White 1970). Despite being modeled on the World Bank, all RDBs have features that aim to distinguish them. While the World Bank is a universal organization open to all sovereign states and operating globally,[2] RDBs are focused on providing financing for economic growth in their regions, although for some of the banks, such as the ADB and EBRD, their conception of their region has broadened considerably. In the late 1950s and 1960s when most of these banks were created (bar the EBRD which emerged at the end of the Cold War), the developing regions of Africa, Asia, and Latin America and the Caribbean were starved of liquidity. Regional member states aimed to create indigenous institutions to raise funds to finance economic growth while recognising the need for extra-regional capital. This informed the decision by most of the architects to base their bank design on the World Bank and to actively seek extra-regional donor funding (African states chose not to seek funding). The banks aimed to generate 'additional' funding for their region to offset pre-existing levels of official development assistance (ODA) and mitigate the political vagaries of bilateral aid disbursements. Other differences are subtle: the AfDB, ADB, and IADB all included provisions in their articles of agreement to support intra-regional projects, although this would prove difficult given the structure of the economies of Africa and Latin America, heightened nationalism, and mistrust among states in Asia (Bull and Bøås 2003; Mingst 1990).

Irrespective of the conservative 'Western' financial structure of these RDBs (Dutt 2001: 249), the banks were imbued with the spirit of regional cooperation. Given the revolutionary fervor of states moving towards or celebrating independence, the possibilities associated with communist, 'Dependencia' and state-led development approaches and the prospects for pan-African and American ideas, these banks epitomised what states in their own regions could achieve. Curiously, the dominance of regional 'ownership' of the banks would not necessarily translate into the formulation of substantially different development ideas but rather influence membership, staffing, and management issues (Mingst 1990). Lending practices were therefore not dissimilar, although the banks emphasized lending to different sectors: the IADB focused significantly on social-sector lending in its first few decades and was well funded, with significant United States (US) support (Dell 1972). The ADB focused on large-scale infrastructure lending and was considered a highly technical institution that was financially conservative (Watanabe 1977). The AfDB had difficulty finding 'bankable' projects and raising funding from the beginning. This stemmed from its refusal to have extra-regional members, making it near impossible for regional members desperate for capital to make use of the institution (Fordwor 1981). Less is known about the lending practices of the sub-regional development banks.

It was not until the 1980s that RDBs shifted towards sectoral lending that was similar to the World Bank's (Culpeper 1997).[3] Yet even when RDBs' portfolios began to look more like those of the World Bank, differences remained. They lagged behind the World Bank considerably in introducing program lending (such as structural adjustment loans) from the 1980s, and lent less than the World Bank for program lending and with less conditionality and oversight. That RDBs have not received the same vitriolic criticism may be because their regional member states have greater ownership and have shielded 'their' bank from criticism or because RDBs do not behave the same way as the World Bank. In sum, the volume breaks new ground by examining the cause of RDB behavior, both independently and with reference to the World Bank. In this volume we argue that RDBs act in accordance with their resource dependence and their legitimacy concerns (detailed below), which lead them to address the same policy issues as the World Bank but at different speeds and with different degrees of interpretation and adoption, from both each other and the World Bank. This in turn creates new sites for the creation and adoption of global development practices, which opens up new fields of investigation for students of global economic governance.

Theorising difference: the resource dependence and legitimacy of RDBs

The volume identifies the source of policy and governance changes initiated by each of the banks in exploring their role and influence in the international political economy. This is important for identifying what drives these international organizations (IOs).[4] Each of the contributions to the book probes the basis for change in the banks with regard to specific policies, strategies, and operations. Theoretical debates over the role of the IMF and the World Bank are based on whether or to what extent these institutions are independent of their member states (Hawkins et al. 2006; Woods 2006; Weaver 2008; Park and Vetterlein 2010). This volume contributes to the scholarly literature by interrogating the ability of RDBs to present their own expert authoritative knowledge of development financing as opposed to acting merely as conduits of their member states' interests and preferences or being shaped by civil society or pressured to emulate the World Bank. The answers highlight the complexity of how power, resources, and ideas interact, requiring multifaceted explanations.

Within the theoretical literature on IOs in general and the Fund and the World Bank specifically, scholars question the extent to which IOs determine their own actions. The rationalist Principal-Agent (P-A) model has been prominent in articulating a framework for IO autonomy within its relationship to member states (Hawkins et al. 2006). This is supported by analyzes of formal power within the banks (Strand 2003, 1999). This approach establishes the puzzle of how, why and when these IOs fail to meet (powerful) members' interests. In this way, the tensions and nuanced relationships between RDBs as relatively autonomous authoritative 'agents' and their 'principal' member states are outlined (Hawkins et al. 2006). This contrasts with the constructivist scholarship on IOs that examines how the relative autonomy of IOs allows these bureaucracies to develop an independent internal culture that shapes their decision-making processes even to the point of becoming dysfunctional and hypocritical (Barnett and Finnemore 2004; Weaver 2008).

Recognising the relative autonomy of the RDBs as bureaucracies run independently by bank management but subject to the demands of their member state executive boards, this book takes up the theoretical concerns regarding why and how RDBs operate the way they do. The volume therefore feeds into debates on whether RDBs like the World Bank can be accused of being foreign policy instruments of powerful states such as the United States (Babb 2009) or whether they are independent institutions that shape member states' interests and preferences, making states 'legible' (Barnett and Finnemore 2004; Broome and Seabrooke 2012). Constructivist accounts recognize the non-state-centric nature of idea and policy formulation within IOs (Park and Vetterlein 2010). In analyzing the IMF and World Bank, constructivists argue that IO behavior is explained by organizational culture, routines and identity, including the role of ideas and the actions of bureaucrats (Chwieroth 2008; Park 2010; Weaver 2008). Constructivists have mapped the policy formulation process in various IMF and World Bank issue areas, demonstrating that ideas with global reach do not necessarily originate within the institutions themselves, or if they do, may have originally been constituted very differently from the final policy product (Park and Vetterlein 2010). As scholars of RDBs we seek evidence that culture influences whether change is more or less difficult, while identifying the key drivers of the banks' development practices.

In demonstrating the cause of each bank's behavior, the contributors thus weigh the role of the internal versus external environment in shaping the organization's actions. Internal influences involve the decision-making of the banks' management teams, which are to differing degrees independent of the member states on their executive boards. This contrasts with the external influences, which may include donor and borrower member states, civil society actors and the World Bank. In investigating the decision-making process, the contributors document which factors best explain each case. This volume therefore adds to the theoretical debate on the basis for IFI behavior. Given that RDBs are structured similarly to the World Bank, it is essential to examine whether what holds for the World Bank holds for the 'other' MDBs.

After identifying the cause of the change, the chapters assess whether the banks are unique in their policy approach, follow the World Bank blindly, or find active or passive ways to resist emulating the World Bank. Beyond examining the extent of World Bank emulation, the volume seeks to investigate the extent to which RDBs are extensions of the World Bank approach to global development, feeding into debates concerning the structure of global economic governance. This is especially important given the larger membership shares and votes that rising powers such as China, Brazil, India, and South Africa have in their regional banks. Alternative theoretical approaches such as world polity and neo-Gramscianism argue that IOs pursue unequal power relations in the international political economy. For example, the latter argue that a hegemonic bloc of global elites in powerful industrialized states and IOs such as the World Bank construct dominant ideas, leaving developing countries with no alternative way to shape their own economic development path (Bøås and McNeill 2004; Goldman 2005). Critical insights from neo-Gramscian approaches can help direct our enquiry into the power dynamics between regional and non-regional interests in the RDBs, and this approach is applied in the case of the European Bank for Reconstruction and Development – the most explicitly liberal of the RDBs (see Shields, this volume). However, the volume also focuses on the extent to which borrower and regional member states' changing geo-economic weight may be altering the international political economy, as discussed in the section below.

The volume produces textured research that explores multiple layers and interactions rather than relying on a single explanation of bank behavior (e.g. formal power relations). This book is firmly committed to theoretical pluralism and so sets the overarching conceptual framework as open to both formal (rule-based material structures) and informal power (both ideational and power-based) mechanisms by member states in examining RDB policy shifts (Kilby 2011). Examining the actions of RDBs includes not only looking at whether change is triggered from out or inside the banks but also identifying the particular competing material and ideational forces that resist or promote change.

To this end we pick up on two central concepts that are seen as driving IFI behavior, *resource dependence* (Babb 2009), and *legitimacy* (Seabrooke 2007). To explain: the RDBs are underpinned by member states' financial and political support. In terms of financing, member states subscribe to each institution through a portion of 'paid-in' capital and 'callable' capital that the banks can draw on if so needed (this has never happened). This provides the banks with the assurance of member states' commitment as well as the capital required for the banks' initial lending and trading activities. All the banks raise further capital through floating bonds and borrowing on international capital markets as well from interest and loan repayments. That sovereign member states underpin the banks' financial capacity assures capital markets of the safety of RDB lending. Financial security is thus both material and ideational, as markets rely on signals from sovereign states regarding the safety of buying bank bonds.[5]

The banks are 'resource'-dependent on the member states in two more ways: first, for periodic increases to their capital through general capital increases (GCIs). These are needed to maintain their capital-to-lending ratios, particularly when the banks want to, or are tasked by their member states to, increase loans to borrowers (particularly after a financial crisis, for example). Thus, despite their relative autonomy in generating income, especially compared with IOs like the specialized agencies and programs of the United Nations, RDBs are still dependent on periodic negotiations among their member states for injections of capital. GCIs vary in frequency among the banks (see Babb 2009: 42). CGIs allow member states to place their policy preferences on the table and identify the direction they want the banks to take as the basis for negotiations over funding. Often, these policy preferences are driven by powerful domestic interests and have led to major changes in IO operations. For some, resource dependence explains why the MDBs have taken on a range of new initiatives in areas such as poverty alleviation, debt relief, gender initiatives, and environment protection (Babb 2009).

Second, all the RDBs except the EBRD have soft loan windows for low-income borrowers or poorest-of-the-poor developing states (although the ADB's soft loan window is due to close in 2017). These soft loan-financing facilities provide low (or zero) interest rate loans and grants for extended periods. As separate funding pots these are voluntarily replenished by member states through frequent negotiation rounds. Like the World Bank's International Development Association (IDA), the RDB soft loan-facilities replenishment rounds occur every three to four years. The IADB has its Fund for Special Operations (FSO), created in 1959, the ADB has its Asian Development Facility (ADF), established in 1973, and the AfDB has its

African Development Fund (AfDF), also established in 1973. The resources available to these special funds are not insignificant: the IADB's FSO, for instance, received almost $10 billion in 2009. Wholly dependent on donor member state contributions, these funds contribute substantially to the work of RDBs in their financing development activities. They have also become the basis for policy demands by donors, with negotiations for replenishing the funds now a determinant of the "direction and content of MDB operational, financial and even internal administrative policies." This has been described as the tail wagging the MDB dog (Mistry 1995: 118).

In addition to these larger soft loan windows, there are numerous special funds that are usually funded by a single member or designed to target a particular policy area. For example, in the 1980s Japan funded a new IADB lending facility to provide grants in the form of technical assistance, the Japan Special Fund. In 2013 the IADB announced that China was creating a new special fund. In the ADB Japan has sponsored several special funds. In fact there are over 50 such funds in the ADB created by either single or several members. In the AfDB there are a number of special funds targeting specific topics, such as the recently created ClimDev-Africa Programme Special Fund. Although these special funds are part of RDB operations, we know very little about how independent – or not – the decision-making of these funds is of their (often single-government) funding sources' interests.

The resource dependence argument is a straightforward explanation for MDB behavior: the banks need capital and will adhere to donor member-state demands in order to receive it. Evidence of MDB's adhering to donor demands in exchange for injections of capital are abundant (Babb 2009; Lavelle 2011). Such an approach may be used not only to describe the behavior of the banks in relation to their member states but also to examine how units, departments, and staff within the banks themselves operate: units and departments compete in turf wars for power and budgetary resources within the organization, while staff vie for promotion (Bebbington et al. 2006; Hall 2007). The resource dependence concept is therefore useful for examining whether RBD behavior is driven from inside or outside the banks.

Moreover, although the concept has not been used in relation to the dependence of the banks on their borrowers, it could equally apply. The utility of the concept therefore works in relation to the banks being dependent on their largest and increasingly discriminating 'middle income' borrowers (Birdsall 2006). In other words, while the neo-Gramscian theoretical approach described above focused on how IFIs provided little or no room for developing states to determine their own approach ('there is no alternative', or TINA), resource dependence is a useful concept that can be applied to examining how changes in the geo-economic balance of power enables middle-income borrowers to determine whether they accept the policy conditionalities attached to MDB loans in comparisons with significant private sector or alternative bilateral development assistance. Moreover, as banks dependent on credit-worthy borrowers, the MDBs may themselves need to reorient their lending practices to be more amenable to borrower interests, as has been witnessed in relation to the World Bank (Birdsall 2006). The concept therefore allows us scope to examine changes in the banks as a result of shifts in the international political economy. While the resource dependence concept fits within the broader rationalist P-A model, it does not have the same conceptual difficulties as the latter when attempting to apply the model down the delegation chain, from donor members to the organization to borrower member states. The P-A model runs into difficulties when it attempts to force the banks to fit the definition of 'Principal' in relation to sovereign borrowers who are cast as 'Agents', when characteristically they do not fit (see the debate between Nielson and Tierney 2005 and Gutner 2005).

The second main concept we take up in the volume is that of legitimacy (Hurd 2007). For the MDBs, "[E]nvironmental pressures and constraints are material in nature (including factors shaping the financial autonomy, competitiveness and viability of the organization), as well as social (factors shaping the legitimacy and authority of the organization)" (Weaver 2008: 26). Member states convey legitimacy on the MDBs through their provision of political support and economic investment. The MDBs and the IMF approach economic growth and development in particular ways. These are based not only on economic theory and ideology but also on what is considered legitimate or accepted by the international community. While there have been shifts over time as to which economic theory should best be applied to facilitate international economic growth and development (from state-led development to harnessing the private sector to supporting institutions), what now constitutes legitimate issues for financing international economic development is far broader than was previously the case and many new issues are now on the MDBs' agenda, including education for young girls, climate change, and HIV/AIDS. Many of these issues emerged in response to the narrow approach to economic development taken by the IMF and the World Bank in the 1980s (Vetterlein 2007).

Legitimacy refers to "the terms by which people recognize, defend and accept political authority" (Bukovansky 2002: 2). The RDBs, like the World Bank, can be considered authorities on international economic development lending, having the technical expertise garnered from decades of lending to their regions (Barnett and Finnemore 2004; Best 2007). Moreover, legitimacy is "where power is acquired and exercised according to justifiable rules, and with the evidence of consent, we call it rightful or legitimate" (Beetham 1991: 3). RDB legitimacy is therefore determined by member states accepting the right of the banks to determine economic development policy approaches and establish conditions on loans to borrower member states. Evidence of consent is with the signing of loan agreements by borrowers. In the case of RDBs this is compounded by the fact that many large borrowers are also significant shareholders, agreeing to establish policies they then contractually accept.

Examinations of the IMF have demonstrated how the Fund lost legitimacy with borrowers and donors during the Asian financial crisis of 1997/8 when its technical authority and rules of lending were exposed as insufficient to grapple with near-instantaneous capital flight, currency devaluation, and political instability in South Korea, Thailand, Indonesia, and Malaysia (Best 2007; Seabrooke 2007). Often the 'output' legitimacy of an institution rests on its ability to provide goods it was mandated to give; without this the organization loses legitimacy (Scharpf 1999). In short, "if an institution exhibits a pattern of egregious disparity between its actual performance, on the one hand, and its self-proclaimed procedures or major goals, on the other, its legitimacy is seriously called into question" (Buchanan and Keohane 2006: 422; Rapkin and Braaten 2009: 125). For the World Bank, questions over the legitimacy of its technical solutions to developing country economic problems were questioned from the 1980s by borrowers, civil society, scholars, economists, policy makers, and other IOs (Vetterlein 2007). As will be shown throughout the volume, many of the practices taken up by RDBs (and the sub-regional development banks or SRDBs) are based on producing policies and practices considered necessary or legitimate by the international development community, including the World Bank. This includes formalising relations with civil society, establishing policies and procedures in relation to gender, human rights and poverty alleviation and the Millennium Development Goals (MDGs).

For the IFIs as a whole, it has not just been a question of whether the operations of the IMF and the MDBs are legitimate but also whether the structure of the institutions themselves is acceptable (Woods 2006). This is also called 'input' legitimacy, or what constitutes accepted participation in decision-making for governing (Scharpf 1999). Much of this discussion is located in the representation of member states in these institutions, with weighted voting according to states' economic power, although changes to the structure of the IFIs have not kept pace with the dramatic shifts in states' standing within the international political economy since the end of the Second World War. In the IMF and World Bank efforts have been limited to redressing the balance and upholding the representative legitimacy or participation of relevant stakeholders. The debate has focused on increasing the representation of emerging middle-income member states (such as Brazil, Russia, India, China, and South Africa, or BRICS) while not diluting the representative power of weak states – or powerful ones! This raises the question of how emerging powers will engage with global economic governance. As discussed in depth in the chapter by Jonathan Strand and Michael Trevathan, rising powers have sought to both engage with RDBs (in subtle ways) and create new institutions such as the New Development Bank (NDB) and the Asian Infrastructure Investment Bank (AIIB), which are discussed further below. The latter may complement or compete with existing MDBs when they begin lending. It is also unclear whether the new institutions will incorporate external input from civil society, as the current MDBs do since civil society actors demanded greater access to information and decision-makers. Whether their technical operational legitimacy (output) or representative legitimacy (input) is pertinent is discussed in relation to RDBs' decisions to alter operations or lending programs. First, however, we must examine in more detail the representation of borrower member states in RBDs and how this affects the banks' standing in global economic governance.

Locating RDBs within shifting global economic governance

The second aim of the volume is to challenge the idea that we can overlook RDBs due to their regional nature. The volume documents the role of RDBs as both agents and structures in the international political economy. It investigates RDBs as agents: analyzing their power to exert pressure on borrower states through the addition of extra-economic concerns such as governance, engagement with civil society, and the MDGs while assessing the political, economic and financial pressures they face from member states and non-state actors. The collection therefore also studies these IOs as structures: examining their project and program-lending practices to identify how they shape international and regional development practice. This is important to document whether the RDBs fit within the broader international development discourse propounded by the World Bank.

In this regard, the book seeks to tease out whether we can differentiate the practices of the RDBs from those of the World Bank or whether RDBs constitute an extension of the post-Washington Consensus. We investigate whether convergence or divergence is occurring in particular policy areas such as environment, accountability, gender equality, and poverty alleviation. Plausible structural explanations for RDB convergence with the World Bank (and with each other) may stem from overlapping member states and bilateral development agency pressure for aid harmonization. Structural causes of divergence may stem from region-specific development issues and political dynamics. Alternatively, agential or organization-specific material and ideational pressures may account for difference among the RDBs, while rotating staff and management among the banks may account for similarities. In sum, this volume investigates the interplay of member states, the bureaucracy and non-state actors. Doing so shows RDBs as both structures and agents in global economic governance as they weigh their resource dependence against their legitimacy concerns.

The book challenges the idea that scholars of global economic governance do not need to examine the regional banks. With dynamic emerging economies in all parts of the world, and with many of them well represented on RDB boards, we question whether the changing geo-economic balance of power changes how we view RDBs. RDBs have power structures that are different from both the World Bank's and each other's, making these institutions primary targets for investigating the degree to which power shifts in the international political economy are played out within these IOs. The changing power dynamics with the rise of the BRICS countries and other emerging economies may provide more room for regionally oriented MDBs to shape regional (and global) development practices. Such influence may also in turn shape the broader international development discourse of the Post-Washington Consensus. The book therefore generates crucial insights into whether RDBs are significantly different from the World Bank and from each other; including whether their practices collectively or individually reinforce or counterbalance the development practices of other international development leaders.

In doing so the book also seeks to probe the strength of the banks' organizational cultures and regional characters. RDBs are informed by a basic assumption in modern economic growth theory that the lack of capital is a major obstruction to economic growth in developing economies. Thus, RDBs are designed to facilitate the flow of capital into developing economies with particular attention on financing projects that may not be viable with only private-sector funding or limited bilateral aid. The RDBs are not identical: they differ in membership, size, mandate, and operational practices. Although RDBs undertake similar activities to the World Bank, their regional mandate determines how the banks identify their role, pursuing a catalytic role in injecting capital into their regions and furthering regional integration (Bull and Bøås 2003; Strand 2014). This mandate also informs their regional character and cognitive authority (Broome and Seabrooke 2012), with scholars and the banks themselves stating that they have unique organizational cultures and doctrines (White 1970; Park 2014).

Moreover, the key players (states, bureaucracies and civil society actors) vary from one RDB to another and this helps shape their development practices. For example, the AfDB faces less civil society criticism than the other banks owing to the collaborative nature of interaction between the voluntary sector and international development lenders on the continent. Other banks have adopted similar policies to the World Bank but have interpreted them very differently (such as the ADB and governance owing to different views in the region on the relationship between state and society). While civil society is robust in Latin America, the focus remains on how well the IADB meets its (larger) borrower member states' needs. Meanwhile the EBRD operates more like a commercial bank in predominantly lending to the private sector in transition economies. In other words, the RDBs are not miniature World Banks, although they may be considered agents of globalization in the same manner as the IMF and the World Bank (Woods 2006; Neumann and Sending 2010). Yet RDBs are less doctrinaire than the World Bank in the application of neoliberal ideas (Mingst 1990; Tussie 1995). The collection assesses the extent to which the banks' organizational cultures and regional character informs whether or not and how they act as a gateway for translating global development practices for their own regions and beyond.

Finally, the greater heterogeneity of international development financing raises the question of whether the RDBs will continue towards policy convergence with the World Bank or whether regionally diverse policies will be accelerated. We aim to locate the RBDs within global economic governance. For this reason, we seek to understand the dynamics between memberstate and non-state actors on these IOs. One fundamental difference between the World Bank and RDBs is that the latter provide more important roles for developing countries in decision-making and policy implementation. Over the past decade the rising importance of emerging markets, such as the BRICS countries, has suggested to many observers that there will be changes to extant global governance mechanisms as India, China, and others seek political influence commensurate with their economic position in the world. There is movement on two fronts to realize this changing reality. As mentioned above, the first is the agreement in July 2014 by Brazil, Russia, India, China, and South Africa to create a New Development Bank or 'BRICS' bank.[6] The second is China's promotion of the new Asian Infrastructure Investment Bank (AIIB), with 20 states signing a memorandum to establish it on 24 October 2014.[7] The trend of creating new multilateral development institutions raises questions since RDBs are designed to have a regional approach to development and give regional member countries greater voice in decision-making. If powerful middle-income countries are choosing to establish new organizations then we need to assess how and why the specific development practices promoted by the regional development banks within their region and extra-regionally are failing to meet their needs. Moreover, there may be greater commonality among RDBs regarding the ways in which they link into their regions (and extra-regionally) that may have broader significance for the literature on regionalism (Acharya and Johnston 2007; Hurrell 1995). To further unpack the role of RDBs in global economic governance, we sketch each bank's characteristics before outlining the contributions to the volume.

Regional development banks: what they are and what they do

Despite being modeled on the World Bank, RDBs nonetheless operate differently: they have different sectoral lending foci; disburse different loan volumes to borrowers in their region compared with the World Bank; and have different ways of interacting with their member states. While the World Bank is considered to be the exemplar IO in international development, RDBs undertake considerable project lending that may exceed the role of the World Bank in specific regions (like the ADB in the Pacific) and specific states (for example, the IADB lends more to small states in Latin America and the Caribbean than the World Bank). It is therefore surprising that RDBs remain understudied when they play such pivotal roles in borrower states. Little academic and policy work has been produced that systematically appraises the place of RDBs in global economic governance. Indeed, scholarly examination of the RDBs in any detail has been infrequent (Culpeper 1997; Head 2005; although Strand, forthcoming, analyzes four of the RDBs). Identifying the main activities and practices of these banks and how they differ from one another and the World Bank is therefore of key concern. Ultimately, the volume demonstrates that RDBs do tackle the same policy concerns as the World Bank but in subtly different ways, acting at different times and speeds and with differing degrees of policy implementation and internalization. This opens wide the research agenda for scholars of global economic governance to examine when and why the MDBs lead and lag one another in producing new international development practices.

While RDBs have a regional flavour they are still subject to the influence of twentieth-century great powers. The chapters identify whether the banks are influenced by broader international development trends such as power shifts in the geo-political economy and the dissemination of ideas of best development practice or whether policy decisions come from inside the banks (staff and management) or from other external actors such as civil society. RDBs may provide evidence that geography matters in ways that theories of IO have not fully contemplated. How the RDBs as regional and sub-regional actors articulate space and place is paramount to our understanding of these institutions (White 1970).

While all the RDBs choose their presidents according to their own procedures, in all cases they must be from the relevant region (an African for the AfDB, a Latino for the IADB, a Japanese national for the ADB, and a European for the EBRD). The remaining governance arrangements for the banks are the same. As with the World Bank, the banks all have a board of governors on which all member states are represented (by member states' treasury or finance ministers). All the banks' boards of governors meet once or twice annually to determine the overall direction of the banks. The governors in turn delegate decision-making power to a sitting board of executive directors. The composition of the board of executive directors is determined by the amount of capital subscribed by the member states, according to a formula of basic and proportional shares. Each RDB allocates a specific amount of shares for its regional members. The president of the bank is chair of the board of executive directors as well as running the bank's daily operations and managing the bank's staff. For many this has led to the assumption that the RDBs are mini-World Banks, despite the differences outlined earlier in the chapter. Whether these differences infuse the banks' development practices in ways previously unstudied is the focus of the volume. In addition, the governance arrangements of the sub-regional development banks are examined in light of the RDB's structural homogeneity.

Outline of the book

The volume thus investigates the activities of RDBs both in general and in relation to particular issues. By casting light on the behavior of RDBs we get a clear and current picture of global economic governance. In section one we look at how RDBs have taken up ideas promoted by donor member states and the World Bank as good development practice. The chapters may be read together or as separate pieces. For the ADB, Yasumasa Komori's chapter demonstrates how the fight against corrupt practices in international development lending has become a major platform for the bank emulating the World Bank in this policy area – with similar implementation problems. This is despite, or perhaps because of, the role corruption was argued to play in the Asian financial crisis of the late 1990s. Nonetheless, the ADB has been careful to clearly differentiate how it defines corruption for the regional context and the timing of the introduction progressed from regional concerns. In chapter three by Kenneth Retzl, the IADB is probed in relation to its adoption of the Millennium Development Goals. Retzl makes the case that the increasing articulation of the MDGs within the IADB accord with the bank's prior focus on social development lending and the emphasis placed on this sector by a former president, Enrique Inglesias. Here again, while the adoption of international norms is evident, these fit within the pre-existing orientation of the organization.

In contrast, the chapter by Anders Uhlin demonstrates how the ADB has opened itself up to civil society by tracing how the latter have influenced the introduction of the bank's safeguard and accountability practices, particularly in their most recent instantiation. This is evidence of a significant change within the ADB to accord more with World Bank practices. In the areas of the environment, gender, engagement with civil society and good governance, Karen Mingst's chapter reveals how the AfDB has adopted similar practices to the World Bank after a time lag of five years or more. She outlines how and why the AfDB has adopted these non-economic policies despite regional member states demanding no such conditionalities when donor states joined the African Development Facility in 1973. Differences do remain, however, as the AfDB has fewer resources and personnel able to ensure implementation. Chapter six by Daniel Braaten returns us to the traditional donor and civil society-led agenda of non-economic concerns to analyze the extent to which RDBs address human rights. He argues that the banks now speak to but do not necessarily act upon human rights, thus revealing similarities among the banks in resisting change.

Section two of the volume addresses how RDBs fit within the international political economy. Despite their longevity, we are only just beginning to identify how these institutions shape how development is understood in their regions and beyond. Chapters in section two investigate how RDBs are part of the structure of the international political economy, reflecting both the changing material relations of powerful states and shifting ideas about development. It therefore examines how the changing material capabilities of the member states may be affecting decision-making processes within the banks, which is analyzed in the chapter by Jonathan Strand and Michael Trevathan. They investigate whether the rise of material power of emerging economies is affecting their position within the RDBs, especially in terms of the banks' governance structures. They demonstrate how little the structures of RDBs are changing despite the rapidly increasing might of the BRICS countries. Chris Humphrey's chapter then examines the dynamics between the IADB, the

World Bank, and the Development Bank of Latin America (formerly known as the Andean Development Corporation or CAF) and their borrowers. The rise of emerging economies now means that the MDBs are dependent on borrowers with the capacity to repay loans in order to maintain their business model, while these same borrowers now have the ability to take their business elsewhere. This has led the MDBs to attempt to modify their lending practices to be more favourable to borrower interests. Humphrey investigates the extent to which the banks have shifted to be more borrower-friendly in relation to the power of borrowers within the banks' governance structure.

Meanwhile, the chapter by Stuart Shields provides a critical approach to the EBRD's legitimacy when he documents how the EBRD, much like the World Bank, maintains a 'common sense' approach to the transition to democracy and free markets in Eastern and Central Europe (ECE). Revealing when and how the banks advance both Washington Consensus and post-Washington Consensus practices reveals both a common defense of MDB practices and the fissures and cracks within any consensus at regional, and even organizational, level. The section also investigates how the sub-regional development banks (SRDBs) take on the governance structures previously established by the larger RDBs, including transparency and accountability mechanisms, as per the chapter by Tina Zappile. For the smaller development banks, different types of legitimacy concerns, technical and operational, are weighed against the desire to maintain exclusive regional representation.

Conclusion

By investigating how RDBs behave, the chapters in this volume attempt to tease out the motivations for specific practices and policy approaches. Through the lens of resource dependence and legitimacy, the collection analyzes how and why they adopt new practices. In doing so, each author identifies whether RDBs are unique in their development practices and regional characteristics. In tracing the origin of the banks' behavior, the authors demonstrate how this compares to the dominant development discourse of the World Bank. Whether the RDBs are as unique as they proclaim is therefore an important empirical question addressed herein. The volume's conclusion then assesses the state of play for RDBs in the twenty-first century. The practices of RDBs across a range of areas are comparable to the current practices of the World Bank, which many see as driving the neoliberal international development lending agenda. For many, this dictating of the current terms through which future lending will apply is a harbinger of a trend in international development financing.

Notes

1 Policy prescriptions included fiscal discipline; reordering public expenditure priorities; tax reform; liberalizing interest rates; establishing a competitive exchange

rate; trade liberalization; liberalization of inward foreign direct investment; privatization; deregulation; and establishing and securing property rights (Williamson 1999).
2 The only major prerequisite to join the World Bank is membership of the IMF.
3 As the youngest of the MDBs the EBRD is the most different in terms of having a political mandate to help the development of market economies in Central and Eastern Europe and to lend primarily (60%) to the private sector.
4 An IO is defined as 'an organization that has representatives from three or more states supporting a permanent secretariat to perform ongoing tasks related to a common purpose' (Barnett and Finnemore 2004: 177).
5 Market confidence is less focused on capital input than it was previously as credit rating agencies' methodologies now examine the internal financial management and loan portfolio quality of MDBs. Nonetheless, should powerful member states withdraw from the MDBs this would have a significant effect on the value of MDB operations.
6 Desi, R. and J. Vreeland. 2014. "What the New Bank of BRICS is All About." *The Washington Post*, 17 July. Available at: www.washingtonpost.com/blogs/monkeycage/wp/2014/07/17/what-the-new-bank-of-brics-is-all-about/.
7 Feng, B. 2014. "Deal Set on China-Led Infrastructure Bank." *New York Times*, 24 October. Available at: www.nytimes.com/2014/10/25/world/asia/china-signs-agreement-with-20-other-nations-to-establish-international-development-bank.html?_r=0.

Bibliography

Acharya, A. and A. Johnston. 2007. *Crafting Cooperation: Regional International Institutions in Comparative Perspective*. Cambridge: Cambridge University Press.

Babb, S.. 2009. *Behind the Development Banks*. Chicago, IL: Chicago University Press.

Barnett, M. and M. Finnemore. 2004. *Rules for the World: International Organizations in Global Politics*. Ithaca, NY and London: Cornell University Press.

Bebbington, A., M. Woolcock, S. Guggenheim and E. O. Olson. 2006. *The Search for Empowerment: Social Capital as Idea and Practice at the World Bank*. Bloomfield, CT: Kumarian Press.

Beetham, D. 1991. *The Legitimation of Power*. London: Macmillan.

Best, J. 2007. 'Legitimacy Dilemmas: The IMF's Pursuit of Country Ownership'. *Third World Quarterly* 28(3): 469–488.

Best, J. 2014. *Governing Failure: Provisional Expertise and the Transformation of Global Development Finance*. Cambridge: Cambridge University Press.

Birdsall, N. (ed.) 2006. *Rescuing the World Bank: A Centre for Global Development Working Report and Selected Essays*. Washington, DC: Centre for Global Development.

Bøås, M. and D. McNeill (eds). 2004. *Global Institutions and Development: Framing the World?* New York and Abingdon: Routledge.

Broome, A. and L. Seabrooke. 2012. "Seeing Like an International Organisation." *New Political Economy* 17(1): 1–16.

Buchanan, A. and R. O. Keohane. 2006. "The Legitimacy of Global Governance Institutions." *Ethics and International Affairs* 20(4): 405–437.

Bukovansky, M. 2002. *Legitimacy and Power Politics: The American and French Revolutions in International Political Culture*. Princeton, NJ: Princeton University Press.

Bull, B. and M. Bøås. 2003. "Multilateral Development Banks as Regionalising Actors: The Asian Development Bank and the Inter-American Development Bank." *New Political Economy* 8(2): 245–261.

Chwieroth, J. 2008. "Organizational Change 'From Within': Exploring the World Bank's Early Lending Practices." *Review of International Political Economy* 15(4): 481–505.
Culpeper, R. 1997. *Titans or Behemoths? The Multilateral Development Banks.* London: Intermediate Technology Publishing.
Dell, S. 1972. *The Inter-American Development Bank: A Study in Development Financing.* New York: Praeger.
Dutt, Nitish. 2001. "The US and the Asian Development Bank: Origins, Structure and Lending Operations." *Journal of Contemporary Asia* 31(2): 241–261.
Fordwor, K. 1981. *The African Development Bank: Problems of International Cooperation.* New York and Oxford: Pergamon Press.
George, S. and F. Sabelli. 1994. *Faith and Credit: The World Bank's Secular Empire.* London: Penguin Books.
Goldman, M. 2005. *Imperial Nature: The World Bank and Struggles for Social Justice in the Age of Globalization.* New Haven, CT: Yale University Press.
Gutner, T. 2005. "World Bank Environmental Reform: Revisiting Lessons from Agency Theory." *International Organization* 59(3): 773–783.
Hall, A. 2007. "Social Policies Inside the World Bank: Paradigms and Challenges." *Global Social Policy* 7(2): 151–175.
Hawkins, D., D. Lake, D. Nielson and M. Tierney (eds). 2006. *Delegation and Agency in International Organizations.* Cambridge: Cambridge University Press.
Head, J. W. 2005. *The Future of the Global Economic Organizations: An Evaluation of Criticisms Leveled at the IMF, the Multilateral Development Banks, and the WTO.* Ardsley, NY: Transnational Publishers.
Hurd, I. 2007. *After Anarchy: Legitimacy and Power in the United Nations Security Council.* Princeton, NJ: Princeton University Press.
Hurrell, A. 1995. "Regionalism in Theoretical Perspective." In *Regionalism in World Politics*, edited by L. Fawcett and A. Hurrell. Oxford: Oxford University Press, pp. 37–73.
Kilby, C. 2011. "Informal Influence in the Asian Development Bank." *Review of International Organizations* 6(3/4): 223–267.
Kuczynski, P.-P. and J. Williamson. 2003. *After The Washington Consensus: Restarting Growth and Reform in Latin America.* Washington, DC: IIE.
Lavelle, K. 2011. *Legislating International Organization: The US Congress, the IMF and the World Bank.* Oxford: Oxford University Press.
Mingst, K. 1990. *Politics and the African Development Bank.* Lexington, KY: University Press of Kentucky.
Mistry, P. 1995. *Multilateral Development Banks: An Assessment of their Financial Structures, Policies and Practices.* The Hague: FONDAD.
Mosley, P., J. Harrigan and J. Toye. 1991. *Aid and Power. The World Bank and Policy-based Lending.* London: Routledge.
Neumann, I. and O. Sending. 2010, *Governing the Global Polity: Practice, Mentality, Rationality.* Ann Arbor: University of Michigan Press.
Nielson, D. and M. Tierney. 2005. "Theory, Data and Hypothesis Testing: World Bank Environmental Reform Redux." *International Organization* 59(3): 785–800.
Onis, Z. and F. Senses. 2005. "Rethinking the Emerging Post-Washington Consensus." *Development and Change* 36(2): 263–290.
Park, S. 2010. *The World Bank Group and Environmentalists: Changing International Organization Identities.* Manchester: Manchester University Press.

Park, S. 2014. "Institutional Isomorphism and the Asian Development Bank's Accountability Mechanism: Something Old, Something New; Something Borrowed, Something Blue?' *Pacific Review* 27(2): 217–239.

Park, S. and A. Vetterlein. 2010. *Owning Development: Creating Policy Norms in the IMF and World Bank*. Cambridge: Cambridge University Press.

Peet, R. 2003. *The Unholy Trinity: The IMF, World Bank and WTO*. London: Zed Books.

Rapkin, D. P. and D. Braaten. 2009. "Conceptualising Hegemonic Legitimacy." *Review of International Studies* 35(1): 113–149.

RIPE (Review of International Political Economy). 2012, "Special Edition Focus on Governing Global Finance and Banking" 19(4).

Scharpf, F. 1999. *Governing in Europe: Effective and Democratic?* Oxford: Oxford University Press.

Seabrooke, L.. 2007. "Legitimacy Gaps in the World Economy: Explaining the Sources of the IMF's Legitimacy Crisis." *International Politics* 44(2/3): 250–268.

Strand, J. 1999. "State Power in a Multilateral Context: Voting Strength in the Asian Development Bank." *International Interactions* 25(3): 265–286.

Strand, J. 2003. "Measuring Voting Power in an International Institution: The United States and the Inter-American Development Bank." *Economics of Governance* 4(1): 19–36.

Strand, J. 2014. "Global Economic Governance and the Regional Development Banks." In *Handbook of Global Economic Governance: Players, Power, and Paradigms*, edited by M. Moschella and C. Weaver. Abingdon and New York: Routledge, pp. 290–303.

Strand, J. Forthcoming. *Regional Development Banks*. Abingdon and New York: Routledge.

Tussie, D. 1995. *The Inter-American Development Bank*. Boulder, CO: Lynne Rienner.

Vetterlein, A. 2007. "Change in International Organisations: Innovation or Adaptation? A Comparison of the World Bank and the International Monetary Fund." In *The World Bank and Governance: A Decade of Reform and Reaction*, edited by D. Stone and C. Wright. New York: Routledge, pp. 144–163.

Watanabe, T. 1977. *Towards a New Asia*. Manila: ADB.

Weaver, C. 2008. *The Hypocrisy Trap: The World Bank and the Poverty of Reform*. Princeton, NJ: Princeton University Press.

White, J. 1970. *Regional Development Banks: A Study of Institutional Style*. London: Overseas Development Institute.

Williamson, John. 1999. "What Should the World Bank Think About the Washington Consensus?' Paper prepared as a background to the World Bank's *World Development Report 2000*. Available at: www.iie.com/publications/papers/paper.cfm?ResearchID=351.

Woods, N. 2006. *The Globalizers: The IMF, the World Bank and their Borrowers*. Ithaca, NY: Cornell University Press.

2 The Asian Development Bank
Joining the fight against corruption?

Yasumasa Komori

Like the World Bank, the Asian Development Bank (ADB) (hereafter "the Bank") had previously considered corruption outside the purview of its mandate because of the political nature of the problem and its charter's prohibition of the Bank's involvement in the political affairs of its members.[1] However, on 2 July 1998 the ADB adopted an anticorruption policy, which was designed to "reduce the burden that widespread, systemic corruption exacts upon the economies of the region and the development of ADB's DMCs [developing member countries]" (ADB 1998a: 10). More specifically, it identified three objectives:

i supporting competitive markets and efficient, effective, accountable, and transparent public administration as part of ADB's broader work on good governance and capacity building;
ii supporting promising anticorruption efforts on a case-by-case basis and improving the quality of our dialogue with the DMCs on a range of governance issues, including corruption; and
iii ensuring that ADB projects and staff adhere to the highest ethical standards.
(ADB 1998a: 7–8)

Drawing on the Bank's governance policy adopted in 1995, the first two objectives of the new policy describe the Bank's efforts to combat corruption in the Asia-Pacific region through the promotion of market liberalization and public sector reform as well as its support for selective anticorruption initiatives. Most importantly, from the standpoint of the organization's integrity, the third objective affirms the ADB's new determination to eliminate corruption amongst ADB staff and in Bank-financed projects, declaring a "zero tolerance" policy (ADB 1998a: 28).

This chapter asks how and why the ADB decided to formulate its anticorruption policy. Was the ADB decision driven externally or internally? Was it triggered by material pressure from the donor countries on which the Bank depends on for its financial resources? Or was it driven by normative legitimacy concerns? Moreover, to what extent has the ADB been successful in mainstreaming the anticorruption norm?

Drawing on the literature on resource dependence theory and constructivist organizational theory, this chapter seeks to explore both external and internal factors that have led to the establishment of its anticorruption policy. It argues that the ADB's decision was, in large part, driven by changes in the organization's *external* environment, both normative and material. By the mid-1990s there was a significant normative shift because of a growing global recognition of corruption's negative impacts on development, the diffusion of anticorruption measures among international organizations (IOs), and the resultant emergence of the global anticorruption norm. At the same time, Western donor countries put material pressure on the ADB to address corruption issues by exercising financial leverage during negotiations over the sixth replenishment of the Asian Development Fund (ADF). In short, the ADB's decision to address corruption can be understood as an attempt both to secure financial resources from the major donor states and to retain its legitimacy in the face of the changing normative environment. Even prior to the Asian financial crisis of 1997/8 there was an increasing awareness within the Bank of the need to combat corruption, especially after its internal portfolio review in 1994. Nonetheless, the crisis served as a major catalyst for accelerating a process already underway. The crisis dramatically increased both normative and material pressures on the Bank to address corruption issues.

The chapter also utilizes the concept of "organizational culture" to explain the ADB's failure to fully embrace the anticorruption norm across different units within the Bank. It argues that, although the ADB has made great strides toward mainstreaming the anticorruption norm, its implementation has been uneven and insufficient because of the persistence of the ADB's internal culture, the lack of incentives to prioritize addressing corruption, and limited resources.

This chapter proceeds in five parts. First, it provides the theoretical framework that is utilized in the chapter. Second, the chapter provides a brief overview of the ADB by focusing on key players and the Bank's organizational culture in shaping the Bank's behavior. Third, the chapter analyzes both external and internal factors that contributed to the ADB's decision to adopt the anticorruption policy. Fourth, it explains the extent to which the ADB has been successful in mainstreaming the anticorruption norm. The final section concludes by considering the relevance of this case for the study of IOs in general and the RDBs in particular.

Theoretical framework

To analyze how and why the ADB adopted its anticorruption policy, this chapter utilizes insights from resource dependence theory and constructivist organizational theory. Resource dependence theory stresses external influences on IOs because of their reliance on external actors for material resources (Pfeffer and Salancik 1978; Babb 2009). As discussed in the introduction of this volume, multilateral development banks (MDBs), including the ADB, rely on member states as well as capital markets for their financial resources.

Thus, the behavior of the MDBs is significantly influenced by the preferences of their major shareholders. It has been widely documented that the United States has frequently used its power of the purse to demand policy changes in the World Bank by exercising "donor leverage" during periodic negotiations over general capital increases (GCIs) and replenishment of its soft loan window, the International Development Association (IDA) (Babb 2009; Woods, 2006). Similarly, in many cases, the ADB's major donors (which overlap those of the World Bank) have used financial leverage to call for policy changes in the ADB through negotiations among member states for its GCIs and the replenishments of the ADF (Babb, 2009; Park, 2014).

While resource dependence theory focuses primarily, though not exclusively, on material resources, constructivist organizational theory emphasizes the role of ideational forces in shaping IO behavior. In doing so, a constructivist account of IOs analyzes the impact of both the *external* normative structure and *internal* organizational culture and identity on IO behavior (Weaver 2008; Park and Vetterlein 2010; Park and Weaver 2012). Externally, the constructivist approach stresses the importance of the normative environment within which IOs operate. It argues that IOs need to be perceived as legitimate and appropriate by a broader community if they are to survive. Thus, IO behavior is guided by the "logic of appropriateness" according to the prevailing international norms. Norms are "shared expectations about appropriate behavior held by a community of actors" (Finnemore 1996: 22). In other words, norms define what is considered a legitimate behavior within the international community.

In analyzing the diffusion of norms, the constructivist approach suggests that IOs themselves play an important role in creating, diffusing, and transmitting new norms in the international community (Finnemore 1996; Park and Vetterlein 2010). New norms emerge either within or outside the organization. Relevant actors may adopt norms that emerged outside the organization because of normative pressure to follow other actors. In particular, actors often emulate organizational leaders primarily out of legitimacy concerns rather than because of the expected material gains (Sharman 2008). In a pioneering work on norm diffusion, Martha Finnemore (1996) argued that as the leader of international development institutions, the World Bank has played a significant role in shaping ways of thinking about development and disseminating new ideas and norms. In her view, the World Bank serves as a norm diffuser, while RDBs, including the ADB, are considered "followers" of the norms (Finnemore 1996: 124). Yet, as discussed below, RDBs should not be viewed simply as miniature versions of the World Bank because they do not necessarily always follow the World Bank (Strand 2014: 593).

Internally, the constructivist organizational theory focuses on the role of organizational culture and identity in shaping IO behavior (Barnett and Finnemore 2004; Weaver 2008; Park 2010). Organizational culture is defined as "the shared ideologies, norms, and routines that shape staff members' expectations about how agendas are set, mandates are operationalized, projects are implemented and evaluated, and what staff behavior will be rewarded or punished in promotions and demotions" (Nielson, Tierney, and Weaver 2006: 109). Organizational culture thus provides the organization with a lens through which staff interprets the organization's central missions, role, and ultimate *raison d'etre*. Although RDBs are modeled after the World Bank, they have developed their own distinctive organizational cultures with a "regional flavor" (Strand 2014), which, in turn, inform which ideas and norms the RDBs learn from the World Bank.

In addition to analyzing the factors that led to the ADB's adoption of the anticorruption policy (material versus ideational as well as external versus internal), this chapter is also concerned with investigating the degree to which the ADB has mainstreamed the anticorruption norm in its core operations. By "mainstreaming," it ultimately means integrating anticorruption into the Bank's policy discourse, strategies, projects, and programs. Some of the indicators of mainstreaming include sufficient allocations of resources in terms of budget and staffing; the incorporation of anticorruption into country partnership strategies (CPS), sector strategies, and projects; careful assessments and mitigation of corruption risks at country, sector, and project levels; observable management and staff commitment to anticorruption; and changes in incentive structures and organizational culture to one in which the norm of anticorruption is valued and given sufficient attention. Organizational culture is useful for explaining the gap between the ADB's efforts to mainstream the anticorruption norm and its actual implementation.

Who shapes ADB policy? Key actors and the ADB's organizational culture

Scholars of IOs have debated the relative importance of their member states and bureaucrats in shaping IO behavior. According to resource dependence theory, the ADB's reliance on financial contributions from donor states for its organizational survival provides the major donor countries with the ability to influence the Bank's operations. In particular, in contrast to the Inter-American Development Bank (IADB), the ADB is characterized as "a donor-dominated bank," in which borrowing countries have little influence in Bank decisions (Babb 2009: 29; Culpeper 1997: 22; Retzl this volume). As the ADB's two largest shareholders, Japan and the United States have held the largest votes in the Bank, each holding 12.8 percent of voting power. The literature on the ADB thus suggests that these two countries have traditionally exerted the largest influence over the Bank's lending policy, day-to-day operations, and its overall evolution (Krasner 1981: 317–320; Kilby 2006). In addition to voting power on board decisions, the United States has also used its financial leverage in negotiations over GCI and ADF replenishment to demand changes in the ADB, just as it has at other MDBs, including the World Bank.

In contrast to resource dependence theory's emphasis on the influence of the Bank's major shareholders, the constructivist organizational theory assumes that the ADB holds a certain level of autonomy independent of its member states not only because of authority delegated by member states, but also because of the technical expertise and professionalism of its management and staff members (Barnett and Finnemore 2004). Presumably the ADB staff's specialized knowledge about the Asia-Pacific economies makes the ADB an authority in the field of economic development and poverty reduction in the region. The ADB management and staff claim that the ADB's comparative advantage lies in being closer to its borrowing countries in the Asia-Pacific than the World Bank and thus being more familiar with local knowledge and experiences (Bøås and McNeill 2003: 36).

As the only established MDB in Asia, the Bank's charter envisions that the Bank would be "Asian in its basic character" (ADB, 1966). To ensure the influence of regional members, the ADB's charter stipulates that at least 60 percent of total voting shares should be held by regional members. Presumably reflecting Asian DMC preferences, the ADB's organizational culture stresses economic growth and values state sovereignty (Park 2014). In contrast with the IADB's emphasis on "social lending," the ADB has traditionally focused on large-scale infrastructure projects, such as energy, transport, and communications, as a means to increase economic growth. Thus, the ADB has been known as one of the most conservative regional development banks (Krasner 1981: 319).

Currently the ADB has approximately 3,000 staff members. As head of the Bank's management team, the president of the ADB plays a significant role in shaping the Bank's agenda and practices. The president is responsible for preparing an agenda for each meeting of the board of directors and chairing the board meetings. It is noteworthy that according to the Bank's rules of voting procedure, unless a formal vote is requested by any director (which, in practice, rarely occurs), the president as chairperson "may ascertain and announce to the meeting the sense of the meeting with regard to any matter" without taking a formal vote (ADB n.d.). Since its foundation, the ADB president has always been Japanese. In addition, Japanese nationals have held many of the ADB's high-level management and staff posts in the departments particularly important for the ADB's overall operations and policy planning, such as the Budget, Personnel, and Management Systems Department, and the Strategy and Policy Department (Yasutomo 1995: 83–86; Wesley 2003: 27). Moreover, Japan has had the largest number of professionals on staff at the Bank, although in the past decade the number of professionals from China and India has increased (see Strand and Trevathan, this volume).

Given Japan's close institutional links with the ADB, some observers contend that the ADB's organizational culture has been greatly shaped by Japanese management styles and economic ideology (Yasutomo 1983, 1995; Wan 1995–1996; Wesley 2003). In terms of decision-making procedures, the ADB has traditionally focused on consultation and consensus (Dent 2008: 768). In terms of economic ideology, some analysts argue that the ADB is strongly influenced by "Japanese developmentalist thinking and ideology," which stresses a positive role of the state in promoting economic growth (Dent 2008: 768–769; Yasutomo 2000: 132). However, other analysts question the extent to which the ADB has been able to offer any unique economic model distinct from neoliberal economic policies promoted by the World Bank (Pascha 2000: 171; Rosser 2009). Ultimately, it is suggested that the ADB, like other RDBs, is more flexible and less doctrinaire than the World Bank in its application of neoliberal economic ideas (Strand 2014).

Explaining the ADB's adoption of the anticorruption policy

In 1998, the ADB adopted the anticorruption policy "as part of its broader work on issues of governance and capacity building" (ADB 1998a: 7). As noted earlier, this represented a major policy shift in that the Bank now entered a new area of operation, which was thought to be outside the purview of its mission. Even the Bank's governance policy three years earlier barely mentioned the word corruption.[2] The following section analyzes both *external* and *internal* factors behind the Bank's policy shift.

External triggers

This section demonstrates that both normative and material pressures from outside the organization contributed to the Bank's decision to adopt an anticorruption policy. It first reveals a significant normative change in the external environment in the mid-1990s as a result of shifts in the discourse on the impact of corruption, the diffusion of anticorruption measures among IOs, and the emergence of the global anticorruption norm. It then shows that there were increasing demands from the Bank's major donor countries that put material pressure on the Bank to address corruption issues. It finally demonstrates that the Asian financial crisis served as the single most important catalyst for the Bank's adoption of an anticorruption policy.

Changes in the discourse on corruption and development

The impact of corruption on economic development has been widely disputed among scholars. Some analysts have argued that certain forms of corruption (e.g. bribery) can have positive effects. Some experts even viewed bribery as "grease for the wheels" of economic growth by circumventing an inefficient bureaucracy and thus enhancing economic efficiency (Leff 1964; Leys 1965; Huntington 1968). Others suggested that corruption is an inevitable part of the process of economic and political modernization (Huntington 1987). In particular, prior to the Asian financial crisis of 1997/8, the economic successes of the countries of East and Southeast Asia led some scholars to claim that corruption was beneficial for economic growth. This is because corruption provides firms and individuals with the means to avoid excessive bureaucratic regulations and ineffective legal systems, thus facilitating investment and economic activity. The combination of rapid economic growth and high level of corruption presented scholars of political economy with what some call the "East Asian Paradox" (Wedeman 2002).

However, the explosion of empirical research during the 1990s showed that corruption has a negative impact on investment and economic growth, denying the East Asian exceptionalism (Gray and Kaufmann 1998). In particular, the ADB's anticorruption policy (1998a: 17–18) cites, among others, IMF economist Paolo Mauro and two World Bank researchers Jose Eduardo Campos and Sanjay Pradhan, who found that corruption is negatively correlated with the investment rate (Mauro 1995; World Bank 1997b). It also refers to Shang-Jin Wei's work, which found a negative impact of corruption on the flow of foreign investment in East Asian economies and concluded that East Asia is not different from other regions (Wei 1997). In the wake of the crisis, as one scholar noted, the "romantic view of corruption" has been replaced by a "more realistic and much less favorable view" (Tanzi 1999: 3). In this respect, the anticorruption policy specifically states that the ADB "rejects the argument that corruption's beneficial effects outweigh its negative consequences" (ADB, 1998a: 19). In summary, by 1998, there was an increasing recognition of corruption's adverse impacts on economic development among both scholars and practitioners.

The diffusion of anticorruption measures among IOs

The mid-1990s witnessed increasing global attention given to the issue of corruption and the adoption of a variety of anticorruption efforts and measures by IOs, including the Organization of American States (OAS), the IMF, the World Bank, the UN, and the OECD. The diffusion of international efforts to fight corruption was promoted by several developments, including the end of the Cold War, the spread of democratization movements, the explosion of NGOs and civil society, and the information revolution (McCoy and Heckel 2002; Bukovansky 2006; Brademas and Heimann 1998). In particular, the creation of Transparency International in 1993 and its first publication of the corruption perceptions index in 1995 had a great impact. Consequently, addressing the issue of corruption was no longer considered taboo among IOs. Against this background, some scholars claim that the mid-1990s witnessed the emergence of a "global anticorruption norm" (McCoy and Heckel 2001).

The most significant development from the perspective of the ADB was a policy shift within the World Bank. Until the mid-1990s, the World Bank had deliberately avoided addressing corruption by arguing that its articles of agreement prohibited it from addressing such political issues. However, in a famous speech at the annual meetings of the World Bank and the IMF in October 1996, the World Bank's president James Wolfensohn denounced "the cancer of corruption" and pledged to make the issue a priority. In 1997, the World Bank published an official anticorruption strategy titled *Helping*

Countries Combat Corruption: The Role of the World Bank (1997). It argued that corruption is "a major barrier to sustainable and equitable development," thus an economic and social issue rather than a political one (World Bank 1997a: 2). As discussed later, this new interpretation of World Bank's role in addressing corruption provided a template for the ADB to follow. In short, the World Bank's move to tackle corruption can be indeed considered a "tipping point" in the emergence of the global anti-corruption norm (McCoy and Heckel 2001), which, in turn, had a significant impact on the ADB's decision to formulate its anticorruption policy.

Calls from donor countries

In the 1990s, the US and other Western donor countries used financial coercion to demand policy changes in the ADB, including the increase of "social sector lending" in areas such as education, health, and environmental protection (Wan 2001) and the establishment of an inspection function (Park 2014). In 1995, the Bank adopted its governance policy in response to increased demand by major Western countries, despite strong opposition from many DMCs, especially China, Malaysia, and Indonesia (Bøås 1998; Jokinen 2004; Bello 2000).

Similarly, major Western donor countries put increasing pressure on the Bank to address corruption issues. During the negotiations over the sixth ADF replenishment (ADF VII), which was concluded in January 1997, donors "stressed the importance of instituting anti-corruption provisions—both in public sector management and the rules and regulations within which the private sector operates—to prevent distorted and inefficient resource allocations" (ADB 1997: 3). Former ADB senior staff members suggest that the Bank's move to address issues of governance and anticorruption was, to an important degree, a response to increased demand by the Bank's major shareholders.[3] In light of the ADB's adoption of an anticorruption policy, Linda Tsao Yang, US executive director of the ADB, suggested that corruption emerged as "a front burner issue," and demanded that the Bank "link progress on anticorruption to overall lending levels to a country, and within a country to a specific sector" (Marozzi 1998: 8). Although it is not clear whether there was an actual threat of opposing the ADF replenishment on the condition of the ADB's adoption of the anticorruption agenda, external pressure from the donor countries provided a direct influence on the Bank's decision to address corruption issues.

The Asian financial crisis

As discussed above, prior to the crisis, the ADB was already under increasing pressure to address corruption issues. However, it was the Asian financial crisis that has provided the most significant boost to the Bank's move to formulate the anticorruption policy. In many ways the crisis was a wake-up call for the ADB.[4] Not only did many of the Asian economies, which were previously thought to present "successful" alternative models challenging the neoliberal orthodoxy, suddenly collapse but the crisis also effectively demonstrated the negative effects of corruption. Therefore, in the wake of the crisis, corruption came to the fore of discussions (ADB 1999: 26). Many observers blamed corruption and cronyism as a major contributing factor to the Asian financial meltdown, particularly in Indonesia, Thailand, and the Republic of Korea. The crisis revealed that close business-government relations, which had once been considered a positive force during the period of high growth, generated corruption, policy bias, and economic mismanagement (Haggard 2000). Consequently, the crisis as well as the corruption scandals involving top government officials contributed to changing the perception of corruption practices in the region (Bhargava and Bolongaita 2004: 1). Although the ADB's management and staff emphasize that the Bank's anticorruption policy was conceived prior to the crisis (Marozzi 1998), the crisis made it urgent for the Bank to adopt the policy.

The Indonesian experience apparently had the most decisive impact on the ADB, not only because of the magnitude of the negative impact of rampant corruption on the country[5] but also because the ADB's "big brother" institution, the World Bank, came under fire for allegedly losing funds to corruption. Right before the crisis spread to Indonesia, at a press conference held in July 1997, a political scientist at Northwestern University Jeffrey Winters alleged that as much as 30 percent of the World Bank's loans to Indonesia had been stolen (Rich 2002: 48; Winters 2002: 126; Mallaby 2004: 184–185). Despite the World Bank's strong denial of the allegation, it was enough to damage the credibility of the organization.[6] Since Indonesia has been an important borrower for the ADB as well, this allegation called into question the integrity of the ADB's operation in the country. Consequently, there was increasing normative pressure on the ADB to combat corruption in its own projects. In sum, the preceding section demonstrated that while there was increasing external pressures in terms of both demands from donor countries and the normative pressure to follow the emerging global anticorruption norm, the crisis provided the Bank with a sense of urgency to formulate its anticorruption policy.

Internal developments

In order to understand how and why the ADB's management responded to the changing normative environment and calls from donor countries, it is necessary to put the ADB's anticorruption policy in the context of the Bank's mission expansion during the 1990s. In response to the growing criticism against the Bank's poor performance in the late 1980s and 1990s, the ADB expanded its mandate into a wider range of issues, such as education, health, gender, environmental protection, and civil society engagement (see Uhlin, this volume). As with the World Bank, the ADB's adoption of an anticorruption policy was driven by its motive to improve the efficiency and effectiveness of Bank lending as well as its strategic attempts to regain organizational legitimacy by responding to the normative shift in the development paradigm.

The ADB's interest in combatting corruption in its lending operations first emerged as a result of the Bank's growing recognition of the need to improve the development impact of its activities. Following the World Bank's lead in conducting its internal portfolio review and releasing its so-called Wapenhans Report in 1992 and spurred partly by the increasing criticism against the ADB from donor countries and NGOs, the Bank became increasing concerned about its performance. As with the World Bank's portfolio review, the ADB's Task Force was internally set up to review Bank operations. The final report, *Report of the Task Force on Improving Project Quality*, released in 1994, recognized the need to improve "accountability for project quality within the Bank" and recommended the Bank's role in supporting the enhancement of institutional capacity building in the DMCs (ADB 1994: iii). It also admitted that the ADB suffered from an "approval culture" (echoing the result of the Wapenhans Report), which stressed achieving lending targets at the expense of careful consideration of local needs, demands, and absorptive capacities (ADB 1994: iii).

Determined to make the Bank a more efficient and effective organization, President Mitsuo Sato (1993–1999) pushed for the ADB's transformation into what the Bank called a "broad-based development institution" (ADB 1998b: 20–21). The 1995–98 Medium-Term Strategy Framework (MTSF) (1995–1998) defined the ADB's expanded role as a "catalyst of policy change and capacity building" in addition to its role as a project financier (ADB, 1995). The establishment of the governance policy in 1995 was an integral part of this transformation (ADB 1999: 30). Given strong reservations among DMCs (Root 1996), however, the authors of the governance policy carefully crafted the document by framing governance as the issue of "sound development management" (ADB 1995: 7). Thus, it assured the DMCs that the policy did not concern itself with political aspects of governance, such as democracy and human rights (ADB 1995b: 21). Building on the World Bank's approach, the ADB's governance policy identified four key elements of governance: accountability, participation, predictability, and transparency.[7] Despite the continuing scepticism, not only among some DMCs but also among some staff members, the ADB successfully adopted the governance policy in 1995, becoming the first MDB to adopt a board-approved policy on governance. This was the first step in incorporating politically sensitive issues within Bank operations.

Three years later, the ADB also adopted the anticorruption policy, not only to maintain the Bank's integrity in the wake of the Asian financial crisis but also to improve the Bank's project quality and thus enhance its development impact on DMCs. In so doing, the ADB self-consciously modeled its anticorruption policy after the approach taken by the World Bank. Robert P.

Beschel, who served as the principal author of the ADB's anticorruption policy, had recently joined the ADB from the Economic Development Institute of the World Bank, where he worked on issues of governance and public sector management. Just as the World Bank started to address corruption "through framing it as an economic development issue" (Park and Weaver 2012: 103), the ADB justified its position on anticorruption issues by arguing that its anticorruption measures "will be grounded solely upon economic considerations and concerns of sound development management" (ADB 1998a: 19).

Building on the approach taken by the World Bank, the ADB did not, however, blindly follow the World Bank. Most notably, the ADB modified the definition of corruption employed by the World Bank. While the World Bank defined corruption simply as "the abuse of public office for private gain," the ADB defined it as "the abuse of public or *private* office for personal gain" (*emphasis added*) (ADB 1998a: 9).[8] The ADB found that the existing definitions of corruption, including that adopted by the World Bank, "do not give adequate attention to the problem of corruption in the private sector or to the role of the private sector" (ADB 1998a: 9). The ADB's anticorruption policy indeed stressed that "the linkage between public and private sector corruption is an area of particular concern for both developed and developing countries in the Asia and Pacific region" (ADB 1998a: 1). This is not surprising, because the Asian financial crisis clearly demonstrated the negative aspect of close ties between the public and private sectors.

Implementation of the ADB's anticorruption policy

While the adoption of the anticorruption policy in 1998 contained three objectives as outlined at the outset, the initial focus was placed to prevent corruption within ADB-financed, administered, or supported activities. For this purpose, the Anticorruption Unit of the Office of the Auditor General (OAG) was created as the designated contact point for allegations of fraud and corruption among ADB projects and staff. It grew into the Office of Anticorruption and Integrity (OAI) in 2009. According to the OAI, the number of firms and individuals debarred by the ADB has increased over time. In 2013, the OAI received a record high of 250 complaints, 92 of which were converted into investigations and 30 individuals and 31 firms were sanctioned by the ADB (ADB 2015a). As of May 19, 2015, 998 firms and 650 individuals have been debarred by the ADB (ADB 2015b). The OAI has also held staff training, workshops, and seminars to raise staff awareness and improve knowledge of the ADB's anticorruption policy and Integrity Principles and Guidelines (IPG).

The ADB has also made efforts to address the issues of governance and corruption more broadly in recipient countries. In 2000, the ADB adopted the Governance Action Plan, which called for the Bank to play a lead role in promoting good governance in the region. In response to a 2006 implementation review of the Bank's governance and anticorruption policies (ADB 2006a), the ADB launched the Second Governance and Anticorruption Action Plan (GACAP II), which called for a more systematic approach to implementing the governance and anticorruption policies through risk assessments and management plans (ADB 2006b). The ADB's commitment to the governance and anticorruption policies has been repeatedly identified as one of the key pillars, priorities, or agendas in its successive strategic frameworks.[9]

The ADB has made great progress toward mainstreaming the anticorruption agenda in its operations. Yet there are still significant limitations to the implementation of the anticorruption policy. In terms of staff resources, there are only 16 international staff members working on governance and public sector management (ADB 2013a: 16).[10] Further, they are spread across regional departments and resident missions. While the number of staff working in the OAI increased from 10 in 2005 to 22 in 2014 (ADB 2014b: 17), it is not sufficient to investigate the growing number of complaints reported to the office.[11] Given the complex and multifaceted nature of corruption issues, the lack of "in-house expertise" poses a significant limitation to implementing governance and anticorruption policies.

In addition to the lack of resources, staff incentive structures are still not fully aligned with the Bank's efforts to curb corruption. The 2006 implementation review mentioned above suggests that there are implicit disincentives for staff to report suspected misconduct, with one member of staff describing it as "likely career suicide" (ADB 2006a: 28–29). Thus, it states that "there remains widespread skepticism among staff both at headquarter and at RMs [Resident Missions]" regarding the governance and anticorruption policies (ADB 2006a: 28). Moreover, there is hesitation on the part of the board members to fully embrace corruption investigations. On the one hand, DMCs' board members wish to avoid their countries being accused of corruption. On the other hand, developed-country board members appear sensitive about admitting their companies' involvement in corruption (ADB 2006a: 28). The review concluded that the implementation of the policies had been insufficient and uneven because of the broad scope of goals with a lack of specific focus, the tenuous ownership of the norm within the ADB, and a lack of resources (ADB 2006a).

Since the 2006 implementation review, the ADB has made some progress, as is evident from the growing number of investigations of fraud and corruption. However, the Bank's incentive structure has not fundamentally changed. The 2013 implementation review of GACAP II acknowledges that "[s]trong incentives still exist to prioritize loan processing over assessing governance risks and implementing and monitoring mitigation measures" (ADB 2013a: 23). On the operational side of the Bank, the "pressure to lend" still remains. Project teams are encouraged to keep the projects to schedule, while careful assessments and mitigation measures of governance and corruption risks could delay the projects. Thus, the 2013 review states that "implementation of risk mitigation measures remains a challenge at the project level" (ADB 2013a: i). It also points to the need to change the Bank's organizational culture to value risk assessments and reduce vulnerability to corruption (ADB 2013a: 23). In short, the persistence of the ADB's internal culture, resilient incentive structures (which prioritize lending), and the limited resources continue to be major obstacles for fully implementing the anticorruption norm.

Conclusion

This chapter argued that the ADB's adoption of an anticorruption policy was largely driven by external forces in the form of both normative and material pressures. By the mid-1990, new empirical research on corruption led to increasing recognition among both scholars and practitioners that corruption poses a serious risk to economic development. At the same time, there was a growing normative consensus among IOs on the need to address the issue of corruption. Most importantly, the World Bank's "framing" of corruption as a development issue set a precedent for the ADB to follow suit. In addition, as a resource-dependent organization, direct demands from major Western donor countries added material pressure on the Bank to address corruption issues. Internally, the ADB was motivated to address corruption issues in order to improve the efficiency and effectiveness of the ADB operations as well as retain organizational legitimacy in the face of the growing criticism against the Bank. Incidentally, the Asian economic crisis, which occurred in the ADB's own backyard, served as the single most important external trigger for the ADB to address corruption, dramatically increasing both normative and material pressures on the Bank. Against this background, the ADB's board of directors approved the anticorruption policy on 2 July 1998—exactly one year after the onset of the crisis.

This chapter also demonstrated that while the ADB has taken many steps to address corruption, especially in its own projects, the Bank's incentive structure and organizational culture have not drastically changed, resulting in uneven implementation across different units within the organization. In particular, pressure to lend still shapes the mindset of project teams engaged in infrastructure operations. Certainly these problems are not unique to the ADB. All the MDBs, most prominently the World Bank, have long been criticized for the "culture of loan approval," pressure to lend, and the incentive structure to prioritize lending over project quality (Weaver 2008). Yet some critics argue that the ADB "is more susceptible to corruption than the World Bank" because of the ADB's distinct internal culture as well as the Bank's external lending environment (Rich 2004: 10). While there is no empirical evidence to substantiate this claim, there is also little reason to believe that the ADB has been more successful than the World Bank in combating corruption. In terms of the ADB's external lending environment, many of the ADB's important clients, including India, China, Pakistan, Indonesia, and the Philippines, have been ranked among the most corrupt countries in the world.[12] As the ADB's recent study shows, despite economic achievements, Asian DMCs' progress in controlling corruption has been slow (ADB 2013b).

As a regional bank, the ADB's organizational culture is presumably more attuned to the Asian DMCs' concerns about state sovereignty and non-interference in domestic affairs (Park 2014). While many DMCs became more open to addressing corruption issues, a few DMCs remain reluctant. At the same time, the ADB's organizational culture emphasizes economic growth as a primary means of poverty reduction, with a traditional focus on infrastructure lending—a sector which has been considered particularly vulnerable to corruption. Consequently, the ADB's efforts to combat corruption have been a very difficult battle.

The case study in this chapter revealed several implications for the study of IOs in general and the RDBs in particular. First, it indicates that IOs operate within broader normative structures. This case study represents an instance of norm diffusion across IOs in which the ADB was a follower in adopting a newly emerging norm outside the organization. Second, an external shock such as the Asian financial crisis can serve as an important trigger for a major policy change in an organization. Third, RDBs like the ADB are subject to the same sort of material and normative pressures from donor countries and the broader international development community as the World Bank. However, the RDBs are particularly responsive to policy changes within the World Bank. In this case study, the ADB emulated the World Bank's move to address corruption issues in a similar attempt to retain organizational legitimacy. Fourth, MDBs suffer from similar problems such as the persistence of organizational culture and incentive structures to prioritize lending. Yet the RDBs are more sensitive to the region's local norms and preferences than the World Bank. The ADB's organizational culture is shaped by Asian DMCs' preferences for economic growth and the principle of state sovereignty. Ultimately, while there are many similarities between the World Bank and the RDBs, each RDB reveals its own unique regional character.

Notes

1 Article 36 of the ADB's charter stipulates that the ADB "shall not interfere in the political affairs of any member, nor shall they be influenced in their decisions by the political character of the member concerned" (ADB 1966).
2 The term "corruption" was used only six times in the document.
3 Interviews with former ADB staff members, September 2014, Washington, DC.
4 Interviews with former and current ADB staff members, September 2014, Washington, DC and October 2014, Manila.
5 According to Transparency International's Corruption Index 1997, Indonesia ranked among the world's top ten most corrupt countries and Asia's second most corruption after Pakistan.
6 The World Bank's internal document later admitted that at least 20–30 percent of the World Bank's lending to Indonesia has been misappropriated (Winters 2002: 127). In August 1998, this secret report was leaked to the *Wall Street Journal*, which again severely damaged the reputation of the organization.

7 These four categories largely followed, but slightly modified the 1992 World Bank report's categorization, which identified the following four elements: public sector management, accountability, the legal framework for development, and information and transparency.
8 It is only recently that the World Bank's official definition of corruption recognized corruption prevalent in the private sector (Weaver 2008: 112).
9 They include: *Poverty Reduction Strategy* (1999), *Long-Term Strategic Framework (LTSF): 2001–2015* (2001), *Enhanced Poverty Reduction Strategy* (2004) and *Medium-Term Strategies II* (2006). The ADB's most recent LTSF, *Strategy 2020*, released in 2008, identified "good governance and capacity development" as one of the five drivers of change.
10 In comparison, according to the World Bank's 2012 updated strategy and implementation plan on governance and anticorruption, the World Bank has over 300 public sector international staff.
11 In contrast, the World Bank's Integrity Vice Presidency (INT) has 94 staff members as of 2012 (World Bank 2013: 50).
12 According to Transparency International's Corruption Perceptions Index (CPI) 2013, which scores 177 countries from the highest rating of 100 (very clean) to 0 (highly corrupt), all of the ADB's five largest borrowers in 2013 (India, China, Pakistan, Indonesia, Philippines) have CPI scores at or below 40 (Transparency International 2013). India, the Bank's largest recipient in 2013, ranks 94 with a CPI of 36. China, the second largest borrower, ranks 80 with a CPI of 40. Pakistan, the third largest borrower, ranks 127 with a CPI of 28.

References

Asian Development Bank (ADB) (n.d.) *Rules of Procedure of the Board of Directors of the Asian Development Bank*. Available at: www.adb.org/BOD/Rules_Procedure_Brd_Dir_ADB.pdf (accessed 5 August 2011).
Asian Development Bank (ADB). 1966. *Agreement Establishing the Asian Development Bank*. Manila: ADB.
Asian Development Bank (ADB). 1994. *Report of the Task Force on Improving Project Quality*. Manila: ADB.
Asian Development Bank (ADB). 1995. *Governance: Sound Development Management*. Manila: ADB.
Asian Development Bank (ADB). 1997. *ADF VII: Report of the Donors*. Manila: Asian Development Bank.
Asian Development Bank (ADB). 1998a. *Anticorruption Policy*. Manila: ADB.
Asian Development Bank (ADB). 1998b. "From Project Financier to Broad-Based Development Institution." In *Annual Report 1997*, ADB. Manila: ADB, pp. 19–39.
Asian Development Bank (ADB). 1999. "Governance in Asia: From Crisis to Opportunity." In *Annual Report 1998*, ADB. Manila: ADB, pp. 15–36.
Asian Development Bank (ADB). 2006a. *Review of the Implementation of ADB's Governance and Anticorruption Policies*. Manila: ADB.
Asian Development Bank (ADB). 2006b. *Second Governance and Anticorruption Action Plan*. Manila: ADB.
Asian Development Bank (ADB). 2013a. *Implementation Review: Second Governance and Anticorruption Action Plan (GACAP II)*. Manila: ADB.
Asian Development Bank (ADB). 2013b. *Asian Development Outlook 2013 Update: Governance and Anticorruption Policies*. Manila: ADB.

Asian Development Bank (ADB). 2014. *Midterm Review of Strategy 2020: Meeting the Challenges of a Transforming Asia and Pacific.* Manila: ADB.
Asian Development Bank (ADB). 2015a. "Overview." *Anticorruption and Integrity.* Available at: www.adb.org/site/integrity/overview (accessed 27 May 2015).
Asian Development Bank (ADB). 2015b. "Sanctions." *Anticorruption and Integrity.* Available at: www.adb.org/site/integrity/sanctions (accessed 27 May 2015).
Babb, S. 2009. *Behind the Development Banks: Washington Politics, World Poverty, and the Wealth of Nations.* Chicago, IL: The University of Chicago Press.
Barnett, M. N. and M. Finnemore (eds). 2004. *Rules for the World: International Organizations in Global Perspective.* Ithaca, NY: Cornell University Press.
Bello, W. (2000). ADB Grapples with Major Problems ahead of Meeting. *Business World*, 2 May: 1.
Bhargava, V. and E. Bolongaita. 2004. *Challenging Corruption in Asia: Case Studies and a Framework for Action.* Washington, DC: The World Bank.
Bøås, M. 1998. "Governance as Multilateral Development Bank Policy: The Cases of the African Development Bank and the Asian Development Bank." *The European Journal of Development Research* 10(2): 117–134.
Bøås, M. and D. McNeill. 2003. *Multilateral Institutions: A Critical Introduction.* London: Pluto Press.
Brademas, J. and F. Heimann. 1998. "Tackling International Corruption: No Longer Taboo." *Foreign Affairs* 77(5): 17–22.
Bukovansky, M. 2006. "The Hollowness of Anti-corruption Discourse." *Review of International Political Economy* 13(2): 181–209.
Culpeper, R. 1997. *Titans or Behemoths? Vol. 5, The Multilateral Development Banks.* Boulder, CO: Lynne Rienner Publishers.
Dent, C. M. 2008. "The Asian Development Bank and Developmental Regionalism in East Asia." *Third World Quarterly* 29(4): 767–786.
Finnemore, M. 1996. *National Interests in International Society.* Ithaca, NY: Cornell University Press.
Gray, C. W. and D. Kaufmann. 1998. "Corruption and Development." *Finance and Development*: 7–10.
Haggard, S. 2000. *The Political Economy of the Asian Financial Crisis.* Washington, DC: Institute for International Economics.
Huntington, S. P. 1968. *Political Order in Changing Societies.* New Haven, CT: Yale University Press.
Huntington, S. P. 1987. "Modernization and Corruption." In *Political Corruption: A Handbook*, edited by A. J. Heidenheimer, M. Johnston and V. T. LeVine. Somerset, NJ: Transaction.
Jokinen, J. 2004. "Balancing between East and West: The Asian Development Bank's Policy on Good Governance." In *Global Institutions and Development: Framing the World?*, edited by M. Bøås. London: Routledge, pp. 137–150.
Kilby, C. 2006. "Donor Influence in Multilateral Development Banks: The Case of the Asian Development Bank." *Review of International Organizations* 1(2): 173–195.
Krasner, S. D. 1981. "Power Structures and Regional Development Banks." *International Organization* 35(2): 303–328.
Leff, N. H. 1964. "Economic Development Through Bureaucratic Corruption." *American Behavioral Scientist* 8(3): 8–14.
Leys, C. 1965. "What is the Problem about Corruption?" *The Journal of Modern African Studies* 3(2): 215–230.

Mallaby, S. 2004. *The World's Banker: A Story of Failed States, Financial Crises, and the Wealth and Poverty of Nations.* New York: Penguin Books.

Marozzi, J. 1998. "Asian Bank Unveils Tough Corruption Policy." *Financial Times,* 9 July.

Mauro, P. 1995. "Corruption and Growth." *Quarterly Journal of Economics* 110(3): 681–712.

McCoy, J. L. and H. Heckel. 2001. "The Emergence of a Global Anti-corruption Norm." *International Politics* 38(1): 65–90.

Nielson, D. L., M. J. Tierney and C. Weaver. 2006. "Bridging the Rationalist-Constructivist Divide: Re-Engineering the Culture of the World Bank." *Journal of International Relations and Development* 9: 107–139.

Park, S. 2010. *World Bank Group Interactions with Environmentalists: Changing International Organization Identities.* Manchester and New York: Manchester University Press.

Park, S. 2014. "Institutional Isomorphism and the Asian Development Bank's Accountability Mechanism: Something Old, Something New; Something Borrowed, Something Blue?" *The Pacific Review* 27(2): 217–239.

Park, S. and A. Vetterlein. 2010. "Owning Development: Creating Policy Norms in the IMF and the World Bank." In *Owning Development: Creating Policy Norms in the IMF and the World Bank*, edited by S. Park and A. Vetterlein. Cambridge: Cambridge University Press, pp. 3–26.

Park, S. and C. Weaver. 2012. "The Anatomy of Autonomy: The Case of the World Bank." In *International Organizations as Self-Directed Actors: A Framework for Analysis*, edited by J. E. Oestreich. London and New York: Routledge, pp. 91–117.

Pascha, W. 2000. "The Asian Development Bank in the Context of Rapid Regional Development." In *Economic Globalization, International Organizations and Crisis Management*, edited by R. Tilly and P. J. J. Welfens. Berlin: Springer.

Pfeffer, J. and G. R. Salancik. 1978. *The External Control of Organizations: A Resource Dependence Perspective.* New York: Harper and Row.

Rich, B. M. 2002. "The World Bank under James Wolfensohn." In *Reinventing the World Bank*, edited by J. R. Pincus and J. A. Winters. Ithaca, NY: Cornell University Press, pp. 26–53.

Rich, B. M. 2004. "Statement of Bruce M. Rich, International Program Manager, Environmental Defense, Washington, DC." In *Combating Corruption in the Multilateral Development Banks*, Committee on Foreign Relations, United States Senate. Washington, DC: US Senate Committee on Foreign Relations.

Root, H. L. 1996. *Small Countries, Big Lessons: Governance and the Rise of East Asia.* Oxford: Oxford University Press.

Rosser, A. 2009. "Risk Management, Neo-Liberalism and Coercion: The Asian Development Bank's Approach to 'Fragile States'." *Australian Journal of International Affairs* 63(3): 376–389.

Sharman, J. 2008. "Power, Discourse and Policy Diffusion: Anti-Money Laundering in Developing States." *International Studies Quarterly* 52: 635–656.

Strand, J. R. 2014. "The Regional Development Banks and Global Governance." In *International Organizations and Global Governance*, edited by T. G. Weiss and R. Wilkinson. London and New York: Routledge, pp. 593–604.

Tanzi, V. 1999. "Governance Corruption, and Public Finance: An Overview." In *Governance, Corruption, and Public Financial Management*, edited by S. Schiavo-Campo. Manila: Asian Development Bank, pp. 1–17.

Transparency International. 2013. "Corruption Perceptions Index 2013." Available at: http://cpi.transparency.org/cpi2013/results/ (accessed 7 July 2014).

Wan, M. 1995–1996. "Japan and the Asian Development Bank." *Pacific Affairs* 68(4): 509–528.

Wan, M. 2001. *Japan Between Asia and the West*. Armonk, NY: M. E. Sharpe.

Weaver, C. 2008. *Hypocrisy Trap: The World Bank and the Poverty of Reform*. Princeton, NJ: Princeton University Press.

Wedeman, A.. 2002. "Development and Corruption: The East Asian Paradox." In *Political Business in East Asia*, edited by A. Gomez. London: Routledge.

Wei, S.-J. 1997. *How Taxing is Corruption on International Investors*, Working Paper 6030. Cambridge, MA: National Bureau of Economic Research.

Wesley, M. 2003. "The Asian Development Bank." In *The Regional Organizations of the Asia-Pacific: Exploring Institutional Change*, edited by M. Wesley. London: Palgrave Macmillan, pp. 19–39.

Winters, J. A. 2002. "Criminal Debt." In *Reinventing the World Bank*, edited by J. R. Pincus and J. A. Winters. Ithaca, NY: Cornell University Press, pp. 101–130.

Winters, J. A. and J. R. Pincus. 2002. *Reinventing the World Bank*. Ithaca, NY: Cornell University Press.

Woods, N. 2006. *The Globalizers: The IMF, the World Bank, and Their Borrowers*. Ithaca, NY: Cornell University Press.

World Bank. 1997a. *Helping Countries Combat Corruption: The Role of the World Bank*. Washington, DC: World Bank.

World Bank. 1997b. *World Development Report 1997: The State in a Changing World*. Washington, DC: World Bank.

World Bank. 2013. *Annual Report: Integrity Vice Presidency Fisca 2012*. Washington, DC: World Bank.

Yasutomo, D. T. 1983. *Japan and the Asian Development Bank*. New York: Praeger.

Yasutomo, D. T. 1995. *The New Multilateralism in Japan's Foreign Policy*. New York: St. Martin's Press.

Yasutomo, D. T. 2000. "Japan's Multilateral Assistance Leadership: Momentum or Malaise?" In *Facing Asia: Japan's Role in the Political and Economic Dynamism of Regional Cooperation*, edited by V. Blechinger and J. Legewie. Munich, Germany: Iudicium, pp. 129–146.

3 The Inter-American Development Bank
Poverty alleviation and the millennium development goals

Kenneth J. Retzl[1]

The original purpose of the Inter-American Development Bank (IADB or Bank) was to provide economic development assistance to member countries in Latin America. More recently, the IADB has updated its purpose to also include social development assistance. This change in focus was formalized a few years after the adoption of the Millennium Development Goals (MDGs) by the international community in 2000. The IADB was not alone; the other regional development banks quickly pledged their support to help their member countries achieve the MDGs. Support by the IADB extended beyond the economic activities and loans it traditionally provided to member countries and meant that many of the MDGs it pledged to support went beyond the regional development bank's initial purview.

This chapter seeks to understand how the MDGs affected IADB operations. To do this, a brief history of the IADB is presented, as well as the events leading up to the creation of the Millennium Development Goals. Following this, a history of the MDGs is presented. Hulme and Fukudu-Parr (2009) argue that the MDGs are an embodiment of poverty alleviation norms that re-emerged in the international arena in the 1990s. To determine how this poverty alleviation norm travels to other organizations, this section includes a brief review of the literature on norm diffusion. The next section analyzes the IADB's social development and poverty alleviation projects. Through this analysis, it is evident that the IADB pursued projects consistent with poverty alleviationprior to the adoption of the MDGs. This section concludes that more important than the prevalent poverty alleviation norms is the fact that the president of the IADB has considerable influence in determining the types of projects the organization funds. Finally, the conclusion summarizes the findings: that the impact of the MDGs on the IADB has been minimal but they continue to emphasize the importance of social development for the IADB.

The Inter-American Development Bank[2]

Created in 1959, the IADB is the oldest of the regional development banks. However, the idea for a development bank in the region can be traced much further back in history. Calls for increasing economic cooperation began in Latin America and the United States in the early nineteenth century (Díaz-Bonilla and del Campo 2010). The original proposal for a regional development bank in the Americas occurred in 1889 at the First Pan-American Conference. The International American Bank was to be a private entity, based in the United States, with branches in several different countries. The creation of the bank was meant to facilitate lending to increase trade between countries without including banks in Europe, as was prevalent at the time (Díaz-Bonilla and del Campo 2010). The delegation sent by the United States supported the creation of the bank, as did President Benjamin Harrison. However, the United States House of Representatives rejected the proposal in 1898 due to concerns about whether the United States' Constitution permitted Congress to create such an institution, as well as a fear that the bank might create branches in the United States that could drive smaller banks out of business (Díaz-Bonilla and del Campo 2010).

Several more proposals for a regional bank serving the Americas were discussed during the early and mid-twentieth century. However, it was the Cold War and fear of Soviet influence in Latin America that pushed the United States to seriously consider a regional bank. As a result, in 1959 a commission made up of several Latin American countries and the United States established a charter for the creation and operation of the Inter-American Development Bank. The same year, the proposal was easily passed in the United States by both the House of Representatives and the Senate. The United States and Argentina were the first countries to sign the agreement in October 1959. Haiti, Venezuela, Guatemala, Paraguay, the Dominican Republic, Chile, Colombia, Ecuador, El Salvador, Honduras, Nicaragua, Panama, Bolivia, Brazil, Costa Rica, Mexico, Peru, and Uruguay signed in late 1959 or early 1960.[3] After several proposed iterations, the Americas finally had a regional development institution. The Inter-American Development Bank began operations on October 1, 1960 and continues to be headquartered in Washington DC.

Originally, the United States was the only non-borrowing member of the IADB. Today, Canada, Austria, Belgium, China, Croatia, Denmark, Finland, France, Germany, Israel, Italy, Japan, South Korea, the Netherlands, Norway, Portugal, Slovenia, Spain, Sweden, Switzerland, and the United Kingdom are all non-borrowing member countries. However, to maintain the influence of the Latin American countries, the voting weight of borrowing member countries cannot fall below 50.005 percent (IADB 1996). The United States continues to have the most voting weight (approximately 30 percent) of any member country.[4] This has led some observers to believe that within the IADB there are "two interacting sets of relationships – the Latin American countries' relationships with each other, and their collective and individual relationships with the U.S.A." (White 1970: 140). However, for most of the IADB's existence, the United States and Latin American countries have been collaborative (Tussie 1995).

The original purpose of the Inter-American Development Bank was "to contribute to the acceleration of the process of economic development of the member countries, individually and collectively" (Organization of American States, 1959). However, over time it has gained a reputation for being the "water and sanitation bank," the "university bank," and the "integration bank" for its respective funding and support of infrastructure, higher education, and regional economic integration projects (Tussie 1995). Additionally, the IADB plays a different role in different countries. Smaller, poorer Latin American countries use the IADB as a development institution, while larger countries use it as a financial intermediary (Tussie 1995).

In terms of social development projects, the IADB has historically been much more involved than the other regional development banks (Culpeper 1997) or even the World Bank (Tussie 1995). This is largely due to the circumstances under which the IADB was created. There was a strong desire to prevent a repeat of the Cuban Revolution elsewhere in Latin America, and social development projects sought to reduce financial inequalities in the region (Culpeper 1997). Throughout the 1960s, approximately 25 percent of all projects benefited social development in Latin America. During this same time, only approximately 5 percent of the World Bank's activities in the region had similar aims (Culpeper 1997).

In 1979, the IADB formalized another social development goal: Fifty percent of its lending program should benefit low-income groups. This requirement was strongly backed by the Carter Administration in the United States (Tussie 1995). This goal was not sector specific (meaning that 50 percent of the projects did not have to fall within the social development sector), and there was little oversight to ensure the progress of such a goal. Because of this, the mandate was largely ignored and did not receive special attention when determining projects to fund (Tussie 1995). However, the IADB recommitted itself to the goal in 1983, and then again in 1989 (IADB 1978; IADB 1989). Unfortunately, in the early 1990s the IADB reported that of the loans that could be assessed, only 40 percent reached the low-income groups they were targeting (IADB 1994). The IADB was improving but still not meeting its targets. At this time, international momentum started to build for formalized poverty alleviation goals.

The Millennium Development Goals

In September 2000, the United Nations Millennium Summit unanimously agreed to a number of poverty alleviation objectives, collectively known as the Millennium Development Goals. However, international concerns regarding social development have a longer history. In the 1960s there were several development summits promising to increase educational opportunities, reduce hunger, and fight drug use. Many of these summits resulted in promises from participant countries without providing a plan to address the issue. Not surprisingly, little progress was made (Hulme 2009).

In the 1980s, numerous developing countries were mired in debt crises that meant they were unable to make their debt service payments to international creditors. During this time, the IMF and World Bank advocated Structural Adjustment Programs (SAPs), which were designed to assist a defaulting government make future debt payments. Generally, these SAPs brought about neoliberal economic reforms: reducing the size of government (by reducing expenditures) and freeing markets from government interference. However, by reducing the size of the government, expenditures for healthcare and education were reduced, as were other policies that targeted the needs of the poor (Hulme and Scott 2013).

It was in this environment that numerous international organizations rediscovered issues of poverty (Noël 2006; Hall 2007). In 1990, the World Bank published the *World Development Report*. Although it had published this report annually since 1978, the 1990 edition stressed the interplay between the provision of economic opportunities and the provision of basic social services (such as education, healthcare, nutrition, and family planning) for the poor (World Bank 1990). Also in 1990, the United Nations Development Programme (UNDP) published its *Human Development Report*. It suggested that impoverished individuals in the developing world were often not enjoying the economic gains their countries experienced. Social safety nets, which were often removed through Structural Adjustment Programs (SAPs), were needed to provide a basic level of service for these individuals (UNDP 1990).

The United Nations and the World Bank were not the only international organizations discussing poverty issues. At a meeting of the OECD's Development Assistance Committee (DAC) in 1995, there was a concern that many summits had made significant promises regarding social development and poverty alleviation but at the same time many developed countries were cutting their aid budgets (Hulme 2009). Poverty alleviation would be much more easily achieved with the financial support of rich countries. Through various meetings, the OECD countries agreed to a 20-year plan to address these issues. These included reducing those in extreme poverty, increasing educational opportunities, increasing gender equality, reducing mortality rates, increasing access to healthcare, and protecting the environment (OECD 1996). Collectively, these became known as the International Development Goals (IDGs), and many were based on commitments from previous UN summits. In 2000, the IMF, OECD, UN, and World Bank published *A Better World for All: Progress Towards the International Development Goals* in which all four organizations voiced support for a near identical iteration of the IDGs. This was done to show solidarity between large international organizations that dealt with development issues (Hulme 2009).

The IDGs became the basis for the Millennium Development Goals (Hulme 2009), which would be formally established in 2001 by the United Nations. In total, there are eight MDGs. To determine whether countries are progressing toward achieving the MDGs, targets are set for each goal that provides the actual development statistics that will be measured. See

Box 3.1 for a listing of the goals and targets that comprise the MDGs. The most recent report from the United Nations indicates that several of the MDGs will be, or are on target to be, attained. Unfortunately, there are several goals that will not be met by the initial 2015 deadline (United Nations 2013).

Box 3.1 - The Millennium Development Goals

Goal 1: Eradicate extreme poverty and hunger

Target 1.A: Halve the proportion of people whose income is less than one dollar a day
Target 1.B: Achieve full and productive employment and decent work for all, including women and young people
Target 1.C: Halve the proportion of people who suffer from hunger

Goal 2: Achieve universal primary education

Target 2.A: Ensure that children everywhere, boys and girls alike, are able to complete primary schooling

Goal 3: Promote gender equality and empower women

Target 3.A: Eliminate gender disparities in all levels of education

Goal 4: Reduce child mortality

Target 4.A: Reduce by two-thirds the under-five mortality rate

Goal 5: Improve maternal health

Target 5.A: Reduce by three-quarters the maternal mortality ratio
Target 5.B: Achieve universal access to reproductive health

Goal 6: Combat HIV/AIDS, malaria, and other diseases

Target 6.A: Have halted and begun to reverse the spread of HIV/AIDS
Target 6.B: Achieve, by 2010, universal access to treatment for HIV/AIDS for all those who need it
Target 6.C: Have halted and begun to reverse the incidence of malaria and other major diseases

Goal 7: Ensure environmental sustainability

Target 7.A: Integrate the principles of sustainable development into country policies and programs and reverse the loss of environmental resources
Target 7.B: Reduce biodiversity loss
Target 7.C: Halve the proportion of people without sustainable access to safe drinking water and basic sanitation
Target 7.D: By 2020, to have achieved a significant improvement in the lives of at least 100 million slum dwellers

> **Goal 8: Develop a global partnership for development**
>
> Target 8.A: Develop further an open, rule-based, predictable, non-discriminatory trading and financial system
> Target 8.B: Address the special needs of the least developed countries, including through tariff and quota free access for the least developed countries' exports; debt relief for heavily indebted poor countries; and more generous ODA for countries committed to poverty reduction
> Target 8.C: Address the special needs of landlocked developing countries and small island developing states
> Target 8.D: Deal comprehensively with the debt problems of developing countries
> Target 8.E: In cooperation with pharmaceutical companies, provide access to affordable essential drugs in developing countries
> Target 8.F: In cooperation with the private sector, make available the benefits of new technologies, especially information and communications

Hulme and Fukudu-Parr (2009) argue the MDGs are an embodiment of a "super-norm" of poverty alleviation that emerged in the 1990s through various international summits. A super-norm is a norm[5] that is comprised of several sub-norms. In the case of the MDGs, the sub-norms relate to health, education, female empowerment, environmental sustainability, and poverty reduction. Taken together, these sub-norms assist in the realization of the super-norm.

Understanding how norms (or super-norms) are accepted and diffused may provide insight into how and why the IADB accepted (or rejected) the super-norm of poverty alleviation. Finnemore and Sikkink (1998) provide three reasons why an organization would accept a norm: to achieve conformity with others, out of a desire for international legitimacy, or out of fear of being shamed by other adopters (i.e. acceptance for "self-esteem" reasons). Similarly, Simmons et al. (2007) believe norms diffuse through coercion, competition, learning, and/or emulation. Still, other scholars find that organizational culture can influence whether norms are accepted. These scholars have noted the power of the leader in affecting change in organizations. Cox (1969) claims that institutional leaders have a certain latitude to advance organizational goals but must do so within the constraints of member states' interests. Barnett and Finnemore (2004) make a similar argument and focus their analysis on the influence of, and constraints on, the United Nations' Secretary General.

In 2003 the IADB stated its commitment to reducing poverty in the region (IADB 2003), and declared its intention to assist member countries achieve the MDGs (IADB 2003). This signals acceptance of the super-norm of poverty alleviation on the part of the IADB but does not indicate why it would do so. There is no indication that the World Bank or any other international organization coerced the IADB, or that the IADB was seeking international legitimacy through its acceptance of the MDGs, or that it was emulating other organizations. A simple answer is that a norm of poverty alleviation has always been present because these types of projects have been undertaken by the IADB since its inception. However, this explanation does not explain why the IADB created several new initiatives that assist member countries achieve development targets after the adoption of the MDGs. To help understand this situation, the following section examines project funding at the IADB to understand what affect poverty alleviation norms and the adoption of the MDGs had on the organization.

The Millennium Development Goals and the Inter-American Development Bank

One way the IADB could engage with the MDGs is to adjust their internal operations. Specifically, it could create new policies and/or business units. Or, the IADB could insert more MDG-related goals in the loans and projects it funds. Another way to incorporate the MDGs into the IADB's operations is to fund more projects relating to poverty alleviation. The following section highlights how the MDGs have affected the IADB, starting with new policies, then moving on to an analysis of project documents prior as well as subsequent to the adoption of the IADBs and an analysis of the project types funded by the IADB.

In terms of formal pronouncements of the IADB as it relates to poverty alleviation and the MDGs, the IADB released a strategy document in 2003 that incorporated the MDGs into the organizational goals of the Bank. Moving forward, the goals of sustainable economic development and poverty reduction/promotion of social equity were to be the "two overarching goals" of the IADB (IADB 2003). While special emphasis was placed on reducing extreme poverty (IADB 2003), the Bank recognized that achieving this would require many other obstacles to be removed first. Hence, the IADB described an action plan that would reduce inequalities relating to access to health and education facilities, reduce the social barriers that hinder women and ethnic minorities, and promote good governance within each country so that money devoted to these goals would not be spent on inefficient or corrupt programs. Additionally, a 2005 report stated that the IADB created an Interdepartmental MDG Group to ensure the MDGs are represented in IADB activities (IADB 2005).

More recent developments at the IADB include the creation of the Division of Social Protection and Health. This segment of the organization focuses primarily on early childhood development (which encompasses healthcare, education, nutrition, and childcare for young children), youth at risk (similar to early childhood development but for older children and young adults), and poverty alleviation (primarily through assistance with conditional cash transfer systems). These objectives of the Division of Social Protection and Health fall in line with many of the MDGs, specifically the goals of eradicating poverty and hunger, achieving universal primary education, and reducing child mortality.

Although the IADB has created new departments and vocalized support for MDG-related issues, there remains a problem with relying solely on pronouncements from the IADB as it relates to the MDGs. The IADB may vocally support the MDGs because it is considered appropriate by the international community, without making any actual changes within the organization.[6] To determine the true effect of poverty alleviation norms on the IADB, several IADB projects were selected at random to determine how well the organization was performing compared to its pronouncements (see Table 3.1 for a list of the projects examined).

Analyzed first is the Honduras 2011 project, which directly targeted preschool aged children in very poor areas and sought to improve the quality of first through sixth-grade education in schools servicing poorer areas. In this project document, the MDGs are explicitly mentioned because of the project's goal of increasing technology in the classroom (Goal 8, Target F). However, of the ten projects selected, it was the only one that specifically mentioned the MDGs. Other projects examined had components that were relevant to the MDGs, but no specific mention was made in the project documents. For example, the Paraguay 2009 project provided technical assistance to better target public spending for social and employment policies within the country (Goal 1, Target B). Additionally, it sought to increase access to healthcare facilities in poor areas of the country (Goals 4–6). Furthermore, the Nicaragua 2011 project sought to increase quality housing options for low and very low-income individuals through the use of direct subsidies, improve water and sanitation facilities (Goal 7, Target C), and restore roadways to informal urban neighborhoods (Goal 7, Target D).

Consistent with the MDGs, the IADB recognizes that inequality of all sorts is prevalent throughout Latin America. Specifically expanding from the traditional conception of socioeconomic inequalities, the IADB acknowledges inequalities related to race and ethnicity factors are present and even includes concerns of indigenous populations (IADB 2010). True to the pronouncement of the organization, several of the projects analyzed included a gender or an indigenous population component. The Paraguay 2009 project included a goal of incorporating a gender element to social policies in the country, as well as being more inclusive of indigenous peoples. Another example is the Venezuelan 2005 project that provided technical assistance for a watershed district. It acknowledged the presence of, and mandated cooperation with, the local indigenous peoples who inhabit portions of the land affected by the project.

What is important to note is that while none of these projects directly relate to the MDGs, they still reflect the larger super-norm of poverty alleviation by seeking the cooperation of women and indigenous people in projects or ensuring access to appropriate resources. It is interesting to note that although the MDGs only include gender equality, the IADB has expanded the understanding of eradicating inequalities to indigenous populations. This indicates the IADB has taken the MDGs as a baseline and tailored it to the realities of Latin America.

Table 3.1 IADB projects

Year	Country	Project title	Project identifier	Sector	Project amount
1997	Brazil	Vocational Education Reform Program	BR-0247	Education	$250,000,000
2011	Honduras	Primary Education and Technology Integration Program	HO-L1062	Education	$37,000,000
1998	Bolivia	Water Quality Management and Control Study for Piraí River	TC9801178	Environment and Natural Disasters	$200,000
2005	Venezuela	Integral Management of the Caroni River Watershed	VE-L1006	Environment and Natural Disasters	$14,000,000
1998	Guatemala	Development of Rural Women's Role in the Consolidation of Democracy	TC9701419	Social Investment	$1,170,000
2009	Paraguay	Support Ministry of "Hacienda" in Social Policy Design	PR-T1078	Social Investment	$1,600,000
1999	Guyana	Low Income Settlements	GY0052	Urban Development and Housing	$27,000,000
2011	Nicaragua	Housing and Comprehensive Habitat Improvement Implementation	NI-L1053	Urban Development and Housing	$20,000,000
1996	Mexico	Sanitation for the Valley of Mexico	ME0179	Water and Sanitation	$365,000,000
2013	Dominican Republic	Potable Water and Sanitation Investment Program	DR-X1005	Water and Sanitation	$35,000,000

The IADB is even getting involved in environmental issues. The IADB realizes the need for sustainability by maximizing "positive environmental and social impacts while minimizing risks to natural and human capital" (IADB 2012). As part of this initiative, the IADB focuses on ensuring that water resources are available and lasting. An example of this type of project is the Venezuela 2005 project that sought to reduce sediment build-up in a river due to improper and/or environmentally harmful agriculture and mining practices in the area (Goal 7, Targets A and C). This sediment can have an adverse effect on the health of the population (as waste products are flowing down the river), as well as decrease hydro-electric power generated by the river.

While it does appear that the MDGs are reflected in the projects analyzed, they are not explicitly discussed in the project documents submitted at the time of project approval (except in the case of the Honduras 2011 project). However, when comparing the above project documents to those completed prior to the adoption of the MDGs, the form and content are nearly identical. For example, women and indigenous issues were present in projects prior to the MDGs. In Guatemala, the 1998 project encouraged more female political participation, especially within the indigenous community. This ranged from encouraging participation in civil society groups to support for running for political office in municipal, regional, and/or national elections. Also, environmental issues were present in a 1998 Bolivian project that sought to reduce water contamination in a river, by both assisting with clean-up and providing education for future prevention (Goal 7, Targets A, C, and D).

Additionally, the Mexico 1996 project sought to improve drainage problems related to wastewater pollution (Goal 7, Target C). It was hoped the project would improve the healthy living conditions of those living in the area, 70 percent of whom were living below the poverty line. Another example is the Brazil 1997 project, which sought to provide educational opportunities that would result in meaningful employment (Goal 1, Target B). This was done by attempting to tailor vocational schools to best meet the demand for labor in each school's immediate vicinity. Finally, projects to provide affordable housing were evidenced by a Guyana 1999 project that provided funding to allow the government to divest large amounts of land and sell it at significantly below market rates to low and very low-income individuals. This provided quality housing to a segment of the population that may not otherwise have had that opportunity (Goal 7, Target D).

Overall, the IADB appears to be successfully implementing plans and programs to assist member countries manage their MDGs. However, based on the project documents examined above, projects approved prior to the creation of MDGs still had components relating to poverty alleviation. This finding indicates that the MDGs did not affect the wording or emphasis of individual projects because MDG-related goals were already being included in project documents.

A final possibility is that the MDGs affected the IADB through its choice of the sectors the organization funded. Tables 3.2 and 3.3 provide project data in five-year increments.[7] Table 3.2 includes the average percentage of projects that relate to each sector (e.g. industry, social investment, and health) for any given year in that time period. Table 3.3 shows the average percentage of funding those projects received (as a function of total project expenditures) in that time period. As is noted within both tables, infrastructure projects comprised most of the projects (in terms of both number and amount) that the IADB completed in the early years. Social services projects have stayed relatively consistent in terms of the number of projects each year. However, the funded amount began to increase in the mid-1980s.

After the adoption of the MDGs, the IADB published *Poverty Reduction and Promotion of Social Equity*, in which the organization restated its goal for both sustainable economic development alongside poverty reduction and the promotion of social equity (IADB 2003). To this end, the IADB recognized that it had a comparative advantage over other organizations to provide assistance for Regional Integration, Competitiveness, Modernization of the State, and Social Development (IADB 2003). The first two relate to sustainable economic development by providing more economic opportunities to the citizens of each country. The latter two seek to improve the social conditions of people. Specifically, modernization of the state seeks to increase democratic governance and promote political participation, especially amongst the poor (IADB 2003).

As is noted in Tables 3.2 and 3.3, these four project types have seen an upsurge in the average number of projects funded, as well as an increase in the allocation of funding. The number of regional integration projects may not have increased much as a percentage of total projects; however, the amount funded has increased significantly. This is especially true between 2006 and 2010. Modernization of the state projects have remained relatively steady in the percentage of projects completed annually; however, these projects have also seen a significant increase in project funding. Social investment projects have seen an increase in both total number of projects compared to other sectors and the amount funded. It appears this increase began in the early 1990s and reached its peak in the early 2000s. These projects fell slightly between 2006 and 2010, but are still much higher now than historically.

Similar to above, where project documents included MDG-related issues prior to the adoption of the MDGs, the IADB began increasing social investment projects prior to the adoption of the MDGs. One possible reason for this might be the history of social development and poverty alleviation projects at the IADB. Additionally, past research suggests that the organization's presidents can have a significant influence on project priorities. Tussie (1995) notes that each of the IADB's presidents has shaped the institution's economic philosophy and lending priorities. More germane to the present study, Culpeper (1997) believes Enrique Iglesias (elected president of the IADB in 1989) was a strong advocate for social sector investment. To investigate the claim that IADB presidents exert significant influence on the types

Table 3.2 Five-year average of total IADB projects by sector

Sector	1961–1965	1966–1970	1971–1975	1976–1980	1981–1985	1986–1990	1991–1995	1996–2000	2001–2005	2006–2010	2011–2013
Agriculture and rural development	24%	24%	25%	30%	22%	18%	11%	5%	5%	5%	5%
Industry	13%	11%	7%	10%	12%	8%	4%	2%	1%	0%	0%
Sustainable tourism	0%	1%	2%	1%	2%	1%	1%	1%	2%	2%	1%
Energy	4%	4%	9%	8%	9%	7%	5%	4%	3%	7%	8%
Transportation	3%	8%	10%	6%	5%	6%	6%	5%	4%	6%	5%
Infrastructure subtotal	44%	48%	53%	55%	50%	40%	27%	17%	15%	20%	19%
Water and sanitation	11%	6%	8%	7%	5%	6%	5%	5%	3%	6%	6%
Education	7%	8%	9%	6%	7%	7%	6%	7%	4%	4%	5%
Urban development and housing	11%	5%	2%	3%	4%	6%	3%	4%	4%	3%	4%
Social investment	0%	2%	0%	1%	1%	2%	4%	12%	17%	11%	10%
Environment and natural disasters	1%	1%	4%	6%	5%	7%	8%	9%	9%	7%	8%
Health	0%	0%	2%	3%	3%	5%	4%	4%	3%	2%	4%
Science and technology	0%	3%	2%	2%	2%	3%	2%	2%	2%	4%	3%
Social services Subtotal	30%	25%	27%	28%	27%	36%	32%	43%	42%	37%	40%
Financial markets and regional integration	4%	3%	3%	4%	4%	2%	7%	1%	3%	5%	7%
Private firms and SME development	0%	0%	0%	0%	0%	0%	7%	10%	16%	17%	9%

Sector	1961–1965	1966–1970	1971–1975	1976–1980	1981–1985	1986–1990	1991–1995	1996–2000	2001–2005	2006–2010	2011–2013
Reform/Modernization of the state	14%	12%	8%	7%	11%	12%	16%	21%	19%	14%	15%
Trade	1%	2%	3%	2%	3%	2%	0%	1%	3%	6%	5%
Other	7%	10%	6%	4%	5%	8%	11%	7%	2%	1%	5%
Economic and governmental subtotal	26%	27%	20%	17%	23%	24%	41%	40%	43%	43%	41%

Source: IADB Project Data, found at www.iadb.org/en/projects/. Compiled by author.

Table 3.3 Five-year average of IADB project amounts by sector

Sector	1961–1965	1966–1970	1971–1975	1976–1980	1981–1985	1986–1990	1991–1995	1996–2000	2001–2005	2006–2010	2011–2013
Agriculture and rural development	24%	32%	20%	23%	20%	20%	6%	4%	3%	3%	3%
Industry	19%	10%	13%	13%	17%	5%	2%	6%	4%	0%	1%
Sustainable tourism	0%	0%	1%	1%	1%	1%	2%	0%	1%	1%	1%
Energy	8%	18%	29%	22%	32%	26%	9%	8%	7%	11%	10%
Transportation	8%	17%	16%	11%	10%	12%	14%	9%	6%	15%	18%
Infrastructure subtotal	59%	77%	79%	70%	80%	64%	33%	27%	21%	30%	33%
Water and sanitation	18%	8%	7%	7%	7%	14%	10%	7%	2%	9%	12%
Education	2%	5%	6%	2%	3%	2%	5%	5%	4%	4%	5%
Urban development and housing	14%	5%	2%	1%	3%	7%	7%	8%	3%	4%	5%
Social investment	0%	0%	0%	0%	0%	0%	6%	13%	39%	11%	8%
Environment and natural disasters	1%	0%	2%	4%	1%	1%	4%	2%	2%	3%	4%
Health	0%	0%	1%	2%	1%	2%	2%	3%	2%	2%	4%
Science and technology	0%	2%	2%	3%	2%	3%	3%	1%	1%	2%	1%
Social services subtotal	35%	20%	20%	19%	17%	29%	37%	39%	53%	35%	39%
Financial markets and regional integration	1%	2%	1%	1%	2%	2%	6%	2%	4%	15%	9%
Private firms and SME development	0%	0%	0%	0%	0%	0%	1%	1%	3%	5%	2%

Sector	1961–1965	1966–1970	1971–1975	1976–1980	1981–1985	1986–1990	1991–1995	1996–2000	2001–2005	2006–2010	2011–2013
Reform/Modernization of the state	0%	0%	0%	0%	0%	5%	21%	31%	17%	13%	14%
Trade	5%	1%	0%	9%	1%	0%	1%	0%	2%	2%	3%
Other	0%	0%	0%	1%	0%	0%	1%	0%	0%	0%	0%
Economic and governmental subtotal	6%	3%	1%	11%	3%	7%	30%	34%	26%	35%	28%

Source: IADB Project Data, found at www.iadb.org/en/projects/, compiled by author.

of projects funded, Table 3.4 presents the average loans by sector during each president's tenure.

The first president of the IADB was Felipe Herrera (1960–1970). From the beginning of his term as president he championed social development projects, especially in education, health, and sanitation (IADB 1997). During Herrera's tenure, infrastructure projects received significant funding, but so too did water and sanitation projects.

In 1971, Antonio Ortíz Mena became the second IADB president. Previously, he was secretary of finance in Mexico, 1958–1970. During his years in the Mexican government, the country experienced increases in gross national product of approximately 6.5 percent per year, industrialization and urbanization increased significantly, and agricultural production rose. Social welfare indicators increased; specifically, life expectancy and literacy rates (Looney 1978). Ortíz Mena is credited as the originator of "stabilizing development" policies in Mexico (Davis 2010), which encouraged both private savings and investment and public spending on projects that would stimulate growth in the private sector (Mena 1969; Looney 1978). Stabilizing development prioritized public spending on projects to benefit the private sector, with decreasing amounts allocated to the social sectors (e.g. health and education).

Given this background, it should not be surprising that Ortíz Mena's tenure with the IADB brought with it an emphasis on projects that would benefit the private sector. Table 3.4 indicates that this is what occurred. Compared to his predecessor, social services projects decreased by the amount that infrastructure projects increased.

Enrique Iglesias was the third president of the IADB and served from 1988 until 2005. Prior to his service with the bank, he was executive secretary of the Economic Commission for Latin America and the Caribbean (ECLAC) as well as foreign affairs minister of Uruguay. At ECLAC, Iglesias wrote that while Latin America experienced strong economic growth historically, the benefits of that growth only benefited a few:

> The development of the last thirty years was thus marked by a basic ambivalence. While on the one hand it revealed the region's capacity for increasing its material output at a fairly high rate, on the other it reflected a flagrant inability to distribute fairly the results of this more rapid material progress.
> (Iglesias 1979: 15)

Under his leadership, the IADB began to focus its projects in the social services sector again. Tussie (1995) notes the emphasis Iglesias placed on poverty alleviation and social development alongside economic development concerns. According to Table 3.4, the IADB nearly doubled the resources to the social services sector during Iglesias' tenure.

Iglesias' successor, Luis Alberto Moreno, took office in 2005 and kept funding levels for projects in the various sectors similar to those of his predecessor. Prior to the IADB, he held various public and private positions in

Table 3.4 Average loans by sector under IADB presidents

Sector	Felipe Herrera 1961–1970	Antonio Ortiz Mena 1971–1988	Enrique Iglesias 1989–2005	Luis Alberto Moreno 2006–2013
Agriculture and rural development	27%	21%	6%	3%
Industry	15%	13%	4%	1%
Sustainable tourism	0%	1%	1%	1%
Energy	13%	27%	11%	11%
Transportation	13%	12%	10%	16%
Infrastructure subtotal	68%	74%	32%	32%
Water and sanitation	13%	9%	6%	10%
Education	3%	4%	5%	4%
Urban development and housing	10%	3%	6%	4%
Social investment	0%	0%	17%	9%
Environment and natural disasters	1%	2%	2%	4%
Health	0%	2%	2%	3%
Science and technology	1%	2%	2%	2%
Social services subtotal	28%	22%	40%	36%
Financial markets and regional integration	1%	1%	4%	12%
Private firms and SME development	0%	0%	2%	4%
Reform/Modernization of the state	0%	0%	21%	13%
Trade	3%	3%	1%	3%
Other	0%	0%	0%	0%
Economic and governmental subtotal	4%	4%	28%	32%

Source: ADB Project Data, found at www.iadb.org/en/projects/, compiled by author.

Colombia, one of which was as a manager for social policies. With the IADB, Moreno has directed his efforts at reforming the internal administration and project management functions (IADB 2014). He has placed special emphasis on improving how the IADB evaluates project results. If Table 3.4 is any indication, it does not appear Moreno has significantly changed the project funding allocation from that of Iglesias.

Again, while it does not appear the actual adoption of the MDGs has had a significant impact on the IADB, the poverty alleviation super-norm present in the 1990s that led to their creation was already present in the organization. Support of this finding is that poverty alleviation projects were undertaken with regularity prior to the adoption of the MDGs. Additionally, this research illustrates the influence that presidents of the IADB have over the types of projects the organization funds. The increase in social services projects beginning in the early 1990s coincided with the election of Enrique V. Iglesias as president of the IADB. His past experience contributed to his understanding of the need for a more holistic approach to development, including more social development projects in the region. Ultimately, if the MDGs have affected the IADB at all, it has provided an opportunity for the Bank to highlight projects and sectoral work it had been engaged in for some time prior to the creation of the MDGs.

Conclusion

The reason provided for the IADB's acceptance of the poverty alleviation norms of the 1990s can be attributed to two factors. First, the IADB has a history of social development projects. While it began primarily as an economic development organization for countries in Latin America, the seeds of social development were planted with the creation of the Bank (Culpeper 1997) and fostered through support from member countries, with major pushes from the United States at times (Tussie 1995). The second reason for the increased focus on poverty alleviation projects in the mid-1990s is the influence of past-president Enrique Iglesias. As this paper has shown, presidents of the IADB have significant influence in determining which sectors will receive increased funding. Additionally, it is interesting to note that all of this appears to have been done independently of the World Bank. Although the two institutions work closely with one another in the region, there is no indication the World Bank placed pressure on the IADB to accept and implement more social development and/or poverty alleviation projects. Tussie (1995) even notes the IADB has been more active with social development and poverty alleviation in the region than the World Bank.

Clearly, the IADB accepted the poverty alleviation norm present in the 1990s, but the fact that it does not explicitly use the language of the MDGs is consistent with past research on the organization. Feinberg (2006) analyzes how the IADB and the Organization of American States adopted mandates from Latin American summits. The author claims the IADB accepts the mandates placed upon them by the summits, but works toward their accomplishment by pursuing activities that are similar to but not the same as those of other international organizations. From the analysis above, it appears the IADB again chose to pursue MDG-related activities independently of other organizations (such as the United Nations and World Bank).

Although the MDGs are set to expire in 2015, there should be little concern that the IADB will be dropping poverty alleviation from its project agenda as long as this emphasis is maintained with current and future presidents of the organization. As noted in Tables 3.2 and 3.3, these types of project were being conducted prior to the creation of the MDGs. In addition, the documents produced by the Bank do not indicate a significant shift away from this area. There have been significant gains in poverty reduction and increased living standards in Latin America (United Nations 2013), but much is still needed. As such, the IADB is ready to continue to provide funding to reduce poverty in the region.

Notes

1 The author would like to thank the editors, the multilateral development bank panel participants at the 2014 International Studies Association, and an anonymous reviewer for their valuable feedback, as well as the Institute for Latin American Studies at the University of Nevada, Las Vegas for their grant support of this research project.
2 For a comprehensive history of the creation of the Inter-American Development Bank, especially for the numerous conferences held in the Americas to discuss the creation of such an institution, see Díaz-Bonilla and del Campo (2010).
3 Originally, only members of the Organization of American States were eligible for membership, but that restriction has since been lifted. Trinidad and Tobago, Barbados, Jamaica, the Bahamas, Surinam, Guyana, and Belize are also now members of the IADB.
4 If looking at voting power (which is the voting strength of an actor when considering the decision rules set forth by an organization), Strand (2003) finds that the United States has approximately two and a half times the voting power than its voting weight suggests. This indicates that the United States has even greater influence than it would initially appear.
5 A commonly shared definition of norms in the constructivist literature is "collective expectations for proper behavior of actors with a given identity" (Katzenstein 1996: 5).
6 In a different international financial institution, Vetterlein (2010) argues that the IMF accepted social development norms but has not internalized them. This is partly due to the economic background of IMF staff and an overall lack of social development expertise within the organization. There is a legitimate concern of publicly acknowledging a popular norm but not altering the behavior of the organization.
7 The sectors listed in the tables come directly from the IADB, while the grouping of sectors into the categories of infrastructure, social services, and economic and governmental are based on similarly presented information in Tussie (1995).

References

Barnett, M. and M. Finnemore. 2004. *Rules for the World: International Organizations in Global Politics*. Ithaca, NY: Cornell University Press.
Cox, R. W. 1969. "The Executive Head: An Essay on Leadership in International Organization." *International Organization* 23(2): 205–230.
Culpeper, R. 1997. *Titans or Behemoths*. Boulder, CO: Lynne Rienner Publishers.

Davis, D. E. 2010. *Urban Leviathan: Mexico City in the Twentieth Century*. Philadelphia, PA: Temple University Press.

Díaz-Bonilla, E. and M. V. del Campo. 2010. *A Long and Winding Road: The Creation of the Inter-American Development Bank*. University of Manchester: Lulu.

Feinberg, R. E. 2006. "Presidential Mandates and Ministerial Institutions: Summitry of the Americas, the Organization of American States (OAS) and the Inter-American Development Bank (IDB)." *The Review of International Organizations* 1(1): 69–94.

Finnemore, M. and K. Sikkink. 1998. "International Norm Dynamics and Political Change." *International Organization* 52(4): 887–917.

Hall, A.. 2007. "Social Policies in the World Bank: Paradigms and Challenges." *Global Social Policy* 7(2): 151–175.

Hulme, D. 2009. "The Millennium Development Goals (MDGs): A Short History of the World's Biggest Promise," Working Paper no. 100. University of Manchester: Brooks World Poverty Institute.

Hulme, D. and S. Fukudu-Parr. 2009. "International Norm Dynamics and 'the End of Poverty': Understanding the Millennium Development Goals (MDGs)," Working Paper no. 96. University of Manchester: Brooks World Poverty Institute.

Hulme, D. and J. Scott. 2013. "Governing Development: Power, Poverty, and Policy." In *Governing the World: Cases in Global Governance*, edited by S. Harman and D. Williams. New York: Routledge, pp. 28–45.

Iglesias, E. V. 1979. "Latin America on the Threshold of the 1980s." *CEPAL Review* 9: 7–44.

Inter-American Development Bank (IADB). 1978. *Proposal for the Sixth General Increase in the Resources of the Inter-American Development Bank*. Report to the Board of Governors. New York: Inter-American Development Bank.

Inter-American Development Bank (IADB). 1989. *Proposal for the Seventh General Increase in the Resources of the Inter-American Development Bank*. Report to the Board of Governors. New York: Inter-American Development Bank.

Inter-American Development Bank (IADB). 1994. *Report on the Eighth General Increase in the Resources of the Inter-American Development Bank*. Report to the Board of Governors. New York: Inter-American Development Bank.

Inter-American Development Bank (IADB). 1996. *Agreement Establishing the Inter-American Development Bank*. New York: Inter-American Development Bank.

Inter-American Development Bank (IADB). 1997. "Felipe Herrera's Enduring Vision." *Inter-American Development Bank*, 1 November. Available at www.iadb.org/en/news/webstories/1997-11-01/felipe-herreras-enduring-vision,7707.html (accessed 25 May 2015).

Inter-American Development Bank (IADB). 2003a. *Poverty Reduction and Promotion of Social Equity: Strategy Document*. New York: Inter-American Development Bank.

Inter-American Development Bank (IADB). 2003b. *Political Consensus Building: The Brasilia International Conference on the Millennium Development Goals in Latin America and the Caribbean*. New York: Inter-American Development Bank.

Inter-American Development Bank (IADB). 2005. *The Millennium Development Goals in Latin America and the Caribbean: Progress, Priorities, and IDB Support for their Implementation*. New York: Inter-American Development Bank.

Inter-American Development Bank (IADB). 2010a. *Report on the Ninth General Increase in the Resources of the Inter-American Development Bank*. Report to the Board of Governors. New York: Inter-American Development Bank.

Inter-American Development Bank (IADB). 2010b. *Operational Policy on Gender Equality in Development*. New York: Inter-American Development Bank.

Inter-American Development Bank (IADB). 2012. *Sustainability Report 2012*. New York: Inter-American Development Bank.

Inter-American Development Bank (IADB). 2014. "Luis Alberto Moreno." July. Available at www.iadb.org/en/about-us/departments/biographies,1347.html?bioid=4 (accessed 25 May 2015).

Katzenstein, P. J. 1996. "Introduction: Alternative Perspectives on National Security." In *The Culture of National Security: Norms and Identity in World Politics*, edited by P. J. Katzenstein. New York: Columbia University Press, pp. 1–32.

Looney, R. E. 1978. *Mexico's Economy; A Policy Analysis with Forecasts to 1990*. Boulder, CO: Westview Press.

Mena, A. O. 1969. *Stabilizing Development: A Decade of Economic Strategy in Mexico*. Mexico City: Ministry of Finance.

Noël, A. 2006. "The New Global Politics of Poverty." *Global Social Policy* 6(3): 304–333.

Organisation for Economic Co-operation and Development (OECD). 1996. *Shaping the 21st Century: The Contribution of Development Co-operation*. Paris: OECD.

Office of Evaluation and Oversight, IADB. 2003. *Poverty Reduction and the IDB: An Evaluation of the Bank's Strategy and Efforts*. RE-288. New York: Inter-American Development Bank.

Organization of American States. 1959. *Agreement Establishing the Inter-American Development Bank*. Treaty Series no. 14. Available at: www.iadb.org/en/news/webstories/1997-11-01/felipe-herreras-enduring-vision,7707.html (accessed 25 May 2015).

Simmons, B. A., F. Dobbin and G. Garrett. 2007. "Introduction: The Diffusion of Liberalization." In *The Global Diffusion of Markets and Democracy*, edited by B. A. Simmons, F. Dobbin and G. Garrett. Cambridge: Cambridge University Press, pp. 1–63.

Strand, Jonathan R. 2003. "Measuring Voting Power in an International Institution: The United States and the Inter-American Development Bank." *Economics of Governance* 4(1): 19–36.

Tussie, Diana. 1995. *The Inter-American Development Bank*. Boulder, CO: Lynne Rienner Publishers, Inc.

United Nations. 2008. *The Millennium Development Goals Report: 2008*. New York: United Nations.

United Nations. 2013. *The Millennium Development Goals Report: 2013*. New York: United Nations.

United Nations Development Programme. 1990. *Human Development Report*. Oxford: Oxford University Press.

Vetterlein, A. 2010. "Lacking Ownership: The IMF and its Engagement with Social Development as a Policy Norm." In *Owning Development: Creating Policy Norms in the IMF and the World Bank*, edited by S. Park and A. Vetterlein. Cambridge: Cambridge University Press, pp. 93–112.

White, J. 1970. *Regional Development Banks: A Study of Institutional Style*. London: Penna.

World Bank. 1990. *World Development Report*. Oxford: Oxford University Press.

4 Civil society and policy reforms in the Asian Development Bank

Anders Uhlin[1]

During the first decades of its existence, the Asian Development Bank (ADB) did not provoke much public criticism despite being a nontransparent and unaccountable international organization (IO) with fundamental impact on the lives of many people across Asia. However, since the 1990s, increasingly well-organized civil society networks have monitored ADB projects, criticized the Bank's approach to development, and challenged its internal policy processes, particularly the lack of transparency and accountability to project-affected people. Beginning in the 1990s, and increasingly so in the 2000s, the ADB has implemented several policies aiming at increasing transparency, strengthening accountability and preventing negative effects of its projects on vulnerable communities and the environment. This raises the question of to what extent civil society organizations (CSOs) have played a role in these reform processes.

The case of the ADB is far from unique. Political decisions with fundamental implications for a large number of people are increasingly taken in governance arrangements beyond the nation-state. The increasing importance of IOs and other forms of global and regional governance raises questions about democratic legitimacy. Most features associated with democracy at the national and local level are absent in global and regional governance. IO officials are not elected and there are few mechanisms for affected people to hold an IO accountable. Decisions are generally taken by a small group of people in a way that lacks both transparency and broader participation. Far from the democratic ideal of political equality, decision-making in global and regional governance is heavily influenced by asymmetric power relations in terms of economic and military resources. Structural inequalities are generally even more pronounced on the global level than within nation-states. Previously, the legitimacy of IOs has to a large extent been based on their perceived problem-solving capacity (see Introduction). IOs have been considered legitimate to the extent that they contribute to solving the problems that made states create them. This performance-based source of legitimacy has increasingly been found inadequate. IOs and other global governance institutions are now challenged not only for perceived shortcomings in their performance but also for their undemocratic nature.

Since the 1990s there has been a strong trend of IOs opening up for civil society participation. Today there are in fact very few IOs that do not provide some form of access for civil society actors, reflecting a genuine "transnational turn in global governance" (Tallberg et al. 2013: 1). Indeed, civil society participation has become a norm in global governance (Reimann 2006; Scholte 2011a). Several observers see increased civil society participation as a potential solution to the lack of democracy beyond the nation-state. Extant research has found many examples of civil society actors contributing to strengthening accountability and increasing transparency of specific IOs (Fox and Brown 1998; O'Brien et al. 2000; Scholte 2011a). In this context, it is of great significance to examine how CSOs can influence policy reforms in IOs. This chapter addresses the question: to what extent have civil society actors influenced policy reforms in the ADB?

The chapter also makes a specific contribution to research on multilateral development banks (MDBs). Examining the complex dynamics of internal and external actors in ADB policy reform processes, it opens up the "black box" of MDBs (Bøås and McNeill 2003: Ch. 4). Extant research has developed a number of theories explaining policy reforms in MDBs (and other IOs). Neoliberal institutionalism privileges the rational design of IOs by states (Koremenos et al. 2001). Critical IPE perspectives emphasize what Gramsci calls "hegemonic power" (Bøås and McNeill 2003). Others have viewed IOs as bureaucracies and emphasized their autonomy from both states and capital (Barnett and Finnemore 2004). Constructivist approaches focus on "policy norms" (Park and Vetterlein 2010). The approach taken in this chapter is distinct from all these theoretical perspectives. Focusing specifically on civil society actors, it is generally in line with constructivist approaches, though it mainly draws on – and contributes to – research on civil society in global governance. It should be stressed that the aim is not to provide a comprehensive explanation to the policy reforms under investigation. The aim of the chapter is limited to providing a deeper understanding of the role of one type of actors in the reform processes. Through its detailed analysis of specific policy reform processes in order to assess civil society influence, the study not only enriches our understanding of the working of the RDBs but also contributes to the broader literature on civil society and the democratization of global and regional governance.

The ADB first introduced policies on information and disclosure in 1994, an inspection function in 1995, and safeguard policies on involuntary resettlement in 1995, on indigenous people in 1998, and the environment in 2002. While briefly covering these early policies, the main focus here is on policy review processes in the 2000s that resulted in a new accountability mechanism (AM) in 2003, a new public communication policy (PCP) in 2005, and a new safeguard policy in 2009. These are the major policies related to transparency and accountability, which has been linked to the democratic credentials of IOs. The selected policy review processes are particularly interesting to examine because they all featured extensive external consultations and very active civil society engagement. Both the AM and the PCP were revised again in 2012 and 2011 respectively, following intense civil society advocacy. Due to space limitations, however, I limit this analysis to the processes leading up to the establishment of the first version of the AM and PCP.

Following this introduction, the next section specifies the meaning of civil society influence on IOs and elaborates on the methodology of the study. The case of ADB is then presented, with a focus on the development of civil society activism targeting the Bank. Then follows three sections tracing civil society influence on the major recent policy reforms of the ADB: the AM, the PCP, and the safeguard policies. The chapter ends with a concluding remark summarizing the main arguments.

Civil society influence on international organizations

In general terms, influence can be defined as "an actor's ability to shape a decision in line with her preferences" (Dür 2008: 561). Hence, influence implies the control over political outcomes (Dür and Bièvre 2007: 3). CSO policy advocacy can have influence in different phases of the policy process, including agenda setting, decision making, implementation, and evaluation. Keck and Sikkink (1998: 25) distinguish between influence on agenda setting, the discursive positions of states and IOs, institutional procedures, policy change, and state behavior. This means that policy advocates can influence both process and outcome (Corell and Betsill 2008: 27).

Extant research indicates that CSOs have most influence on agenda setting (Friedman et al. 2005: 160; Joachim and Locher 2009: 173; McKeon 2009: 132). In a study of NGO advocacy at UN-sponsored world conferences Friedman et al. (2005: 160) concluded that NGOs influenced agenda setting, but governments controlled decision making and determined the extent of NGO-access. Similarly, McKeon (2009) claims that the increasing civil society access to the UN system mainly means episodic participation instead of meaningful involvement in global governance. Nevertheless, CSOs can have policy influence that goes beyond having an impact on agenda setting. Based on comparative case studies of interaction between the World Bank, NGOs and grassroots movements, Fox and Brown (1998: 2) conclude that "the Bank has to a small and uneven but significant degree become more publicly accountable as the result of protest, ongoing public scrutiny, and empowering effect on insider reformists". The role of CSOs in strengthening the accountability of the World Bank has been relatively thoroughly researched (Fox and Brown 1998; O'Brien et al. 2000, Chs 2, 4; Clark 2002; Clark, Fox and Treakle 2003; Park 2010b; Pallas 2013). Regional development banks have received less scholarly attentions (but see Tussie and Casaburi 2000; Bøås and McNeill 2003).

Proving an actor's influence on a specific process or outcome is methodologically very difficult. In addition to the general problem of proving causality, there are several more specific methodological problems, including the complexities of different channels of influence (inside, outside, structural power), the presence of counter-lobbying, and the possibility of influence on different stages of the policy process (Dür 2008: 561). Moreover, civil society influence on IOs often works through the power of states (Pallas and Uhlin 2014). Established methods for measuring civil society/interest group influence include *preference attainment, process-tracing*, and *attributed influence* (Dür 2008). Following the logic of methodological triangulation, I will use all three. I will interpret as an indication of a civil society actor's influence on ADB if a) I find similarities between initiatives from the actor and decisions on, and implementation of, ADB reforms (preference attainment), and b) it can be established that the sequence of events was such that civil society initiatives preceded the decision on ADB reform (process-tracing), and c) there are testimonies about the actor's influence by several different actors involved in the process (attributed influence) (Corell and Betsill 2008; Scholte 2011b: 83). It should also be stressed that the aim of this research is to further our understanding of the dynamics of civil society engagement with IOs in light of possible democratic implications – not to specify the relative influence of CSOs compared to other actors within or outside IOs.

This methodology of analyzing influence requires several different kinds of empirical material. The study draws on extensive empirical data, including relevant ADB and CSO documents, accessed on various websites or acquired during fieldwork, as well as more than 50 qualitative interviews with representatives of ADB and a broad spectrum of regional civil society actors.

Civil society advocacy targeting ADB[2]

The limited previous research on civil society engagement with ADB has either taken a bottom-up perspective focusing on specific protests (Tadem 2003) or a top-down perspective analyzing the way ADB has granted access to a broad set of transnational actors in order to gain functional benefits (Tallberg et al. 2013: Ch. 6). While both studies provide important insights, they have clear limitation from the perspective of the present study. The former study is limited to one specific social movement campaign and, hence, does not cover the full spectrum of civil society advocacy targeting ADB. The latter study draws entirely on ADB sources. It contains no reference to CSO documents or interviews with civil society activists and thus underestimates the amount of contestation and protest.

Civil society advocacy targeting the ADB has emerged since the late 1980s. One of the first civil society campaigns on ADB was carried out in 1988 by the Asian NGO Coalition (ANGOC) and the US-based Environmental Policy Institute (later Friends of the Earth). In 1989 CSOs began to attend ADB annual meetings. In 1992 representatives of a number of mainly Philippine-based CSOs decided to create a "NGO Working Group on ADB" with a secretariat in Manila. An important civil society campaign in the early 1990s focused on the Masinloc coal-fired thermal power plant project in the Philippines. Protests by the local population and transnational NGOs delayed

64 *Anders Uhlin*

the project for several years, but finally the power plant was built. However, the negative publicity shifted the balance in favor of reformers within ADB (Bøås and McNeill 2003: 94).

The NGO Working Group also criticized a number of other policies and projects during ADB annual meetings, through letters and other publications and in direct dialogue with ADB management and staff. In 1998 and 1999 the NGO Working Group was restructured and renamed the NGO Forum on ADB. Since then, most civil society advocacy targeting ADB has been coordinated by the NGO Forum on ADB.[3] With a secretariat in Quezon City, the Philippines, the NGO Forum has established regional working groups all over Asia. There is also participation from Europe, Japan, Australia and the United States. Members of the NGO Forum include national CSOs as well as grassroots groups and communities, including mass based movements such as vendors and farmers' associations. Focusing on social justice, gender, and the environment, members of the NGO Forum unite in a struggle against specific ADB policies, projects and programs that they believe threaten people's lives and the environment. The main goal of the NGO Forum is to make ADB responsible and accountable for the impacts of its projects and policies. The NGO Forum criticizes both ADB's development paradigm, which is described as top-down, pro-market and oriented toward economic growth, and the lack of accountability of the institution. The NGO Forum tries to influence ADB to adopt "poverty reduction focused and grassroots-based policies for sustainable development" and demands a thorough democratization of policy-making processes within the Bank.

Generally speaking, there are three critical civil society positions toward ADB (in addition to the uncritical partnership position of many project-implementing NGOs). First, some CSOs focus on shortcomings of specific projects that they think should be corrected. Second, the most active advocacy CSOs argue that ADB policies should be reformed. This might refer to both substantive development policies and internal governance policies. Third, some radical social movement activists believe that ADB should be abolished. The NGO Forum on ADB, in a sense, bridges all the three critical positions. While excluding CSOs having too close connections to ADB, and in particular those being funded by the Bank, its basic position is reformist in the way activists make use of the formal channels for engagement and focus on policy reform within ADB. Nevertheless, the NGO Forum also facilitates and supports a number of protest activities carried out by movements and associations with a more radical, uncompromising agenda.

The ADB accountability mechanism[4]

Like the other MDBs, ADB cannot be subject to any judicial proceedings. No legal action can be taken in a court against ADB in any of its member countries. Hence it is very difficult to hold the Bank accountable if it violates international declarations or national laws. ADB's own AM is therefore the

Table 4.1 Comparison between key civil society demands and final AM

Civil society demands in review of Inspection Panel	AM May 2003
Institutional structure	
Establish permanent Inspection Panel and abolish Board Inspection Committee.	Demand met. Inspection Panel and Board Inspection Committee replaced by a) Special Project Facilitator (SPF) and b) Compliance Review Panel (CPR), both permanent bodies.
Inspection function should be independent of management and board of directors.	Demand to some extent met. SPF should have integrity and independence from ADB operations departments and CPR should have integrity and independence from ADB management.
Scope	
Include private sector loans.	Demand met. Private sector loans included.
Accessibility	
Create a more user-friendly process assisting complainants. No requirements for citing non-compliance.	Demand to some extent met. Easier process. Outreach program. Advice should be provided to prospective complainants. No requirements for citing non-compliance.
Complaints should be accepted in local languages and information on inspection function made available in local languages.	Demand met. English working language, but complaints in any of the "official or national languages" of ADB's developing member countries accepted. Information available in languages other than English.
Quality of process	
The process should be transparent.	Demand to some extent met. Information disclosure concerning major aspects of the processes, but SPF and CRP will "exercise discretion" and not give any media interviews during any stage of the consultation and compliance review.
Site visits should be mandatory.	Demand not met. Site visits "in consultation with the borrowing country." Not mandatory, but "ADB expects that site visits will be a routine and non-controversial aspect of the accountability mechanism."
Ensure implementation of remedial measures.	Demand to some extent met. SPF and CRP will monitor implementation, but no details provided.

Sources: Bank Information Center 2002; ADB 2003.

only way people affected by ADB projects can hold the Bank accountable. In this section I trace the development of the ADB AM with a specific focus on possible civil society influence on this process. In particular I examine the review of the ADB Inspection Function and the establishment in 2003 of a new AM with a problem solving and a compliance review component. I begin with a process-tracing approach and then analyze preference attainment. I also refer to interviews with representatives of CSOs and ADB in order to track attributed influence.

In the 1990s there were increasing demands from civil society as well as donor governments that international financial institutions (IFIs) should become more accountable. As a reaction, the World Bank introduced an Inspection Panel in 1993 (Park 2010a). Other MDBs followed suit, partly modelling their AMs on the World Bank's Inspection Panel (Park 2014). In 1995 ADB introduced an Inspection Panel similar to that of the World Bank. From 1995 to 2003 ADB received eight requests for inspections. Only two were deemed eligible – the Samut Prakarn Wastewater Management Project in Thailand and the Chasma Right Bank Irrigation Project in Pakistan (ADB 2012: 2). Experiences from the two cases handled by the Inspection Panel were largely negative and indicated a number of problems. In 2001 ADB set up an internal working group to review the Inspection Function, with CSOs, including the NGO Forum on ADB, invited to take part in the review process. Taking advantage of this opportunity, a 40-page document, inclusive of detailed recommendations concerning the ADB Inspection Function, was submitted in March 2002 by the Washington-based Bank Information Center (BIC), the NGO Forum on ADB, Oxfam, International Rivers Network, and a number of NGOs from Pakistan and Sri Lanka (Bank Information Center et al. 2002). Additionally, BIC and the NGO Forum also organized a seminar on the Inspection Function at the ADB Annual Meeting in Shanghai in May 2002. The NGO Forum and other CSOs also participated in ADB's formal review process and submitted detailed recommendations for reform. Activists involved also stress the importance of informal contacts with reform-oriented representatives of the ADB Board of Directors, especially those representing Western governments. However, more radical strategies were also important in putting pressure on ADB and strengthening reformers within the Bank, for example the demonstrations at the ADB Annual Meeting in Chiang Mai in May 2000 (Bøås and McNeill 2003: 118–119; Tadem 2003).

The NGO Forum on ADB claims to have played an important role in shaping the new AM. Assessing preference attainment, a closer examination of the demands and recommendations put forward by CSOs indicates that many of these were indeed incorporated in the AM policy document.

Civil society demands concerning the ADB AM broadly fall into four categories. First, some demands focused on the institutional structure of the mechanism, in particular a set up that would guarantee the permanence and independence of the mechanism. Second, aspects of the scope of the mechanism were also discussed. Third, the accessibility of the AM for project-affected people was a major concern of CSOs. Fourth, several demands pertaining to the quality of the process were also put forward.

The old Inspection Panel was not a permanent body with inspection requests being handled by the Board Inspection Committee, consisting of ADB board members. Hence the process lacked independence. CSOs demanded that the Board Inspection Committee should be abolished and a permanent Inspection Panel independent of management and the board of directors should be established. The new AM included a consultation phase and a compliance review phase. People believing they were negatively affected by ADB-sponsored projects could submit complaints to the Office of the Special Project Facilitator (SPF), which reviewed the complaint and proposed a problem-solving method, including consultation with the complainants and ADB staff. If complainants were not satisfied with the outcome of this process, complaints could be submitted to the Compliance Review Panel (CRP). If the Panel considered the complaint eligible and received authorization from the board of directors it conducted a compliance review, in which all stakeholders were consulted. This eventually resulted in a report from the CRP to the board of directors, which made a final decision on the recommendations in the report. We can conclude that civil society demands have been met, at least to some extent, as the AM featured permanent and more independent bodies compared to the previous Inspection Panel.

Concerning the scope of the mechanism, only one specific civil society claim can be identified; the demand for the AM to apply to private sector loans too. This demand was met. The old Inspection Function was criticized for being too complicated, in practice preventing most affected stakeholders from using it. Communications were to be made in English, and complainants were required to cite what specific ADB policies they claimed the Bank did not comply with. CSOs demanded a more user-friendly process, assisting complainants instead of placing a burden on them. They suggested there should be no requirements for citing non-compliance. These demands were also met, at least to some extent. CSOs also demanded that complaints should be accepted in local languages and that information should be available in local languages. This demand on accessibility was also met.

Concerning the quality of the process, CSOs wanted more transparency. This demand was partly met as the final policy document states that there should be information disclosure concerning the major aspects of the processes, although it also states that the SPF and CPR will "exercise discretion" and not give any media interviews during any stage of the consultation and compliance review. CSOs also demanded that the implementation of remedial measures should be ensured by ADB. The final policy document states that SPF and CPR will monitor implementation, but it does not provide any further details.

One important CSO demand related to the quality of the process was not met, however. Based on the negative experiences of the Samut Prakarn case, CSOs suggested that site visits should be mandatory in the compliance review. On this aspect, the sovereignty claims of developing country governments were respected as ADB stated that site visits should be made "in consultation with the borrowing country" (ADB 2003: 14).

On balance, it can be concluded that most civil society demands and recommendations appeared in the final policy document. This finding, however, cannot on its own be taken as proof of civil society influence on ADB. Other actors also put forward demands similar to the CSOs. The review of the Inspection Panel took place in a general context of demands for increased accountability of IFIs. There was pressure from the G7 on all MDBs to create compliance mechanisms (ADB 2003: 42). ADB donor governments specifically demanded a strengthened and more independent and transparent inspection function and the inclusion of private sector projects (ADB 2000: 36–37). The consultation process indicated broad support for an independent AM, including a compliance review panel as an improved version of the World Bank panel (ADB 2003: 15). Hence, some of the CSO demands were shared by donor governments.

In addition to civil society advocacy and pressure from Western governments, clearly the World Bank was influential as a model. The ADB "borrowed" the idea of an Inspection Panel from the World Bank (Park 2014). The World Bank Inspection Panel was a permanent and independent unit separate from management and it reported directly to the board of directors, characteristics that were valued by CSOs and donor governments. The problem-solving approach of the Special Project Facilitator was partly inspired by the Compliance Advisor and Ombudsman of the International Finance Corporation and Multilateral Investment Guarantee Agency handling private sector projects within the World Bank group (ADB 2003: 38). While it would be too simplistic to think that the regional development banks just emulate World Bank policies (Bøås and McNeill 2003: 47), some diffusion effects seem obvious. However, even when acknowledging the influence of the World Bank as a model, we find indirect civil society impact, as pressure from civil society was behind the establishment of the World Bank Inspection Panel (Park 2010a). Unless there had been strong civil society campaigns, on the democratic deficits of IOs in general as well as specifically targeting ADB, it is highly unlikely that donor governments would have forced ADB to strengthen its accountability to non-state stakeholders.

The ADB public communications policy

The lack of transparency of the MDBs was rarely questioned during the first decades of their existence. Transparency is in tension both with norms of confidentiality in banking and state sovereignty as emphasized by the governments owning the MDBs (Nelson 2001: 1835). However, in the 1990s public demands for more transparency in global governance in general, and the MDBs in particular, were raised. CSOs protested against the secrecy that characterized decision-making as well as project implementation in the World Bank and the regional development banks. Under pressure from CSOs and donor governments, all the major MDBs adopted new information disclosure policies in the 1990s. The World Bank took the lead and Nelson (2001: 1838) assessed its transparency reforms as slightly more liberal than those of ADB and the other RDBs. The World Bank implemented its disclosure policies as a result of pressure from Western governments and NGO critics, in particular US-based environmental NGOs.

ADB established an Information Policy and Strategy and a Policy on Confidentiality and Disclosure of Information in 1994 (ADB 2005: i). As indicated in the name of the second policy, much emphasis was on confidentiality and CSOs generally considered ADB to remain highly non-transparent. While a lot of information was disclosed the most important information necessary for meaningful participation in the development of policies and projects were kept secret. A representative of the transnational CSO Focus on the Global South, commenting on the public communication policies of the World Bank and ADB, argued that "the primary aim of these practices appears to be to keep the public occupied with sometimes interesting, but largely irrelevant, information while the institutions go on with business as usual" (Guttal 2002: 105). She concluded that ADB and the World Bank are "highly non-transparent in their policy-programme formulation and decision-making" (Guttal 2002: 105).

Under pressure from CSOs and certain governments, ADB began a review of its information disclosure policy in August 2003. Process tracing shows that while criticizing ADB's consultation process for not being inclusive enough and calling for the inclusion of project-affected people (ADB 2004), CSOs participated in the review process by submitting reform proposals and taking part in consultations arranged by ADB. Public consultations on a draft policy were conducted in March/July 2004. At the consultation on ADB's draft PCP, New Delhi, India, 14 July 2004, 18 representatives of Indian CSOs participated. One participant, who was also a key member of the NGO Forum's team lobbying ADB on the transparency policy, argued that to the extent that there was support from governments for civil society demands for more openness, this support did not follow any particular pattern. There was no specific country that systematically promoted transparency and even China occasionally made positive contributions to the PCP (Interview, civil society activist, 4 November 2010).

A transnational civil society network headed by Article 19 (UK), the Bank Information Center (USA), and the Commonwealth Human Rights Initiative (India) provided detailed comments on the ADB's second PCP draft. The 14-page document dated November 24, 2004, was endorsed by 39 other NGOs and NGO networks, including the NGO Forum on ADB. The document notes "progressive elements" of the second draft, including recommendations from CSOs that had been incorporated in the new draft policy. Such "progressive elements" which have been important demands from CSOs were the disclosure of board of director schedules and minutes, a translation strategy, and transparency during project implementation. The document then lists previous civil society demands that have not been incorporated in the second draft. They include an independent appeals mechanism, more disclosure of private sector information, and disclosure of all board documents (Article 19 et al. 2004).

Following the preference attainment approach, I compare key civil society demands with the final version of the PCP established in 2005 and find some striking similarities (Table 4.2). Nelson (2001: 1838) identifies several dimensions of transparency: fullness and timeliness of disclosure, accessibility of documents, and mechanisms for recourse and influence. These categories are useful when providing a more systematic account of civil society demands in the review of ADB's information disclosure policy. The fullness and timeliness of disclosure were of central concern to CSOs. The point of departure for CSOs lobbying ADB was that public disclosure should be the rule. Exemptions should be few and clearly motivated. CSOs demanded the public disclosure of many more documents than was the case under the old policy. Types of documents specifically mentioned included draft Poverty Reduction Partnership Agreements, rehabilitation and replacement documents, review and monitoring reports, project reports submitted by borrowers, project audit reports (including complete budget breakdown), private sector financial information, tentative schedules and minutes of meetings with the board of directors, and voting records of executive directors. The overall demand was met as the PCP clearly stated that "/i/n the absence of a compelling reason for confidentiality, there shall be a presumption in favor of disclosure of information" (ADB 2005: 6). Disclosure was extended to some of the documents listed by CSOs, (including tentative schedules and minutes of board meetings), but the final version of the PCP still included many more exemptions than CSOs wanted. For instance, proceedings from board meetings and audit reports were not to be disclosed. On the timeliness of disclosure, CSOs demanded that board documents should be disclosed at least 30 days before board meetings. This demand was only partly met, as ADB made a difference between documents submitted to the board for information and for consideration. The PCP stated that:

> unless restricted by other provisions in the Policy, documents submitted to the board for information shall be disclosed no later than upon circulation to the Board, and documents submitted to the Board for consideration shall be disclosed no later than upon approval or endorsement by the Board.
>
> (ADB 2005: 7)

Moreover, CSOs demanded that information to affected people should be provided throughout all project stages. This demand was partly met as ADB committed to post on its website project documents produced from the early concept stage through implementation and evaluation.

Table 4.2 Comparison between key civil society demands in review of ADB information disclosure policy 2003–2005 and ADB PCP 2005

Civil society demands in review of information disclosure policy 2003–2005	PCP 2005
Fullness and timeliness of disclosure	
Public disclosure should be the rule. Exemptions should be few and clearly motivated. More should be disclosed, including draft Poverty Reduction Partnership Agreements, rehabilitation and replacement documents, review and monitoring reports, project reports submitted by borrowers, project audit reports (including complete budget breakdown), private sector financial information, tentative schedules and minutes of meetings with the board of directors, voting records of executive directors	Overall, demand met as PCP is based on a presumption in favor of disclosure, unless there is a valid reason for non-disclosure. Disclosure of some of the documents listed by CSOs, (including tentative schedules and minutes of board meetings), but still more exemptions than CSOs wanted. E.g. proceedings from board meetings and audit reports not disclosed.
Information to affected people should be provided throughout all project stages.	Demand to some extent met. ADB commits to post on its website project documents produced from the early concept stage through implementation and evaluation.
Board documents should be disclosed at least 30 days before board meetings.	Demand partly met. Documents submitted to the board for *information* disclosed no later than upon circulation to the board. Documents submitted to the board for *consideration* disclosed no later than upon approval or endorsement by the board.
Accessibility of documents	
Communication plans should be mandatory for all projects.	Demand not met. Communication plans only for certain projects and programs.
Resident missions should be responsible for information in local languages.	Demand met. Resident missions and representative offices will coordinate the translation of documents and review the accuracy of translations.
Mechanisms for recourse and influence	
There should be an independent appeals mechanism for those who believe their requests have been unreasonably denied.	Demand partly met. Appeals mechanism created, but not independent from management. Public Disclosure Advisory Committee (PDAC) will review requests for information that have been denied, but this is not an independent body. Chaired by the managing director general and reports directly to the president.
There should be feedback mechanisms to ensure two-way communication.	Demand to some extent met. PCP mentions importance of feedback and two-way communication, but provides no details on how this should be implemented.

Sources: ADB 2004; NGO Forum on ADB 2004; ADB 2005.

Concerning the accessibility of documents, CSOs recommended that communication plans should be mandatory for all projects. However, ADB was only willing to have communication plans for certain projects and programs. CSOs also suggested that resident missions should be responsible for information in local languages. This demand was met as the PCP states that resident missions and representative offices will coordinate the translation of documents and review the accuracy of translations.

An important civil society demand was that there should be an independent appeals mechanism for those who believe their requests have been unreasonably denied. The PCP contained the establishment of a Public Disclosure Advisory Committee (PDAC) as an oversight body to interpret, monitor, and review the disclosure requirements of the PCP. This body was to be chaired by the Managing Director General and only include ADB staff and report directly to the President (ADB 2005: 28–29). Hence, like similar mechanisms in other IOs, it was an internal appeal mechanism not independent from ADB management. Finally, CSOs argued in favor of feedback mechanisms to ensure two-way communication. This demand was partly met. The PCP mentions the importance of feedback and two-way communication, but provides no details on how this should be implemented.

This analysis indicates that transnational civil society actors played an important role in shaping ADB's new information disclosure policy. The systematic comparison of civil society demands and the final version of the PCP reveals striking similarities. The NGO Forum on ADB and other CSOs involved in the campaign claim to have been influential and interviewed ADB staff and management also stress the influence of CSOs. Hence, the method of attributed influence also point in the direction of civil society influence on ADB's policy reform. However, it should be noted that CSOs were not the only stakeholders arguing in favor of reform of ADB's information disclosure policy. There were also demands from donor governments and to some extent also from the private sector. Moreover, the review of ADB's transparency policy took place in a context of increasing demands for more transparency in global governance. In its 2005 PCP, ADB itself refers to a "global trend toward greater openness" as a background to its new policy (ADB 2005: i). Both CSOs and ADB made references to information disclosure policies in other IOs and states. For instance, references were made to freedom of information laws of Mexico and South Africa and a specific World Bank project (Swajal) was highlighted as a good example of transparency (ADB 2004).

The ADB safeguard policies

In order to avoid, minimize or mitigate adverse environmental and social impacts that may result from development projects, ADB developed three safeguard policies: Involuntary resettlement Policy (1995), Indigenous Peoples Policy (1998), and Environment Policy (2002). In 2005 ADB initiated a safeguard policy update. For this purpose a website was set up as a forum for stakeholder feedback. Two consultation drafts and the draft working policy paper were published here together with comments from various stakeholders and ADB response. Some documents were translated into selected languages, including Russian and Indonesian. Between October 2007 and April 2008, 14 multi-stakeholder workshops were held in several Asian countries as well as in North America and Europe. Most participants represented governments (45 percent) followed by CSOs (34 percent), the remaining coming from the private sector, development agencies and academia (ADB 2009b: 82). In May 2009, the ADB Board of Directors approved the Safeguard Policy Statement.

Process-tracing shows that the NGO Forum on ADB and other CSOs lobbied very actively concerning the safeguard policies. They had frequent formal and informal discussions with ADB directors and staff, but they also organized demonstrations and tried to influence public opinion through media (Interview, civil society activist, 10 December 2010). In 2006 the NGO Forum on ADB published detailed documentation on how ADB's existing safeguard policies had been violated in Bangladesh, India, Laos and Pakistan (NGO Forum on ADB 2006). The NGO Forum on ADB provided very detailed and technical input in the review process. Comments on the second draft of the Safeguard Policy Statement is a 263-page document, which in a matrix form goes through page by page of the draft policy document, suggesting changes in virtually every paragraph and also providing reasons for the proposed changes (NGO Forum on ADB 2008). The complexities of the safeguard policies and the extent and level of detail of civil society suggestions makes it difficult to present a comparative analysis in a table, the way preference attainment was analyzed concerning the AM and PCP. What is covered in Table 4.3 is a selection of significant civil society demands.

The overall concern of CSOs was to avoid dilution of existing safeguard policies. Reading the first draft policy statements, CSOs suspected that the outcome of the policy review would be weakened safeguards. Many civil society activists were so upset about the content of the first drafts that they boycotted the consultations. In February 2008 the major regional and international CSOs withdrew from consultations with ADB in order to demonstrate their disappointment with the draft consultation paper. In March 2008 CSOs from Vietnam, Cambodia, Thailand and Burma refused to attend the ADB Safeguard Policy Update consultations in Hanoi, referring to major weaknesses of the draft. The second draft, according to the NGO Forum on ADB, meant "a significant dilution of the Bank's existing safeguards" and "a marked decrease in transparency" (NGO Forum on ADB 2008). However, moving from the second draft paper to the Review Paper of Safeguard Policy Statement, ADB made significant revisions in line with civil society demands. Commenting on the ADB Review Paper of Safeguard Policy Statement, the NGO Forum on ADB welcomed the revisions and stated that "the ADB is close to achieving President Kuroda's goal of 'no dilution' from existing

74 *Anders Uhlin*

Table 4.3 Comparison between key civil society demands in the review of ADB's safeguard policies 2005–2009 and ADB Safeguard Policy Statement 2009

Civil society demands in review of safeguard policies 2005–2009	Safeguard Policy Statement 2009
Avoid dilution of existing safeguards.	Significant dilution in consultation drafts, but not in final policy document.
Scope should be widened to include core labor standards.	Demand not met, but ADB claims this is already addressed in social protection strategy.
There should be an explicit reference to UN Declaration on the Rights of Indigenous Peoples concerning principle of "free, prior, and informed consent."	Principle recognized, but for the purpose of operationalization ADB refers to "broad community support."
Involuntary resettlement policy should cover other impacts than those related to land acquisition.	Demand met.
No country safeguard systems.	Country safeguard systems used, but only in a limited number of countries and not for highly sensitive and complex projects.
Gender mainstreaming.	Demand met.

Sources: NGO Forum on ADB 2008, 2009a, 2009b.

policy" (NGO Forum on ADB 2009b: 1). Hence, the overall concern about avoiding policy dilution was to a large extent satisfied.

Many civil society comments focused on widening the scope of the safeguard policies. One example was the demand that core labor standards should be included. This demand was not met, but ADB claimed that this was already addressed in its social protection strategy. Another important demand was that there should be an explicit reference to the UN Declaration on the Rights of Indigenous Peoples concerning the principle of "free, prior, and informed consent". ADB did recognize the principle in the final policy statement, but for the purpose of operationalization the Bank maintained its reference to the more diffuse "broad community support". Yet another important demand was that the involuntary resettlement policy should cover other impacts than those related to land acquisition. In this case the document was revised in line with civil society suggestions. Another major civil society criticism was related to the use of Country Safeguard Systems (a country's legal and institutional framework rather than general ADB safeguards), which CSOs suspected would weaken safeguards as most countries have insufficient regulations on environmental and social issues. Hence, the NGO Forum on ADB suggested that the Country Safeguard Systems should not be part of the ADB Safeguard Policy. The final policy document maintained references to Country Safeguard Systems, but clarified that these should be used only in a limited number of countries and not for highly sensitive and complex projects.

Gender was a key concern for several of the CSOs most active in the policy review process. Many civil society demands focused on the need for a systematic gender analysis and awareness in all aspects of the safeguard policy. In this respect, CSOs were strikingly successful in influencing the Bank. Commenting on the final review paper, the NGO Forum praised ADB stating that "the R-paper sets an example for other IFIs in regard to explicitly requiring gender sensitive and responsive application of the safeguards policies" (NGO Forum on ADB 2009b: 1).

The method of attributed influence also provides indications of civil society influence in this case. Representatives of the NGO Forum on ADB who were most active in the Safeguard Policy campaign were satisfied with the outcome. One activist argued that though CSOs did not achieve everything, the very intense campaign was worth the effort as CSOs had real influence. "If we do not push it, Western governments would close their eyes," she argued (Interview, civil society activist, 10 December 2010). Another representative of the NGO Forum, reflecting on the Safeguard Policy campaign, said:

> It was a wonderful experience because the board members and the safeguard units and Forum had a lot of exchanges and Forum had very concrete, [...] very voluminous submissions. And we achieved most of the things. But now it's a question of how the safeguard policies has to be implemented.
> (Interview, civil society activist, 17 November 2011)

As stressed by the cited civil society activist, influencing the formulation of the policies is not enough. Implementation has to be monitored too. However, while essential for an overall assessment of the legitimacy of the ADB, this goes beyond the scope of the present study.

Conclusion

The analysis of ADB policy reform processes – using the methods of process-tracing, preference attainment and attributed influence – indicates significant civil society influence resulting in improved accountability, more transparency, and broadened participation. The NGO Forum on ADB and other CSOs have both engaged in protest activities and taken part in formal consultations with very detailed and specific demands on ADB policy reforms. Many civil society demands and suggestions are reflected in ADB's policy documents and interviewed representatives of ADB and CSOs testify to the substantial civil society input in the processes. However, we should be careful not to overstate the influence of CSOs. It should be noted that both civil society activists and ADB representatives might have good reasons to exaggerate the impact of CSOs. CSOs might have a tendency to overstate their own influence in order to prove their success to members, supporters and funders and ADB itself might exaggerate civil society influence on its policies as a way to provide increased legitimacy for its activities and policies. Moreover, CSOs have not been the only actors promoting accountability, transparency and participation. In all three cases examined here – the ADB AM, PCP and Safeguard policy – CSOs had aligned interests with Western donor governments. The World Bank has also served as an inspiration, particularly in the case of the AM, but ADB has not simply copied institutional solutions from the World Bank.

Of the three cases under investigation, civil society influence on the Safeguard Policy was probably most extensive. This review process featured the most detailed civil society input, but also a quite confrontational civil society approach in the initial phases of the process. The fact that there are substantial indications of civil society influence on all three policies raises the question if these policies are exceptional or if the cases are likely to reflect a more general trend of civil society influence in global governance. These policy reforms strengthening the transparency and accountability of the ADB to non-state stakeholders can be conceptualized as a process of political liberalization (Uhlin 2011). Civil society actors promoting political liberalization may have relatively strong influence on MDBs and other IOs because they do not challenge capitalist interests and state sovereignty in a fundamental way. Promoting transparency and accountability, they can even find some aligned interests with powerful state and business actors. There is no indication of direct influence by civil society groups voicing more fundamental criticism against neoliberal development policy (even if such radical criticism may open up space for reformers to promote political liberalization). The NGO Forum on ADB and other CSOs certainly disagree with ADBs focus on economic growth and state sovereignty, but their influence on these fundamental issues has been very limited. Focusing on the more modest agenda of political liberalization, they have been able to gain significant influence.

Do these policy reforms related to transparency and accountability matter? Writing on the ADB AM, Park (2014: 231) concludes that "the AM has not penetrated the consensus-oriented hierarchical culture of the ADB, which favors economic growth and state sovereignty." The present study supports this conclusion. CSOs have influenced specific policies, but these policy reforms have not led to cultural change within ADB. The AM, PCP and Safeguard Policy are more about form than norm. The dominant ADB norm focusing on large infrastructure projects for economic growth and respecting the sovereignty of member states has not changed with the implementation of the new policies. However, this process of political liberalization is not insignificant. The Bank is now a completely different IO than it used to be before the 1990s. It has become more liberal in the sense of protecting some rights of affected people. Project-affected stakeholders, with the help of CSOs, have been able to make use of the AM, PCP and safeguard policies in order to protect their interests against the powerful Bank.

Notes

1 I would like to thank Morten Bøås, Sara Kalm, Susan Park, and Jonathan Strand for constructive comments on previous versions of this text. Research for this chapter was carried out within the Transdemos research program funded by Riksbankens Jubileumsfond.
2 The analysis of ADB–civil society relations draws on Kalm and Uhlin 2015: Ch 5. See also Uhlin 2011).
3 Unless otherwise stated, all information on the NGO Forum on ADB in this section is found at the organization's website www.forum-adb.org/index.php (accessed 15 February 2013).
4 Part of the analysis in this section draws on Uhlin 2011.

References

Asian Development Bank (ADB). 2000. *Seventh Replenishment of the Asian Development Fund (ADF VIII). ADF VIII Donors' Report: Fighting Poverty in Asia.* Available at: www.adb.org/sites/default/files/institutional-document/32436/files/adfviii-donors-report.pdf (accessed 1 June 2015).

Asian Development Bank (ADB). 2003. *Review of the Inspection Function: Establishment of a New ADB Accountability Mechanism.* Available at: www.adb.org/sites/default/files/institutional-document/32108/adb-accountability-mechanism.pdf (accessed 1 June 2015).

Asian Development Bank (ADB). 2004. *Consultation on ADB's Draft Public Communication Policy*, New Delhi, India, 14–15 July: Summary of Participant Recommendations. Available at: www.forum-adb.org/docs/delhi-wkshp-summary-fin.pdf (accessed 10 April 2013).

Asian Development Bank (ADB). 2005. *Public Communications Policy: Disclosure and Exchange of Information.* Available at: www.adb.org/sites/default/files/PCP-R-Paper.pdf (accessed 10 April 2013).

Asian Development Bank (ADB). 2009a. *Safeguard Policy Statement*, June. Available at: www.adb.org/sites/default/files/pub/2009/Safeguard-Policy-Statement-June2009.pdf (accessed 13 February 2014).

Asian Development Bank (ADB). 2009b. *Working Paper: Safeguard Policy Statement*, January. Available at: www.adb.org/Documents/Policies/Safeguards/Safeguard-Policy-Statement.pdf (accessed 5 April 2013).

Asian Development Bank (ADB). 2012. *Accountability Mechanism Policy 2012.* Available at: www.adb.org/sites/default/files/accountability-mechanism-policy-2012.pdf (accessed 5 April 2013).

Article 19, Bank Information Center, Commonwealth Human Rights Initiative. 2004. *Civil Society Comments on Second Draft Public Communication Policy of the Asian Development Bank*, 24 November. Available at: www.forum-adb.org/docs/Comments_on_2nd_draft_PCP.pdf (accessed 10 April 2013).

Bank Information Center (BIC), et al. 2002. *Strengthening Public Accountability. Recommendations to the Asian Development Bank (ADB) for Revising its Inspection Policy*, 18 March. Available at: www.forum-adb.org/pdf/strengthening-public-accountability-200203.pdf (accessed 1 June 2015).

Barnett, M. and M. Finnemore. 2004. *Rules for the World. International Organizations in Global Politics.* Ithaca, NY and London: Cornell University Press.

Bøås, M. and D. McNeill. 2003. *Multilateral Institutions: A Critical Introduction.* London: Pluto Press.

Clark, J. 2002. "The World Bank and Civil Society: An Evolving Experience." In *Civil Society and Global Finance*, edited by J. A. Scholte and A. Schnabel. London: Routledge, pp. 11–127.

Clark, D., J. Fox and K. Treakle (eds). 2003. *Demanding Accountability: Civil Society Claims and the World Bank Inspection Panel.* Lanham, MD: Rowman & Littlefield.

Corell, E. and M. M. Betsill. 2008. "Analytical Framework: Assessing the Influence of NGO Diplomats." In *NGO Diplomacy. The Influence of Nongovernmental Organizations in International Environmental Negotiations*, edited by M. M. Betsill and E. Corell. Cambridge, MA: MIT Press, pp. 19–42.

Dür, A. 2008. "Measuring Interest Group Influence in the EU: A Note on Methodology." *European Union Politics* 9(4): 559–576.

Dür, A. and D. de Bièvre. 2007. "The Question of Interest Group Influence." *Journal of Public Policy* 27(1): 1–12.

Fox, J. A. and L. D. Brown. 1998. *The Struggle for Accountability: The World Bank, NGOs, and Grass-Roots Movements.* Cambridge, MA: MIT Press.

Friedman, E. J., K. Hochstetler and A. M. Clark. 2005. *Sovereignty, Democracy, and Global Civil Society: State-Society Relations at UN World Conferences.* Albany, NY: State University of New York Press.

Guttal, S. 2002. "Disclosure or Deception: Information Access in the World Bank and the Asian Development Bank." *Development Dialogue* 1(2002): 104–116.

Joachim, J. and B. Locher. 2009. "Transnational Activism in the EU and the UN." In *Transnational Activism in the UN and the EU*, edited by J. Joachim and B. Locher. London and New York: Routledge.

Kalm, S. and A. Uhlin. 2015. *Civil Society and the Governance of Development: Opposing Global Institutions.* Basingstoke: Palgrave.

Keck, M. E. and K. Sikkink. 1998. *Activists Beyond Borders: Advocacy Networks in International Politics.* Ithaca, NY and London: Cornell University Press.

Koremenos, B., C. Lipson and D. Snidal. 2001. "The Rational Design of International Institutions." *International Organization* 55(4): 761–799.

McKeon, N. 2009. *The United Nations and Civil Society: Legitimating Global Governance – Whose Voice?* London and New York: Zed Books.

Nelson, P. J. 2001. "Transparency Mechanisms at the Multilateral Development Banks." *World Development* 29(11): 1835–1847.

NGO Forum on ADB. 2004. *Civil Society Comments on Second Draft Public Communications Policy of the Asian Development Bank.* Available at: www.forum-adb.org/docs/Comments_on_2nd_draft_PCP.pdf (accessed 27 August 2014).

NGO Forum on ADB. 2006. *Untold Realities: How the ADB Safeguards have been Violated in Bangladesh, India, Lao and PDR Pakistan.* Manila: NGO Forum on ADB.

NGO Forum on ADB. 2008. *Comments to the Safeguard Policy Statement Second Draft of October 2008*, 4 December. Quezon City: NGO Forum on ADB.

NGO Forum on ADB. 2009a. *Detailed Recommendations for Improvement of the SPS R-Paper: An Attachment to Forum's Submission on Comments to the Safeguard R-Paper*, 15 July. Available at: www.forum-adb.org/docs/Detailed_SafeguardsRecommendations.pdf (accessed 13 February 2014).

NGO Forum on ADB. 2009b. *Significant Progress Made in R-paper at Risk if Remaining Dilutions not Addressed: Comments of the NGO Forum on ADB on the*

Review Paper of Safeguard Policy Statement of the Asian Development Bank, 14 July. Available at: www.forum-adb.org/docs/Comments-SafeguardsRPaper_July14.pdf (accessed 13 February 2014).

O'Brien, R., A. Marie Goetz, J. A. Scholte and M. Williams. 2000. *Contesting Global Governance: Multilateral Economic Institutions and Global Social Movements.* Cambridge: Cambridge University Press.

Pallas, C. 2013. *Transnational Civil Society and the World Bank: Investigating Civil Society's Potential to Democratize Global Governance.* Basingstoke: Palgrave Macmillan.

Pallas, C. and A. Uhlin. 2014. "Civil Society Influence on International Organizations: Theorizing the State Channel." *Journal of Civil Society* 10(2): 184–203.

Park, S. 2010a. "Designing Accountability, International Economic Organisations and the World Bank's Inspection Panel." *Australian Journal of International Affairs* 64 (1): 13–36.

Park, S. 2010b. *World Bank Group Interactions with Environmentalists: Changing International Organisation Identities.* Manchester: Manchester University Press.

Park, S. 2014. "Institutional Isomorphism and the Asian Development Bank's Accountability Mechanism: Something Old, Something New; Something Borrowed, Something Blue?" *The Pacific Review* 27(2): 217–239.

Park, S. and A. Vetterlein (eds). 2010. *Owning Development: Creating Policy Norms in the IMF and the World Bank.* Cambridge: Cambridge University Press.

Reimann, K. D. 2006. "A View from the Top: International Politics, Norms and the Worldwide Growth of NGOs." *International Studies Quarterly* 50(1): 45–67.

Scholte, J. A. (ed.). 2011a. *Building Global Democracy? Civil Society and Accountable Global Governance.* Cambridge: Cambridge University Press.

Scholte, J. A. (ed.). 2011b. "Civil Society and IMF Accountability." In *Building Global Democracy? Civil Society and Accountable Global Governance*, edited by J. A. Scholte. Cambridge: Cambridge University Press, pp. 78–104.

Tadem, T. S. E. 2003. "Thai Social Movements and the Anti-ADB Campaign." *Journal of Contemporary Asia* 33(3): 377–398.

Tallberg, J., T. Sommerer, T. Squatrito and C. Jönsson. 2013. *The Opening Up of International Organizations: Transnational Access in Global Governance.* Cambridge: Cambridge University Press.

Tussie, D. and G. Casaburi. 2000. "From Global to Local Governance: Civil Society and the Multilateral Development Banks." *Global Governance* 6(4): 399–403.

Uhlin, A. 2011. "National Democratization Theory and Global Governance: Civil Society and the Liberalization of the Asian Development Bank." *Democratization* 18(3): 817–841.

5 The African Development Bank
From follower to broker and partner

Karen A. Mingst

The slogan "African solutions to African problems" has dominated development policy discourse in the first decade of the twenty-first century. Yet the call for "African solutions" and "African institutions" is not new. When the African Development Bank (AfDB) was established in 1964, it was founded as an African institution, celebrating the virtues of "going it alone." The belief was that an all-African bank management and reliance on African donors would be able to fashion development alternatives uniquely suited to Africa. Has the AfDB been an innovator and an independent entity, providing African solutions? Or has the institution been a follower of the trends and demands of the international development community? Why has the AfDB adapted to newer development practices? How is the institution repositioning itself for the future?

This paper comes to three conclusions. First, the goal of Africanicity proved illusionary: incorporating international donors has been a necessity. Second, in terms of development ideas, the AfDB has been a follower, lagging behind other development actors like the World Bank by as much as five to ten years before incorporating key development issues: environmental sustainability, civil society organizations, gender, and good governance. Why the AfDB responded to those external demands is explained by the need for both external resources and international legitimacy; there is little evidence of these policy changes emanating from within the organization. Third, the AfDB is attempting to reposition itself as a leader among African institutions and among external donors. That reorientation includes promotion of regional and sub-regional integration, serving as a knowledge hub for innovation and technology and an institutional broker for an increasing number of partnerships among other IGOs, CSOs, and the private sector. This chapter begins by considering the historical context of Africanicity of the AfDB and then examines how the AfDB responded to changing norms and policy priorities in development assistance after the Cold War. Recent efforts by the AfDB to provide solutions to Africa's unique problems are then surveyed.

"Africanicity": the goal vs. reality

When the African Development Bank was founded, the wounds of colonialism were fresh and the desire to be independent was too strong to consider Western country membership. Membership and participation was limited to African states and its secretariat was entirely African. This "Africanicity," a key part of the organizational culture, was important symbolically; it was, in the view of the Libyan executive director, "our strength. We feel that speaking as an African to an African is better than if you send a Dutchman or a German to talk to an African" (quoted in Thurow 1989: 11). As AfDB president Fordwor (1981: 116) described, that "was an expression of African determination to help itself ... ." Some at the time feared that Africanicity might undermine its financial credibility, though that view was dismissed.

Yet it soon became apparent to most members that additional external resources were necessary. In 1972 the African Development Fund (AfDF) was established, admitting 20 nonregional member states, and in 1982 the AfDB opened to nonregional membership – a necessity in the resource-constrained environment. That decision was controversial, with strong opposition from states such as Nigeria, Libya, Egypt, and Algeria. The compromise reached was that the "African character" of the institution was to be preserved in terms of leadership and personnel. Nonregionals were limited to one-third of the votes in the AfDB and one-half of voting in the AfDF. And only one nonregional state, the United States, was given its own executive director, although as Strand (2001: 208) has calculated "voting weights ... do not denote voting power." With excellent ratings from the international investor services industry, the number of loan commitments grew quickly, in the bank's "honeymoon period" (Sherk 1999: 64).

Still administered by an African staff from an African location, the AfDB sought to continue the policy of using only economic criteria in its loan decisions. But gradually, more pre-loan conditions, more financial accountability measures, and more discussion of loans to the private sector crept in, all advocated by nonregional members. These decisions were accepted rather reluctantly by the African states, but nonregional resources were essential to the functioning of the bank. At the beginning, such conditionality was not attached to particular strategies of economic development or to broader economic development goals. When conditions were discussed, the decisions were framed tentatively – using words like *suggesting, leading*, and *eventually including* – but follow-up investigations were rare and the conditions applied in a lax fashion. This approach is consistent with Babb's hypothesis (2009: 230) that resource-dependent organizations tend to adopt the substantive suggestions made by external actors but choose to ignore the form. These changes did not reflect African initiatives or unique African approaches.

External influences for change were evident, with both the U.S. and the World Bank (WB) pressuring the AfDB. The U.S. wanted the MDBs to treat all individual borrowers the same to avoid competition among MDBs and to expedite co-financing. Since the AfDB in the 1990s co-financed more than 80 percent of its projects with the WB, that made organizational sense (Babb 2009: 152–3). The World Bank's pressure was subtle: it "would expect AfDB to support, through its resources and dialogue ..." (World Bank 1985), its policy reform goals. The AfDB could be a useful "go-between" with African governments, muting criticism of policy reforms, even "cushioning conditionalities." The challenge for the AfDB was to maintain what it viewed as the basis for its legitimacy, its Africanicity, quietly not opposing, but not enforcing, limited conditionalities. As a non-committed follower, AfDB sought to soften the effects of the demands of the international financial institutions while maintaining its more general hands-off approach to states – providing, in its view, a stronger sense of borrower ownership (English and Mule 1996: 5).

But African states were experiencing real economic decline and the need for resources became greater. The 1990s were the "lost decade," with major economic decline in Africa. Total international aid dropped from $17.2 billion in 1990 to $12.3 billion in 1999 and aid in per capita terms fell from $32 to $19. Per capita income dropped from $552 to $474 and there was an increase in the percentage of the population living on less than $1 a day. HIV/AIDS became recognized as not only a health care crisis but also an economic crisis, affecting wage earners in the prime of life. And the 1990s added a new category, failed state, for Somalia, Liberia, Zaire, and Rwanda. Under such conditions, opportunities for the AfDB to chart its own African approach to development or even resist the WB or large donor states became even fewer.

The AfDB was in no position to begin to provide viable development alternatives. On the contrary, the organization itself was in crisis. Things came to a head in 1994 with the Task Force on Project Quality, or the so-called Knox Report. This "critical and hard hitting" (Sherk 1999: 66) report identified critical problems in the quality of lending, much of it to uncreditworthy borrowers, leading to an unsustainable ratio of debt to usable capital. The bank's ratings in the international capital market plummeted. Financial difficulties were compounded by arguments between some long-serving African executive directors and the bank's former president, resulting in an immobilized organization. Major nonregional donors postponed funding to the AfDF.

Both the continent-wide stagnation and the organizational crisis led to crucial reforms. The loan portfolio was reviewed and many loans were cancelled; lending criteria were instituted; external auditors were appointed; and the AfDB staff was cut by 20 percent and 70 percent of the management replaced. The voting share of the nonregional members of the bank was raised from one-third to 40 percent (Babb 2009: 154, 30–31). These organizational reforms not only undermined the "African character" of the bank in terms of regional member ownership but also resulted in increased surveillance by those outside the bank, making it less likely that the bank could approach development differently.

This combination of dire economic conditions, severe resource constraints, and diminished organizational legitimacy caused by poor management compelled the AfDB to accept changes in the thinking of the international development community and the approaches adopted by other development institutions. These changes were initiated by transnational activists and non-regional donor states and exercised by the latter during negotiations for periodic replenishments of the AfDF. There was little discernable pressure in favor of these changes from either the bank bureaucracy or regional member states. Why the AfDB changed may be due in part to mimicry, when, as Park and Vetterlein (2010: 17) explain, "actors copy organizational leaders in their field to gain legitimacy ... ." Re-establishing organizational legitimacy in the eyes of international actors – including the private financial institutions – became essential after the disastrous 1990s. But adoption of different priorities followed by institutional adaptation also occurred because the bank recognized that there would be material gains.

The changing landscape of development aid and the AfDB response

By the 1990s, the ideas and policies of the international development community had begun to change, and this was occurring outside the offices of the AfDB – to the chagrin of African member states. We examine four of these change areas in turn; environmental sustainability; civil society engagement; gender; and good governance in member states and the bank. In each case we compare the timing and source of the changes in the World Bank with those in the AfDB. The initiatives confirm the argument that English and Mule (1996) suggested but could not prove at the time: that the AfDB follows, often with a time lag of years. But as demands by the international development community on the AfDB became greater, the former U.S. executive director Donald Sherk (1999: 72) warned of a potential danger: "that the U.S. [and the rest of the international development community] was overloading the influence 'circuits' by trying to obtain too many changes and not allowing for new policies to make themselves part of the Bank's permanent landscape." Institutionalization of these changes would take years; internalization within the organizational culture longer still.

Sustainability and the introduction of environmental criteria

The push by the international development community to broaden its conception of development to include sustainability and environmental issues was introduced and supported by transnational activists. As Park (2010) explains, it was these groups rather than individual states or World Bank management that fought for the shift to sustainability. The World Bank became the focus of activist discontent in the aftermath of the Amazon project in northwest Brazil when the devastating effects of deforestation became apparent. Public pressure for change came during the 1983 negotiations for replenishment of the International Development Association in the U.S. Congress. The WB's hiring of a Scandinavian environmental advisor in the mid-1980s was one perfunctory response. In 1987 a Socio-Environmental Division was created as part of a general reorganization, but in three years it included just a single staff environmentalist and assistants, despite the bank's pledge to integrate environmental work into country development strategies. In 1991, Operational Directive 4.01 required environmental impact assessments for all projects having potential environmental effects. And the number of environmental projects did increase.

Continuing to respond to external pressures, the Independent Inspection Panel was established in 1993 to hear complaints from people living near projects that suffered from harm. Yet the change was limited; the panel could only hear cases approved by the Board of Executive Directors and borrowing governments. The World Bank has published ten social and environmental safeguard policies that promote inclusive and environmentally sustainable development and have added compliance procedures to ensure that safeguard policies are followed.

According to Weaver (2008: 24), however, there was still major opposition from both client governments and members of the WB bureaucracy. As recently as 2013, one of the bank's harshest critics of its destructive environmental policy supports this view. Rich (2013) contends that the bank has not stopped environmental destruction but hastened the process. He concludes that the bank's culture may not be able to change; others disagree.

The AfDB was resistant to incorporating environmental considerations into project lending, fearing that such an assessment would prevent approval of some projects and inflate the costs of all projects. In 1991, the U.S. Treasury used the occasion of the sixth replenishment of the AfDF to demand that the bank prepare environmental impact statements and increase the number of projects for energy conservation. But a year later only "limited progress" had been made. And the U.S. Treasury reported that they therefore would not support the bank's lending program (Babb 2009: 190–191). By 1992, systems for evaluating environmental impact had been initiated in the WB, the Inter-American Development Bank, and the Asian Development Bank, but the AfDB had no established procedures.

The AfDB did set up the Environment and Sustainable Development Unit and a public information center in 1996. As NGOs began to be involved in bank activities, as explained below, bank officials did meet with NGO representatives, enhancing accountability and transparency. Yet the bank still did not carry out, much less require, environmental impact statements. Throughout most of the 1990s, the strategy from the U.S. administration, the main backers of the reforms, was that the RDBs – and the AfDB in particular – needed to follow the same direction as the World Bank; pressure continued to be particularly intense during negotiations for fund replenishments.

Environmental issues were only a marginal consideration during the early years of the new millennium. While civil society organizations pushed the agenda, another external influence, the emergence of climate change, spurred a substantive AfDB response. In 2013, the AfDB approved new environmental and social safeguard policies. These new safeguards are intended to protect local populations, vulnerable groups, and the environment against negative effects of AfDB projects. And the safeguards will for the first time be applied to all the bank's lending operations. All loans will be screened for environmental and social risks. The "green growth" rhetoric, so central to the 2013 strategy, committed the bank to building resilience to climate shocks with infrastructure and natural resources protection. To that end, the AfDB established a new climate change fund in 2014, with initial funding from Germany. Climate readiness projects will be funded, enabling members to apply for additional UN funding. The AfDB itself serves as the implementing agency for the UN's Global Environment Facility, managing 23 projects across the continent, more than half in 2013 alone.

AfDB change is actually occurring before the WB updates its own safeguard policies, leading the World Bank's Information Center to claim that "the African Development Bank safeguards coverage sets standard for the World Bank to emulate" (www.bicusa.org). For once, the AfDB may be at the forefront of international development policy change. AfDB leadership is yet to be duplicated in the other policy areas.

Adoption of civil society engagement

In 1981 the World Bank published its first note on relations with NGOs. Establishing an NGO-WB committee, regular consultative meetings were held. As pressure from NGOs, other civil society organizations, and member states on environmental issues mounted, CSOs sought more direct roles, in particular exerting pressure after the 1988 annual meeting of the WB and IMF. By 1990 the bank reported consultations with CSOs in 21 percent of its projects, from design and planning to implementation and monitoring. By 2010, that number had increased to 86 percent.

The World Bank continues to deepen those relationships. The 1993 Inspection Panel provided limited opportunity for private individual inputs. But since 1994 the bank has provided information for accountability and transparency purposes. As the bank tells the story, the "breadth and quality" of bank–CSO relations intensified in the mid-1990s when specialists in civil society were hired for work in bank offices all over the globe.

The AfDB held its first consultative meetings with civil society in the early 1990s, followed by a manual on "Procedures, Mechanisms, and Guidelines" for cooperation with NGOs. But it was ten years later, in 2000, before a revised policy provided for greater CSO involvement in project implementation (AfDB 2000). This has occurred through the preparation of Poverty Reduction Strategy Papers, Country Strategy Papers, and its Fragile States initiatives, with sub-contracts to CSOs. In 2010 that commitment was once again enhanced, this time with explicit recognition that inclusive growth could only be achieved through collaboration with CSOs, specifically connected with environmental and social safeguards systems, the Independent Review Mechanism (the AfDB's version of the WB Inspection Panel), and in fragile states (AfDBG 2012c). In the *Civil Society Engagement Framework*, bank officials admitted that despite the increase in CSO participation in policy development and implementation (CSOs were engaged in about 78 percent of projects in 2008, up from 19 percent in 1996), CSO engagement was still ad hoc and unsystematic. The bank needs to engage with a greater diversity of CSOs and not rely on the same organizations, and also needs to forge more contacts with locally based associations. The bank's regional departments and country offices need to work more broadly, including increasing the capacity of CSOs to participate through training sessions and education. These priorities developed, in part, as the result of a bank survey of 40 CSOs with experience of working with the bank.

Illustrative of the rising importance of African CSOs is the fact that they have organized themselves to monitor the AfDB. The Civil Society Coalition on the African Development Bank is an African-led network of 35 NGOs (four of which are from Western Europe and the U.S.) that seeks to improve the capacity of African CSOs to engage the bank, make the bank's operations more transparent, improve public accountability, and serve as a liaison with local communities. Funded by the Open Society Foundation and Oxfam Novib, the Dutch affiliate of Oxfam International (which is based in Tunis, the temporary headquarters of the AfDB), the coalition provides assistance to CSOs to evaluate AfDB projects seen as problematic. The coalition's major direct success has been in its lobbying for the new Disclosure and Access to Information Policy to increase communication and transparency.

In short, although CSO involvement with the AfDB came later compared to other MDBs, CSOs are now more actively enhancing their own capacity to participate in AfDB activities. These changes in the AfDB again reflect exogenous factors: there has been an explosion of CSO activity in all areas of African life and the AfDB continues to follow the practices of the other MDBs in this area.

Focusing on gender

The World Bank came late to the gender and development norm, well after other institutions had adopted the perspective. In 1977, a Women in Development (WID) office was established within the World Bank, but no policy papers or sectoral guidelines were issued on how to integrate women's roles. Seven years later, under "Sociological Aspects of Project Appraisal," women were discussed along with other targeted groups, including minorities and resettled populations (Mingst and Warkentin 1997). Guidelines were presented in the 1984 Operational Manual Statement (OMS 2.20) requiring more gender analysis during the appraisal phase; however, no training was conducted on how this was to be done.

Meanwhile, with the global feminist movement, the UN Decade for Women, and the UN world conferences on women, the women in development (WID) agenda emerged and became institutionalized. For example, the UN reported over 20 separate UN agencies and 11 specialized agencies sponsoring activities for the advancement of women in 1988/9. That does not mean that women were targeted as explicitly as under the WID agenda, or that the projects were effectively implemented to mainstream women into economically productive roles, or that the broader reformulated view of gender and development (GAD) was widely accepted. Gender and development uses gender analysis to examine the nature of gender differences and employs the concept of gender mainstreaming, bringing in gender issues to resource allocation, structuring institutions, and framing development goals.

What is clear is that by 1994 the agenda had become integrated into the WB's analysis and operations, coinciding with the Beijing World Conference on Women. Its 1994 paper "Enhancing Women's Participation in Economic Development" articulated a policy more clearly. And in 2001 the Gender Mainstreaming Strategy was approved. In 2004, Operational Policy 4.20 "Gender and Development" was revised, although it was limited to investment projects. Institutional changes occurred under the Gender and Development Group and analytical work on gender improved.

Weaver (2010: 78, 89) attributes the bank's embracing of the gender component and its institutionalization to the support of both the bank's top leadership, a few core people in the bureaucracy, and strong activist pressure. As she explains, a group of "a small yet very proactive and dedicated core of gender advocates" within the Bank led the "remarkable mainstreaming effort." They did so in a way that did was consistent with the practices of the bank's operational cultures without antagonizing skeptical member states.

The AfDB was both slower to respond to the external pressures for a gender and development perspective and lacked vocal supporters within the bank. Between 1986 and 1990, the African Development Bank changes toward a WID program began with the AfDB hosting seminars, appointing a senior WID advisor in 1987, and establishing a WID unit with two gender experts in the same year, primarily with external funding from UNDP. Those actions took place almost a decade later than similar initiatives at the WB. The AfDB's first WID policy paper was published in 1990, outlining the bank's need to integrate women's concerns into bank operations; well after similar policies were elucidated in the WB and across other development institutions.

A 1995 evaluation of the AfDB's WID activities (AfDB 1995) finds that the activities had not resulted in mainstreaming gender issues. WID expertise at the bank was limited to the policy level, with little integration into the project level; the activities were almost all funded by external donors; there was lack of ownership of the program by the bank itself. Not surprisingly, given the other criticisms, there was no institutional mechanism to ensure compliance or implementation. These omissions are not surprising given the chaotic state of the AfDB during this time.

The AfDB's *New Vision* (1999) represented an attempt to reposition the organization following its identity crisis, singling out gender as a priority cross-cutting issue for the reorganization. Special attention was given to three areas relevant to women: more functional literacy programs; more attention to women in primary and secondary education; and reduction of infant and maternal mortality. To meet these goals, the WID Unit was disbanded and its personnel redeployed: a reorganization consistent with what had occurred in the other development agencies previously. Under a unit focusing on sustainable development, gender concerns were grouped with the environment, population and civil society participation. The 2002 study *The Gender Policy* conducted a few years later (AfDB 2002) was optimistic that this reorganization was resulting in a better integration of cross-cutting issues. That included a broad commitment to women's economic empowerment, institutional knowledge building, and support for regional member states to themselves make gender mainstream (Aasen 2009).

In 2011 the AfDB's own evaluation team, together with an independent consultant, conducted a detailed assessment of gender mainstreaming programs in various development agencies including the UN's specialized agencies, the World Bank, the ADB, and donor states (Risby and Todd 2011). The study considered 25 evaluations from various gender-specific programs sampled from the first decade of the new millennium. This report reached key conclusions about development institutions overall: leadership had not consistently supported gender mainstreaming; incentive systems for gender integration was limited; financial and human resources were insufficient; policies adopted lapsed very quickly; monitoring and evaluation was carried out in an inconsistent manner. Interestingly, *no program of the AfDB was included*. That study might be viewed as a justification for AfDB's relative inactivity; gender projects were not working effectively in other organizations. But the same year as that study, AfDB established a new gender program related to gender-based violence in fragile states.

The AfDB has now developed an institutional commitment under its Gender and Social Development Monitoring Division for gender-targeted initiatives, as pressed by external constituencies. "Gender Strategy 2014–2018" (AfDBG 2013/2014) calls for both internal changes in the bank's staffing and work environment and external support for enhancing female property rights, economic empowerment, and capacity building in member states. Whether these goals became institutionalized and financially supported remains an open question.

Good governance: governance of member states and the development banks

Policy-based lending, adopted widely by both the IMF and World Bank in the 1980s, provided the opening for a broader development agenda that included institutional reforms. Ironically, interest in governance had actually been expressed in the mid-1970s by WB employees in the African division, but it fell on deaf ears. By the end of the 1980s, however, there was increasing concern that the economic reforms integral to the Washington Consensus were not achieving their intended affects. The World Bank's 1989 report *Sub-Saharan Africa: From Crisis to Sustainable Growth* called not only for economic reforms consistent with structural adjustment reform but also for "good governance." Lack of "good governance," it argued, might be the reason that economic reforms were not leading to the intended outcomes (World Bank 1989).

At that time, good governance was narrowly defined as an efficient public service. For the World Bank, an economic institution whose articles of agreement committed it to political neutrality, the term was purposefully chosen to be limiting and vague. However, debate ensued, pitting economists, the overwhelmingly number of WB employees, viewing poor governance as inefficiency of the public sector versus social scientists hired during the 1980s, who saw good governance as including political dimensions like democratic pluralism and human rights.

The politically neutral language of "good governance" was adopted. What governance meant gradually expanded as participatory approaches to development brought in CSOs and women, among others. While governance was permanently on the agenda, it was only in 2005 that governance began to include anticorruption, as introduced by the then WB president, Paul Wolfowitz.

The African Development Bank came to governance later. In the Agreement Establishing the African Development Bank, political neutrality was explicit: "the Bank ... shall not interfere in the political affairs of any members, nor shall they be influenced in their decisions by the political character of the member concerned. Only economic conditions shall be relevant ... ." Yet as early as 1994 the bank's African Advisory Council suggested that the bank needed to be involved in democracy promotion and governance. There was talk of developing an African approach to governance different from the liberal democratic model implicit in the good governance lexicon. But the bank, paralyzed by institutional crisis, was unable to deliver an alternative (Bøås 1998: 121–122).

Instead, nonregional donors began to link capital increases of the AfDB and replenishment of the AfDF with imposition of governance criteria. For example, in the fifth capital increase in 2000, AfDB had to agree to allocate funds according to indicators of governance performance. In the ninth replenishment in 2002, AfDF agreed to limit or end lending in the face of serious governance issues. Until 2001 there was no staff or policy paper on the subject.

By the time the 2001 *African Development Report* was forthcoming, the bank's position had changed, with bank officials and member states acknowledging the necessity of good governance for economic growth. A broader range of institutional reforms was necessary to ensure accountability of the public sector, transparency in budgets and expenditures, greater participation by the beneficiaries, and the building of management capacities for greater efficiency. The report concedes that "its efforts should, wherever possible, build on the national authorities' own willingness and commitment to address governance issues, recognizing that its involvement is more likely to be successful when it strengthens the hands of those in the government seeking to improve governance." Yet the bank may be limited, cognizant of "the different axioms of good governance, country circumstances, the state of dialogue with the country and budgetary and staff constraints." The conclusion hedges again, pledging to address "specific issue of poor governance, including corruption, when they have been judged to have a significant macroeconomic impact" (AfDB 2001: 37–38).

The bank's *Development Effectiveness Review on Governance* (AfDB 2012) details improvements across 18 countries in governance indicators related to revenue and tax systems. Time required to start a business was halved; time taken by businesses to pay taxes was down by 10 percent; and average time required to enforce a contract was shorter by 50 days. Through Contract Watch, the AfDB, along with CSOs, governments, and the private sector, works with 12 African countries to more effectively monitor contracting processes, aimed at curbing corruption and improving public sector efficiency. Stakeholders are encouraged to offer further suggestions through the implementation of its 2013 web-based platform.

These initiatives still represent a narrow conception of governance, namely bureaucratic effectiveness. This is more restricted than the understanding of good governance of other development institutions. For African states the issue remains a very politically sensitive topic, especially the issue of corruption in member state governments. Since state representatives in the AfDB often return to their home governments, they are reluctant to push member states on the issue. Although the bank allocated more than 22 percent of its resources to governance, broadly defined, between 2008 and 2011, specific categories are not reported and corruption is not singled out. The bank is still walking "a tightrope between consensus and controversy" which Bøås (1998: 118) identified more than a decade ago.

The 2001 report also addressed internal governance issues: enhancing sectoral effectiveness by encouraging more participation by borrowing countries and other stakeholders, strengthening financing management, and enhancing management system through performance evaluations. Improving internal governance of the bank itself was strongly support by the U.S. Thus, under pressure from the nonregional members during the ninth replenishment, the AfDF agreed to a strategy with specific indicators to evaluate progress toward meeting development goals and assess the effectiveness of the institution (Babb 2009: 222).

In all four policy areas the AfDB trailed the World Bank in the introduction of new development practices – whether environmental sustainability, incorporation of CSOs and gender concerns, or good governance. An analysis of the respective banks' timelines indicates that the AfDB lagged behind the

WB by at least five years before the issue was discussed in written documents and there was another lag period before greater policy clarity was offered and the institution reorganized around the new agenda. Despite the goal to be an African institution, the bank was reacting to what was occurring in the external environment. There is little evidence that the regional member states had a uniquely African strategy, were able to advocate for a different approach, or had the capacity to resist the strong voices of those supporting dominant development practices. After the turbulent years of the 1990s, the AfDB had little choice but to re-establish its legitimacy by following the demands of those articulating what had become the dominant development practices. Given the bank's resource dependency, it is still beholden to major donor states and the WB, its partner in co-financing.

The struggle for organizational autonomy: African solutions to African problems

As well as accepting the dominant development practices, the AfDB also recognized the new reality that it is just one among many African institutions in a continent crowded with potential financiers, from new development banks like the New Development Bank and new major donor states like China, India, and Brazil to private capital and private equity firms. No longer is the bank just a development finance institution, even though since 2008 it has surpassed the World Bank in amount of lending to the continent. In this new role, the AfDB has revived its commitment to regional integration, returning to one of its original mandates. The bank is also repositioning itself. To be a leader, the bank aims to be a knowledge hub for innovation and technology and an institutional broker for an increasing number of partnerships.

Leader in regional integration: revival of an old approach

The AfDB founders saw the promotion of regional projects as its niche; projects involving at least several African countries should have high priority. Regional projects, however, never represented but a small percentage of the ADB lending portfolio during the first decades, reflecting both opposition from geographically disadvantaged states and acknowledged organizational weaknesses in managing and implementing multinational projects. Most admit the organization's failure to make a significant contribution in this area (see Mingst 1990).

The 1999 AfDB *New Vision* statement reinvigorated its commitment to regional integration and systematized the focus. This led in 2006 to a department dedicated to regional integration. But during the interim, African-led sub-regional initiatives were expanding at a fast pace (see Zappile, this volume). Examples include the free trade area of the Economic Community of West African States and the common external tariff of the West African

Economic and Monetary Union, both solidified in 2000; the formalization of the Economic and Monetary Community of Central African States and the free trade area within the Common Market for Eastern and Southern Africa; the East African Community established in 1999; and the movement toward a free trade area for the Southern African Development Community. Yet the emergence of these sub-regional institutions has not led to a more efficient and broader trading group. Indeed, a major study by the World Bank (2012) argues that Africa's regional trade is still inefficient, undermined by the high costs of moving goods between countries, long transit times, and unnecessary rules and regulations. Cross-border infrastructure needs improvement, but changing restrictive rules and licensing procedures and facilitating financial services is also necessary. Hence, given the clear bottlenecks, the AfDB is returning to regional integration as a top priority, strengthening the capacities of the regional economic organizations and stimulating inter-regional cooperation. This commitment is greater than exhibited in other MDBs.

The AfDB adopted a Regional Integration Strategy in 2009 that focused on infrastructure connections, prioritizing cross-border projects. In 2012, for example, 25 percent of total investments went to regional integration projects, including those in energy, transportation, finance, agriculture, and water/sanitation, leading to financing for cross-border roads and feeder roads and cross-border transmission lines. This has occurred through the bank leveraging its financial support by mobilizing additional resources and using public–private partnerships. With a mandate from the Heads of States of the African Union in 2012, the bank leads efforts to develop key regional infrastructure.

Working with partners with the sub-regional groups, the AfDB supports regional payment systems in the West African Monetary Zone and works to harmonize public procurement systems within the Common Market for Eastern and Southern Africa. And it works with ECOWAS to mainstream West African trade facilitation. Leadership in this area also includes partnering with various regional economic organizations on cross-border projects in agricultural trade and border-crossing procedures. Much of AfDB's contribution is in terms of leadership and ideas, for resource and capacity constraints remain.

Equally as important, the AfDB has taken on more of a leadership role, chairing the Infrastructure Consortium for Africa, an Africa-wide initiative begun at G-8 meetings in 2005. The AfDB provides an institutional home for NEPAD's Infrastructure Project Preparation Facility, supporting grants to design regional infrastructure projects. The mandate for AfDB's leadership of development of key regional infrastructure was reiterated at the 2012 meeting of the Heads of States of the African Union, showing a convergence of development priorities. That convergence may be just as important as the coalescence around the Millennium Development Goals.

The importance of the regional integration agenda is illustrated in the *Development Effectiveness Review 2012: Promoting Regional Integration*

(AfDBG 2012b). The document provides a detailed assessment by category on how well Africa is integrating regionally, how well the bank is doing in promoting integration, and how effective and how efficient the banks programs are. This is one of the most thorough evaluation documents produced by any of the development banks, in terms of breadth. But regional integration is not the only initiative.

Knowledge hub for innovation and technology

The bank seeks to be a knowledge hub, particularly in innovation and technology. While not an innovator or developer of technology (AfDBG 2012a), the bank increasingly sees itself as a knowledge hub and broker to promote innovation and technology. As a knowledge hub, the bank is positioning itself as broker among states, educational establishments, and businesses, supporting entrepreneurship in schools and facilitating vocational education and job training. Consistent with this thrust, in 2013 the AfDB agreed to create a Pan-African University, consisting of five institutes. The thematic institutes are spread over the continent. That particular project meets several key objectives: responding to the request of the African Union for such a network in innovation and technology; meeting the human development capacity-building initiatives; encouraging regional integration; incorporating green development. This is undoubtedly an ambitious agenda and will not be institutionalized in the short term, but it sets positive goals of working with other institutions.

Another example of AfDB initiatives in innovation and technology shows the way AfDB is leveraging its relationships with states. In 2013 the "Transform Africa" conference was hosted by Rwanda with the bank's financial backing. Following on from a 2007 conference with a similar objective, the aim of the thousand or so public and private participants was to push for the development of technologies like broadband to transform social and economic development. The AfDB report (2013) *Connecting Africa: An Assessment of Progress Towards the Connect Africa Summit Goals* was timed to coincide with the conference. The program was also designed to encourage entrepreneurial businesses and facilitate online collaboration. In this case, the AfDB did not take the initiative but responded to a strong push from the Rwandan president, Kagame, who had already made Rwanda a leader in technology. But the "Africa Smart Manifesto" again represents a partnership approach, involving not only the AfDB and ITU but also the World Bank and the private sector.

The bank is also a compiler of knowledge. The AfDB Group (2011) in *Africa in 50 Years' Time* laid out a sophisticated analysis of the drivers of change over the coming half century, compiling the report from 11 major scholarly papers commissioned by the bank. What is interesting is that the report did not delineate what the AfDB's role might be or should be. Rather, the intention was to present a continent-wide assessment useful for all institutions.

Vital to an economic analysis is the statistical gathering capacity of states. Through the bank-led African Symposium on Statistical Development in 2014, the bank offered both technical assistance and capacity building to support national statistical systems in 40 regional member states. This initiative serves to increase state capacities in a key area. Perhaps most innovative is its goal to adapt international standards to meet African conditions. This revival of statistical capacity building may be a response to widespread criticisms about the quality of data in African states and points to the World Bank and UN institutions as partly responsible for the poor data methods and reporting (see Jerven 2013).

The AfDB's role in statistics generation is vital as the bank manages a number of key data-dependent programs, including the Africa Information Highway, the Africa Infrastructure Knowledge program, Statistical Business Registration, the International Comparison Program for Africa, and the Harmonized Consumer Price Index, among others. And the bank manages the *African Statistical Journal*.

The AfDB is trying to improve that statistical base is two ways. Data on remittances from African migrants to their home countries, exceeding $60 billion in 2012, is poor. The goals are to both track the amount of remittances and reduce the transfer costs. Such remittances, already an important source of investment capital, can be mobilized and expanded if the data were more reliable. Another initiative concerns the informal sector. While it is estimated that about 55 percent of sub-Saharan Africa's GDP and 80 percent of labor comes from the informal sector, the data is unreliable or invisible in official statistics. The AfDB leadership is exploring ways to help governments formalize some segments of this sector, thus facilitating data collection for planning purposes. Both of these initiatives are clearly "doable," relatively low-cost programs with potential for greater rewards.

The AfDB is the first regional development bank to participate in the Green Growth Knowledge Platform, a multistakeholder knowledge network. Through this platform, the AfDB is sharing its reports on African green growth needs. In this way, the bank is framing the issue of green growth in the African context. And the bank is hosting the African Water Facility website for sharing knowledge and information about grants to different stakeholders, with financial support from the AU and donor governments and foundations as well as the AfDB.

AfDB as institutional broker and partner

Perhaps foremost in the repositioning is the AfDB's role as institutional broker, recognizing that the organization must not only partner with the traditional institutions – the World Bank Group and major bilateral Western donors – but also with the revitalized African-based institutions, the African Union and NEPAD, the UN's Economic Commission for Africa, the UNDP Regional Bureau for Africa, and the sub-regional trading groups.

Partnerships need to include CSOs, private businesses, and states from emerging economies (China, India, Brazil), sovereign wealth funds and pension funds, as well as financing from African sources, more efficient tax collection, royalties from extractive industries, remittances from migrants, and rich African philanthropists. With this expected new finance base, the bank can leverage its role as institutional broker (AfDB Group 2013).

Since 2007 the AfDB has specified the various ways that partnerships leverage resources and knowledge. Partners can cooperate through traditional means like trust funds and co-financing, but it can also mean technical cooperation, the secondment of officials between organizations or staff exchanges, special initiatives for limited purposes, or research or knowledge partnerships. Partnerships help to reposition the bank as an institutional broker and demonstrate positive results to internal and external stakeholders. Yet the AfDB has not yet embraced the more encompassing view of partnerships as articulated in the World Bank. In *The World Bank and Aid Effectiveness* (2011), the WB has developed indicators of levels of partnership: harmonization of aid practices by joint missions to the field and joint country analytic work; coordination at country level with other aid donors; coordinating with wider stakeholders like parliaments (something AfDB does not do) and civil society; and partnering with the private sector.

Some examples of the partnerships detail the ways that AfDB serves as an institutional broker. The Multi-donor Water Partnership Program comes closest to a traditional partnership, the AfDB working with donor states like the Netherlands, Canada, and Denmark since 2006. The objective, however, is not to co-finance specific projects but to enhance the operational capacity of the bank in its rural water and climate initiatives. The partnership carried out studies of best water practices in 32 countries, specified guidelines for various policies, including water-user fees, rainwater harvesting, and management of wetlands. As a result of the partnership, the bank has the capacity and expertise to exercise leadership.

Partnerships increasingly include non-traditional partners, creating new entities. Two examples illustrate the trend. The Health in Africa Fund brought together the WB (most notably the International Finance Corporation), the AfDB, the Bill and Melinda Gates Foundation, and the German development finance institution (DEG) to create a new private equity fund. Managed by Aureos Capital, the Health in Africa Fund invests in small and medium-sized African companies, private health clinics and diagnostic centers serving low-income Africans. This partnership is part of a concerted effort to harness the private sector for national health goals, with the AfDB the second largest contributor after the IFC. Similarly, the African Guarantee Fund for Small and Medium-sized Enterprises (AGF) is also a public/ private partnership designed to finance small and medium-sized enterprises, often a neglected segment. Funded by the AfDB, with Danish and Spanish support, they provide financial guarantees to partner-lending institutions, which then, in turn, support businesses. This partnership is consistent with AfDB's support of regionalization and the pooling of resources to avoid duplication and inefficiencies. Whether the AfDB is able to enhance its capacity to be a reliable partner for development will depend on both its prudent management of scarce economic resources and its ability to harness the resources and expertise of its partners.

Conclusion: from follower to broker, partner, and leader?

While many of these initiatives are relatively young and their success and sustainability are not assured, they do provide an indication of how the AfDB is trying to position itself more broadly in the African landscape of development. The initiatives with the greatest probability of success are the partnerships with multiple actors whose participation strengthens all parties and activity around developing and refining statistical services. The initiatives less likely to be successful in terms of effectiveness are those that call for the creation of more African institutions. Rather than creating more institutions and new programs, the bank needs to integrate institutions and strengthen the most effective.

After more than two decades of following the initiatives of the donor community, be it the World Bank or nonregional member states, and after two decades of being unable to fashion unique African solutions for African problems, the AfDB has adopted the dominant development practices in terms of sustainability, civil society involvement, gender programs, and good governance. They have adopted new practices as a result of both external forces and internal need for change and have done so both to garner external resources and to enhance legitimacy. Ultimately this means that the AfDB remains a follower of international development trends, responding to donor-led demands. At the same time, it is struggling to exert a degree of autonomy and leadership by reinvigorating its traditional commitment to regional integration and providing leadership to and fostering partnerships with both established institutions and the new development actors on the continent. Its success at those tasks will determine its future.

References

African Development Bank (AfDB). *Annual Reports* (various years). Available at: www.afdb.org/en/documents/publications/annual-report/ (accessed 5 June 2015).
African Development Bank (AfDB). 1995. *Mid-Term Review of ADB-WID Programme and Proposal of a Strategy.* Tunis, Tunisia: AfDB.
African Development Bank (AfDB). 1999. *New Vision.* Tunis, Tunisia: AfDB.
African Development Bank (AfDB). 2000. *Co-operation with Civil Society Organisations: Policy and Guidelines.* Tunis, Tunisia: AfDB.
African Development Bank (AfDB). 2001. *African Development Report.* Available at: www.afdb.org/en/documents/document/african-development-report-2001-8786/ (accessed 5 June 2015).

African Development Bank (AfDB). 2002. *The Gender Policy.* Available at: www.afdb.org/fileadmin/uploads/afdb/Documents/Policy-Documents/10000003-EN-THE-GENDER-POLICY.PDF (accessed 5 June 2015).

African Development Bank (AfDB). 2012. *Development Effectiveness Review 2012: Governance.* Available at: www.afdb.org/fileadmin/uploads/afdb/Documents/Project-and-Operations/Development%20Effectiveness%20Review%202012%20-%20Governance.pdf (accessed 5 June 2015).

African Development Bank (AfDB). 2013. *Connecting Africa: An Assessment of Progress Towards the Connect Africa Summit Goals.* Available at: www.afdb.org/fileadmin/uploads/afdb/Documents/Project-and-Operations/Connecting_Africa_-_An_Assessment_of_Progress_Towards_the_Connect_Africa_Summit_Goals_-_Main_Report.pdf (accessed 5 June 2015).

African Development Bank Group (AfDBG). 2011. *Africa in 50 Years' Time: The Road Towards Inclusive Growth.* Available at: www.afdb.org/fileadmin/uploads/afdb/Documents/Publications/Africa%20in%2050%20Years%20Time.pdf (Accessed 5 June 2015).

African Development Bank Group (AfDBG). 2012a. *Briefing Notes for AfDB's Long-Term Strategy.* Supporting Innovating and Entrepreneurship for Socioeconomic Development Briefing Note 2 (7 March). Available at: www.afdb.org/fileadmin/uploads/afdb/Documents/Policy-Documents/FINAL%20Briefing%20Note%204%20Africas%20Demographic%20Trends.pdf (accessed 5 June 2015).

African Development Bank Group (AfDBG). 2012b. *Annual Development Effectiveness Review 2012: Promoting Regional Integration.* Thematic Review. Tunis, Tunisia: AfDB.

African Development Bank Group (AfDBG). 2012c. *Framework for Enhanced Engagement with Civil Society Organizations.* Available at: www.afdb.org/fileadmin/uploads/afdb/Documents/Policy-Documents/Framework%20for%20Enhanced%20Engagement%20with%20Civil%20Society%20Organizations.pdf (accessed 5 June 2015).

African Development Bank Group (AfDBG). 2013. *At the Center of Africa's Transformation: Strategy for 2013–2022.* Available at: www.afdb.org/fileadmin/uploads/afdb/Documents/Policy-Documents/AfDB_Strategy_for_2013%E2%80%932022_-_At_the_Center_of_Africa%E2%80%99s_Transformation.pdf (accessed 5 June 2015).

African Development Bank Group (AfDBG). 2013/2014. *Investing in Gender Equality for Africa's Transformation.* Available at: www.afdb.org/fileadmin/uploads/afdb/Documents/Policy-Documents/2014-2018_-_Bank_Group_Gender_Strategy.pdf (accessed 5 June 2015).

Aasen, B. 2009. "Gender Equality and the Multilateral Development Banks (MDBs): How the World Bank, the African Development Bank, the Asian Development Bank and the Inter-American Bank Work on Women Empowerment and Gender Equality." Working Paper no. 123. Norwegian Institute for Urban and Regional Research, Oslo.

Babb, S. 2009. *Behind the Development Banks. Washington Politics, World Poverty, and the Wealth of Nations.* Chicago, IL: The University of Chicago Press.

Bøås, M. 1998. "Governance as Multilateral Development Bank Policy: The Cases of the African Development Bank and the Asian Development Bank." *The European Journal of Development Research* 10(2): 117–134.

English, F. P. and H. M. Mule. 1996. *The African Development Bank.* Boulder, CO: Lynne Rienner Publishers.

Fordwor, K. D. 1981. *The African Development Bank: Problems of International Cooperation.* New York: Pergamon Press.

Jerven, M. 2013. *Poor Numbers: How We Are Misled by African Development Statistics and What to Do About It.* Ithaca, NY: Cornell University Press.

Mingst, K. A. 1990. *Politics and the African Development Bank.* Lexington, KY: University Press of Kentucky.

Mingst, K. A. and C. P. Warkentin. 1997. "The Politics of Women and Development in the United Nations." In *Swords and Plowshares: The United Nations in Transition,* edited by R. Wheeler and H. McConnell. Toronto: Canadian Scholar's Press, pp. 157–174.

Park, S. 2010. *The World Bank Group and Environmentalists: Changing International Organization Identities.* London: Manchester University Press.

Park, S. and A. Vetterlein. 2010. "Owning Development: Creating Policy Norms in the IMF and the World Bank." In *Owning Development: Creating Policy Norms in the IMF and the World Bank,* edited by S. Park and A. Vetterlein. Cambridge: Cambridge University Press, pp. 3–26.

Rich, B. 2013. *Forecasting the Future: The World Bank and The Politics of Environmental Destruction.* Washington, DC: Island Press.

Risby, L. A. and D. Todd. 2011. "Mainstreaming Gender Equality: A Road to Results or a Road to Nowhere? An Evaluation Synthesis." Report undertaken by the AfDB principal evaluation officer and a consultant.

Sherk, D. R. 1999. "The African Development Bank: A Rare Success on a Troubled Continent." Prepared for the International Financial Institution Advisory Commission. Published in U.S. House of Representatives, Committee on Financial Services, Hearings (25 April 2001) "U.S. Policy Towards the African Development Bank and the African Development Fund." Washington, DC: US Government Printing Office.

Strand, J. R. 2001. "Institutional Design and Power Relations in the African Development Bank." *Journal of Asian and African Studies* 36(2): 203–223.

Thurow, R. 1989. "Development Bank in Africa Transcends the Region's Despair." *Wall Street Journal,* 16 May.

Weaver, C. 2008. *Hypocrisy Trap. The World Bank and the Poverty of Reform.* Princeton, NJ: Princeton University Press.

Weaver, C. 2010. "The Strategic Social Construction of the World Bank's Gender and Development Policy Norm." In *Owning Development: Creating Policy Norms in the IMF and the World Bank,* edited by S. Park and A. Vetterlein. Cambridge: Cambridge University Press, pp. 70–89.

World Bank. 1985. "Outcome of Discussions with AfGDB Delegation." Consultation meeting of 14–16 January on Aid Coordination. Unpublished document.

World Bank. 1989. *Sub-Saharan Africa: From Crisis to Sustainable Growth; A Long-Term Perspective Study.* Available at: www.gbv.de/dms/zbw/256156794.pdf (accessed 5 June 2015).

World Bank. 2011. *The World Bank and Aid Effectiveness: Performance to Date and Agenda Ahead.* Available at: www1.worldbank.org/operations/aideffectiveness/documents/OPCS_Aideffectivenes_IssuesBrief.pdf (accessed 5 June, 2015).

World Bank. 2012. *De-Fragmenting Africa: Deepening Regional Trade Integration in Goods and Services.* See especially P. Brenton and G. Isik, "Introduction: Linking African Markets: Removing Barriers to Intra-Africa Trade," pp. 1–22.

6 Ambivalent engagement

Human rights and the multilateral development banks

Daniel B. Braaten[1]

The World Bank has received significant criticism for the negative impact its lending activities have on human rights and for its ambivalence in incorporating human rights into its policies and procedures. Scholars have analyzed the negative impact of the World Bank's lending policies, particularly structural adjustment, on human rights in recipient countries (Abouhard and Cingranelli 2006, 2008; Eriksen and de Soysa 2009). Additionally, many argue that the World Bank is subject to various human rights obligations under international law (Skogly 2001; Darrow 2003; De Feyter 2004; Crippa 2010). Finally, scholars have critiqued the World Bank for its lack of incorporation of a comprehensive human rights policy (Sarfaty 2009; Fujita 2013, 2010). What has received less attention, however, is an overview of the human rights impact of all of the multilateral development banks (MDBs), which include the regional development banks (RDBs) – the African Development Bank (AfDB), the Asian Development Bank (ADB), the European Bank for Reconstruction and Development (EBRD), and the Inter-American Development Bank (IADB) – and the World Bank. As the contributors to this volume acknowledge, the global lending capacity of the RDBs is significant and their impact is worldwide.

This chapter examines the existing procedures and policies at each of the five MDBs and how they either promote human rights or try to prevent human rights abuse. More specifically, this chapter will analyze reforms the MDBs have undergone in two areas: social development lending and the development and implementation of safeguard policies. While these changes were not meant to provide comprehensive promotion and protection for the entire range of human rights as recognized by international law, they do have relevance for certain human rights, both directly and indirectly. For example, the safeguard policy all MDBs have on involuntary resettlement can have an impact on people's rights to adequate housing as defined in the International Covenant on Economic, Social, and Cultural Rights (ICESCR) and the right to liberty of movement and freedom to choose one's residence as defined in the International Covenant on Civil and Political Rights (ICPSR), among other rights (Martin 2011).

The rest of the chapter will proceed as follows. The first section will describe the impact the MDBs can have on human rights, both positive and negative. This will be followed by a brief overview of the charters of the MDBs and how they have been interpreted with regard to promoting and protecting human rights. The next two sections will examine the amount and types of social development lending that occurs at each MDB and the safeguard policies instituted at each. The safeguard policies section will also contain a brief discussion of the accountability mechanisms at the MDBs and how they work to hold the banks accountable to their own safeguards. Finally, the conclusion will discuss whether MDB actions on human rights are more rhetoric or reality.

The primary finding in this chapter is that the MDBs are ambivalently engaged with human rights. Rhetorically, the banks have expressed some support for human rights, especially social, economic, and cultural rights. However, this support is almost exclusively couched in terms of promoting rights that will in turn lead to greater economic growth and development. In terms of actions taken to protect and promote human rights, the MDBs have made a piecemeal attempt to ensure that some economic and social rights are promoted but have not addressed the promotion or protection of civil and political rights in any significant manner.

Human rights and the multilateral development banks

The impact of the MDBs on human rights can be both positive and negative. On the positive side, the MDBs provide much-needed financing for economic development projects. These projects aim to facilitate economic growth and the alleviation of poverty, one of the greatest contributors to increased enjoyment of human rights. Overall, economic growth and development is positive for the enjoyment of human rights, and to the extent that development institutions such as the MDBs contribute to this they can have a positive impact on the human rights of millions of people (Howard-Hassmann 2005). More specifically, development financing can have a direct positive impact on the realization of many economic and social rights as defined by various human rights treaties, including the ICESCR. Access to basic rights such as clean water, food, shelter, essential medicine, and education are all listed in human rights treaties such as the ICESCR, the Convention on the Rights of the Child, and the International Convention on the Elimination of Discrimination Against Women (CEDAW) among others. These rights are also the target of much of the social development lending that the MDBs undertake, therefore contributing directly to the realization of specific rights.

Conversely, institutions like the MDBs can have a decidedly negative impact on human rights through their lending activity, both directly and indirectly. The indirect negative impact from MDB lending can come in the form of support for rights-repressing regimes. Lending support from the MDBs to rights-repressing governments (which can abuse both civil and political rights and economic, social, or cultural rights) can potentially prolong this type of repression by providing economic support to such governments.

Secondly, MDBs can have a direct negative impact on human rights through the types of development projects they finance. Large infrastructure projects, which for many years have been the bread and butter of the World Bank and the RDBs, can cause massive disruption to the lives of local people in the path of these projects. These disruptions can lead to local populations losing their traditional sources of income without adequate compensation, as well as other problems. Additionally, many of these projects displace already marginalized people such as indigenous groups, ethnic minorities, women, and children (Clark 2002).

The MDBs, particularly the World Bank, have rhetorically claimed to promote human rights, particularly economic and social rights. However, even this level of rhetorical support indicates an ambiguous engagement with human rights since the institutions do not show the same level of support for civil and political rights. The actual realization of rights from their activities is also unclear. One of the major factors that complicate the MDB position on human rights is the foundational charter for each institution. The mandates for all the MDBs, except the EBRD, explicitly forbid the use of political factors in the decision-making processes of the institutions (where the promotion of human rights is considered political and stems from the traditional understanding of state sovereignty protecting the rights of states to determine the fate of the people within their territories). The mandates of the AfDB, ADB, and IADB all follow the lead of the World Bank, whose articles of agreement state in Article IV, Section 10:

> The Bank and its officers shall not interfere in the political affairs of any member; nor shall they be influenced in their decisions by the political character of the member or members concerned. Only economic considerations shall be relevant to their decisions, and these considerations shall be weighed impartially in order to achieve the purposes stated in Article I.
> (IBRD 1945)

Because of this language, the World Bank and other RDBs have argued that they are prohibited from incorporating direct political issues such as human rights into their lending activity. Of course, many have argued – including some World Bank staff members themselves – that the mandate can be interpreted more broadly to include political issues such as human rights, especially as they may affect economic development.[2] Despite this, neither the World Bank nor the African Development Bank, Asian Development Bank or Inter-American Development Bank has a comprehensive human rights policy that guides its operations and lending practices.

The EBRD is an outlier here in terms of political factors influencing its lending decisions. The EBRD's charter states that political affairs can influence lending decisions. The EBRD takes on, as part of its mandate: democracy promotion, promotion of the rule of law, and respect for human rights. The preamble of the EBRD charter states that the institution is:

> Committed to the fundamental principles of multiparty democracy, the rule of law, respect for human rights and market economics … . Welcoming the intent of Central and Eastern European countries to further the practical implementation of multiparty democracy, strengthening democratic institutions, the rule of law and respect for human rights and their willingness to implement reforms in order to evolve towards market-oriented economies.
>
> (EBRD 1991)

Although the preamble does not create a legally binding obligation it does signal the overall values of the treaty. Furthermore, Chapter 1, Article 1 of the EBRD charter also states:

> In contributing to economic progress and reconstruction, the purpose of the Bank shall be to foster the transition towards open market-oriented economies and to promote private and entrepreneurial initiative in the Central and Eastern European countries committed to and applying the principles of multiparty democracy, pluralism and market economics.
>
> (EBRD 1991)

After the EBRD became operational it set out guidelines for the political aspect of its mandate. The memorandum points to other regional organizations and treaties such as the Council of Europe and the European Convention on Human Rights as reference points for the bank to use when implementing its own political mandate (EBRD 2013). The memorandum also couches the EBRD's support for democracy in terms of its simultaneous support for a country's transition to a market economy. Finally, the EBRD measures a country on its political progress (i.e. its transition to democracy) based on its adherence to those rights that are essential to multi-party democracy, pluralism, and market economics. This means a focus specifically on civil and political rights (EBDR 2013). This focus is understandable given the bank's mandate to assess progress in countries in Eastern and Central Europe moving to multi-party democracy in the post-Cold War era.

The EBRD is unique amongst development banks in that it explicitly embraces political factors in its lending decisions, specifically issues dealing with democracy and the rule of law that are highly intertwined with protecting civil and political rights (see Shields, this volume). However, because the EBRD focuses on a country's transition to democracy (and a market economy), the institution can be fairly loose in what it considers transitioning activity and therefore still within the mandate. The NGO CCE Bankwatch Network has criticized the EBRD for not having consistent democracy promotion criteria and defining transitioning to democracy so broadly as to include all but the most repressive regimes (CCE Bankwatch Network 2011). Regardless of its approach to promoting democracy, the EBRD's mandate only focuses on a narrow promotion of certain civil and political rights and does not employ similar language in relation to economic, social, and cultural rights; it thus does not embrace human rights comprehensively. The other RDBs follow the lead of the World Bank and their charters explicitly prohibit political factors, including the whole panoply of human rights, from influencing their lending decisions. Just looking at the mandates of each of the MDBs, human rights play no role in the operations and lending decisions of the MDBs with the exception of the EBRD's inclusion of civil and political rights. Additionally, none of the MDBs have developed a comprehensive human rights policy to guide their operations and lending decisions.

Despite the lack of a comprehensive approach to promoting and protecting human rights, these institutions have over time, at least rhetorically, taken a piecemeal approach to human rights through social development lending and the development of safeguard policies. These developments have indirectly, and in some cases directly, sought to promote and protect certain human rights despite the general ambivalence of the banks regarding human rights. The rest of this chapter will analyze how the MDBs seek to promote and protect human rights (or fail to do so) by focusing on their social development lending and their safeguards policies. As a point of comparison, the World Bank's approach to human rights will serve as a focal point for the RDBs to see how they rate on human rights issues compared with each other. Do they exceed the World Bank in respect for human rights or do they fall short of the World Bank example? Additionally, how do the RDBs compare to one another? Are any of the RDBs better on human rights than the others or do they all have roughly the same approach?

Social development lending

Social development lending is lending for sectors outside the MDBs' traditional lending sectors, which include energy, agriculture, transportation, and urban development. Social lending is lending for education, health, and expanding safety nets (Lyne et al. 2009). This type of lending can have a direct impact on human rights, particularly social and economic rights such as the right to health and the right to education. Traditionally, MDB lending has focused on large-scale development projects. Some examples include large-scale infrastructure projects like the building of major highways or dams. Over the last few decades, however, the MDBs have engaged in more social development lending and more specifically targeted anti-poverty lending (Retzel, this volume; Culpeper 1997). This type of activity can have a more direct positive effect on human rights than the more vaguely argued idea that economic growth and development will lead to better human rights protection overall. Lyne et al. (2009: 418) argue that from the mid-1980s there was a general trend of increased social development lending in the MDBs, but there was also considerable variation across the banks in how much each one emphasized social development lending.

Social development lending has become a larger part of the World Bank's lending profile. Lyne et al. note that:

> Total dollars lent for social development at the World Bank in 1998 – in education, health, and safety nets – exceeded loans for the traditional sectors of energy, industry, mining, oil and gas, irrigation, transportation, and urban development combined. Given that such "traditional" sectors had dominated the Bank's portfolio since 1945, this change marked a major shift in lending behavior.
>
> (ibid.: 408)

In 2005 the World Bank placed social development as a core element in its development strategy, and while social issues have been a part of World Bank lending since the 1970s, this shift made social issues central to the strategy for the first time. Vetterlein (2007) argues that social policy in the World Bank has changed over time, from the 1970s, when social development policies were an important component of World Bank lending, to the 1980s when they were downplayed, to the 1990s when they were seen as components of economic growth, and to the 2000s when they resumed their position as a core component of the development strategy of the World Bank. The World Bank has recently funded a number of projects that fulfill a social development agenda, including a Global Program on Forced Displacement and Regional Centers of Excellence in Social Development. According to the World Bank, between 2008 and 2012 the IBRD and IDA lent $4.9 billion for social development projects. These projects were focused on themes of participation and civic engagement as well as conflict prevention and gender equality (World Bank 2013a).

The African Development Bank's focus on social development lending has led to the launch of a number of programs. These include the New Partnership for Africa's Development (NEPAD) and the Fragile State Facility established in 2001 and 2008 respectively. The NEPAD's stated goals are to: "promote accelerated growth and sustainable development, to eradicate widespread and severe poverty, and to halt the marginalization of Africa in the globalization process." It hopes to accomplish these goals through six sectoral strategies: bridging the infrastructure gap; building human resources, which includes reducing poverty; bridging the education gap; reversing the brain drain; improving health; developing sustainable agriculture; protecting the environment; supporting culture; and finally, developing science and technology (AfDB 2014c). The Fragile State Facility (FSF) is an autonomous entity within the AfDB and its goal is to provide support for states emerging from conflict or crisis. Its goals for eligible countries include "consolidating peace, stabilizing their economies, and laying the foundation for sustainable economic growth" (AfDB 2014a). This is to be accomplished by the FSF through supplemental support, debt arrears clearance, and targeted support. Although the FSF does not explicitly advocate social development lending, that type of lending does fall within its purview. Additionally, fragile states are places that often have terrible human rights records, so in providing specific support to those states the AfDB can indirectly support human rights.

The African Development Bank also has a specific policy on mainstreaming gender promotion in its activities as a means of supporting economic growth and gender equality on the continent (AfDB 2001; see Mingst, this volume). Recently, the AfDB outlined its objectives for mainstreaming gender promotion in its activities for 2014–2018. The strategy has three pillars: improving legal status and property rights for women, economic empowerment, and knowledge management and capacity building (AfDB 2014b). The idea here is to make economic growth more inclusive by allowing women a greater role and stake in it and also to increase economic growth through the contributions of women.

The stated goal of the ADB in its social development agenda is:

> To reduce poverty, inequality and vulnerability among poor and marginalized persons by transforming institutions to enable them to foster inclusiveness and equitable access to services, resources and opportunities; empower people to participate in social, economic and political life; and provide security to help individuals cope with chronic or unforeseen and sudden risks.
>
> (ADB 2014e)

The Asian Development Banks has identified five areas to focus on in its social development agenda: poverty reduction, social protection, health, education, and gender. In 2004 the ADB reviewed and updated its poverty reduction strategy to incorporate the Millennium Development Goals and create a broader and more inclusive poverty reduction strategy. This enhanced poverty reduction strategy has three pillars: pro-poor sustainable economic growth, inclusive social development, and good governance. The enhanced poverty reduction strategy also incorporates issues that indirectly affect poverty such as environmental sustainability, gender equity, private sector development, and regional cooperation (ADB 2014d). In terms of social protection, the ADB has focused on three main areas: labor market policies, social insurance, and social assistance. The goal here is to protect people during crises and provide an investment for future development (ADB 2014f). Additionally, the ADB has created a Social Protection Index that can serve as a single indicator guide for governments to help them assess the level of social protection in their country (Handayani 2014). With regard to health, the ADB has sought to increase lending for projects associated with maternal and child health, communicable diseases, pandemics and emerging diseases, and strengthening health services in general (ADB 2014c). For education, the ADB has sought to fund projects focusing on access to primary and secondary education as well as technical and higher education. It has also sought to fund projects that promote equity in education and ensure education is financially sustainable (ADB 2014b). Finally, with regard to gender, the ADB has tried to promote gender through mainstreaming gender in all its operations (from project planning to implementation and review) and also explicitly promoting and monitoring gender equality in its member countries (ADB 2014a).

With its ninth general capital increase in 2012, the Inter-American Development Bank's board of governors mandated the institution to pursue two main goals: poverty reduction and inequality reduction along with sustainable economic growth. To achieve these goals the IADB identified five sectoral priorities, the first one of which was social policy for equity and productivity. This social policy for equity and productivity contains five specific priorities: safety nets for the poor, labor market reform, education, health, and gender and diversity (IADB 2014a). These five priorities exemplify social development lending and now constitute a main plank of IADB lending activity. Additionally, the IADB has specific policies on gender and indigenous issues. In 2007 the IADB created a gender and diversity division with a goal of promoting gender equality and support for those in the region of African or indigenous descent. The gender action plan commits the bank to support gender equality by mainstreaming it in its activities as well as supporting it through direct investment. The IADB also states that, through its Gender and Diversity Fund, it tries to mainstream race into its activities as part of supporting the African-descendant population in Latin America and the Caribbean, in addition to direct lending and the implementation of lending safeguards (IADB 2014b).

Finally, the EBRD has laid out its commitment to social development lending in its 2008 statement on environmental and social policy, which is the same policy statement that outlines its safeguard policies detailed below. The 2008 report states that the EBRD is "committed to promoting 'environmentally sound and sustainable development' in the full range of its investments and technical cooperation activities" (EBRD 2008: 2). The policy outlines the social dimensions of sustainable development as including labor standards, working conditions, and community impacts that include public health and safety, gender equality, impact on indigenous peoples and culture, involuntary resettlement, and affordability of basic services. The EBRD hopes to ensure these are promoted by mainstreaming them throughout their activities and by selecting projects for funding that promote them as well. The EBRD, however, also outlined a desire to directly promote social development through direct lending. This is to be done through technical assistance, stand-alone investment projects, and pilot program, among other mechanisms (EBRD 2008).

Social development lending can have a direct positive impact on human rights if done effectively. Lending that is targeted at helping the most vulnerable and providing basic social services such as health care and education can lead to the fulfillment of those rights as outlined in the ICESCR. Each of the MDBs considers social development lending as part of its mandate to foster economic development, which indicates that a consensus has emerged among the MDBs about the necessity of social development lending. Lyne et al. (2009) argue that the increase in social development lending seen over the last few decades in the MDBs is driven by coalition politics in the executive boards of the MDBs. Western donor states, tired of funding large infrastructure projects, and some developing states formed voting coalitions to support social development lending projects.

In addition to including social development lending in their portfolios, most of the MDBs have adopted specialized plans or funds that try to target money at groups in particularly dire circumstances; the Fragile State Facility of the AfDB is an example. Despite the prevalence of social development lending in the MDBs, these institutions still mostly finance more traditional development projects within traditional development sectors, and while greater economic growth can lead to greater protection of human rights, this type of lending is a circuitous means of promoting human rights compared with social development lending, which can have direct targeted impact.

Safeguard policies

All the MDBs have safeguard policies meant to protect vulnerable people and the environment from exploitation by the banks' ongoing operations. However, the level of protection and what is protected varies across institutions. Safeguard policies in the context of this chapter refers to operations policies established in each MDB that are designed to eliminate or minimize the negative aspects of MDB lending activities, which can include environmental damage and harm to affected communities that may violate individual rights. In the MDBs, operational policies are rules that establish the requirements of the bank itself and of its borrowers, and these requirements apply to all the banks' activities. Additionally, each bank has established its own accountability mechanisms to hold the institution accountable to its own safeguard policies.

In 2013 the World Bank began the process of revising and updating its safeguard policies. Part of the purpose of this revision is to consolidate its various safeguard policies into one comprehensive policy. As of 2015, the World Bank's social and environmental safeguard policies include: Environmental Assessment, Natural Habitats, Pest Management, Involuntary Resettlement, Indigenous Peoples, Forests, Physical Cultural Resources, and Safety of Dams. In 2005 the World Bank introduced a pilot program which would help borrowing countries develop their own policy safeguard systems and allow them to take on a larger role in implementing the safeguard policies (World Bank 2013b). Table 6.1 lists all the social and environmental safeguard policies for each MDB.

The proposed revision of the World Bank safeguards has not been without controversy: various NGOs have criticized these changes as weakening the current safeguards rather than strengthening them. The World Bank has

Table 6.1 MDB Safeguard Policies 2015

Bank	World Bank	AfDB	ADB	EBRD	IADB
Involuntary Resettlement	x	x	x	x	x
Indigenous Peoples	x		x	x	x
Gender					x
Environmental and Social Assessment	x*	x	x*	x	x*
Natural Habitats	x				
Pest Management	x				
Forests	x				
Pollution Prevention		x		x	
Biodiversity		x		x	
Cultural Heritage				x	
Health		x		x	
Labor		x		x	
Safety of Dams	x				

Note: * Environmental Assessment only.

undertaken the re-evaluation of its safeguard policies after an internal evaluation documenting how the safeguards have performed. The evaluation recommended harmonizing standards across the entire World Bank Group and also for the World Bank specifically to consolidate its environmental policies and strengthen its country safeguard pilot program (Independent Evaluation Group 2010). It is this latter measure that has engendered much of the criticism from NGOs. The Bank Information Center (BIC), an NGO that monitors the World Bank, argued that the proposed revisions would weaken the Indigenous Peoples policy by creating a loophole allowing governments to circumvent it. According to the BIC, the new proposal "allows governments to "opt out" of previously guaranteed protections for indigenous peoples, citing discomfort among certain African governments with the term "indigenous peoples" and the rights it confers" (BIC 2014). Additionally, the World Bank acknowledged a need to more clearly define peoples who are vulnerable or disadvantaged and include age, disability, gender, and sexual orientation, but the new proposal does not do so and only refers to those categories in a general way (BIC 2014). The World Bank's re-evaluation of its safeguard policies has also uncovered serious problems with the institution's involuntary resettlement safeguard. After an internal evaluation, the World Bank acknowledged that because of poor record keeping and documentation the institution had no idea how many people had been forced off of their land because of projects it financed, or to what extent those individuals were compensated, if at all. World Bank president Jim Yong Kim promised that the institution "must and will do better" in terms of accounting for the impacts World Bank projects have on involuntary resettlement, and also released a new action plan to improve the performance of its involuntary resettlement safeguard policy (Yukhananov 2015; World Bank 2015).

In 2013 the African Development Bank created a unified safeguard policy called the Integrated Safeguards System (ISS). ISS contains five operations safeguards: Environmental and Social Assessment; Involuntary Resettlement, Land Acquisition, Population Displacement and Compensation; Biodiversity and Ecosystem Services; Pollution Prevention and Control, Hazardous Materials and Resource Efficiency; and Labor Conditions, Health and Safety (AfDB 2013). The AfDB acknowledges in the preamble to the ISS statement that it:

> Views economic and social rights as an integral part of human rights, and accordingly affirms that it respects the principles and values of human rights as set out in the UN Charter and the African Charter of Human and Peoples' Rights. These were among the principles that guided the development of the Integrated Safeguards System.
>
> (AfDB 2013: 1)

This acknowledgment of human rights makes the AfDB one of the only MDBs to mention human rights explicitly with respect to its safeguard policies. The AfDB states that the motivation for revising its safeguard policies was to align them with the bank's 2013–2022 overall lending strategy and to harmonize their standards with those of other IFIs (AfDB 2013).

The AfDB's new social safeguard system has not been met with universal support, especially with regard to its perceived lack of support for indigenous peoples' rights. The NGO Forest People's Program (FPP) criticized the new AfDB standards for not including a standalone operational policy on indigenous rights as the other MDBs do. It is expected that potential negative impacts on indigenous communities will be considered under the first operational safeguard of the ISS, Environment and Social Assessment. The Forest People's Program acknowledges that this inclusion of indigenous rights considerations under the Environmental and Social Assessment operational safeguard is a positive first step but worries that it will lead to "weak implementation" (FPP 2013).

In 2009 the Asian Development Bank developed its Safeguard Policy Statement (SPS). The SPS is a single policy statement that integrates the ADB's three established safeguard policies on Involuntary Resettlement, Indigenous Peoples and Environmental Protection into one comprehensive policy statement. The SPS maintains these three safeguard policies but provides more detail and clarification on the scope and objectives of each policy.

The SPS also contains four sets of requirements for the ADB's clients to ensure they are compliant with these policies. Three of the sets of requirements map to the three safeguard policies (Involuntary Resettlement, Indigenous Peoples, and Environmental Protection), while the fourth is a set of special requirements for different finance modalities. This last set of requirements is for alternative finance approaches outside of the standard project loans (ADB 2009).

The ADB stated that its desire to update its policy safeguards was driven by the changing international environment. Specifically, it mentions that borrowing country members have been enhancing their own social and environmental protections and other international financial institutions such as the World Bank, the International Finance Corporation (which is part of the World Bank Group), and the EBRD have been modifying their own policy safeguards, and that the ADB seeks to harmonize its standards with those of its peers (ADB 2009). Critics took this to mean that the ADB was seeking to weaken its policy safeguards to placate borrowing member countries and streamline their safeguard polices to make them less burdensome. NGOs and civil society organizations, fearing that the review process would lead to a weakening of the safeguards, became heavily involved in the review process, causing the ADB president to issue a statement saying the review process would lead to "no weakening" of the safeguards (Rosien 2010).

As detailed above, the EBRD adopted its Environment and Social Policy in 2008. The policy notes that "the EBRD is committed to promoting 'environmentally sound and sustainable development' in the full range of its investment and technical cooperation activities" and "the Bank (EBRD) recognizes that financing sustainable development must rank among the highest priorities of the EBRD's activities" (EBRD 2008: 2). The Environment and Social Policy outlines how the EBRD will implement its commitment to sustainable development, which includes environmental and social sustainability. In keeping with this goal the EBRD's Environment and Social Policy lists ten performance requirements its clients are expected to meet and the EBRD's role is to review and assess its clients' actions to ensure that they are in line with the ten requirements. The ten performance requirements are: Environmental and Social Appraisal and Management; Labour and Working Conditions; Pollution Prevention and Abatement; Community Health, Safety and Security; Land Acquisition, Involuntary Resettlement and Economic Displacement; Biodiversity Conservation and Sustainable Natural Resource Management; Indigenous Peoples; Cultural Heritage; Financial Intermediaries; and Information Disclosure and Stakeholder Engagement (EBRD 2008).

Finally, the Inter-American Development Bank does not have a comprehensive policy statement unifying its operational safeguards but it does have individual operational safeguards for Environment and Safeguard Compliance, Involuntary Resettlement, Indigenous Peoples, and Gender and Development. As with the other institutions, the IADB's operational safeguards commit its clients to abiding by safeguards and the bank to monitor its clients to ensure adherence to the policies. The IADB safeguard policy on indigenous peoples is different from similar policies in the other MDBs because it has two main goals: to promote the economic development of indigenous communities – specifically, to promote "development with identity" – and to create safeguards that minimize exclusion and adverse impacts the IADBs operations might have on indigenous peoples (IADB 2006). The IADB defines "development with identity" as:

> a process that includes strengthening of indigenous peoples, harmony and sustained interaction with their environment, sound management of natural resources and territories, the creation and exercise of authority, and respect for the rights and values of indigenous peoples, including cultural, economic, social and institutional rights, in accordance with their own worldview and governance.
> (IADB 2006: 20)

In general the IADB hopes to realize this policy by mainstreaming indigenous issues in its development operations with a variety of more specific measures, such as support for indigenous peoples governance and support for appropriate consultation with indigenous peoples with regard to natural resource management. The IADB's indigenous policy safeguard is considered to be the strongest of all the banks (see Humphreys, this volume).

Across the MDBs the safeguard policies have developed in an ad hoc manner, again highlighting MDB ambivalence about human rights. The initial creation of such measures seems to have been driven by pressure from a constellation of environmental NGOs and donor states, specifically the United States, which led to the creation of environmental policies in the MDBs and to environmental safeguards (Babb 2009). The more recent re-evaluations of safeguard policies that have occurred, and are occurring, in the various MDBs seem to be driven by what some of the MDBs refer to as a "changing international environment." This can be seen in both the World Bank and ADB responding to borrowing countries with more streamlined safeguard implementation and country-level safeguard responsibilities and in the AfDB's desire to harmonize its safeguards with those of other MDBs and IFIs. Additionally, NGO pressure has been applied to both try to prevent any rollbacks in safeguards policies and enhance the current policies.

Reviewing the safeguard policies in the MDBs, again in Table 6.1, one can see several key areas that relate to human rights, including involuntary resettlement, indigenous peoples protection, health, labor conditions, and gender discrimination. Not every MDB has an operational policy that covers these areas but they are all covered by at least one MDB. For example, all of the MDBs have an operational policy on involuntary resettlement. This is perhaps not surprising since it is an issue that is intertwined with development lending – especially the large infrastructure projects that the MDBs finance in large volumes. Involuntary resettlement is a situation in which an individual or group of individuals does not have the right to refuse land acquisition for development activity. It is a situation that can be ripe for the abuse of human rights, which can include civil and political rights along with economic rights (Clark 2002).

As was mentioned above, each of the MDBs has an accountability mechanism that serves to hold the institution accountable to its own safeguard policies. In 1993 the World Bank created an Independent Inspection Panel (WBIP) that is meant to serve as a mechanism for people adversely affected by WB projects to air their grievances and seek redress (Bissell and Nanwani 2009). The WBIP was the first accountability mechanism created by an MDB and has served as a model for the RDBs in creating their own mechanisms. The WBIP is composed of three members appointed by the executive board of the World Bank, all serving a fixed five-year term while reporting directly to the executive board. The Bank's management is then required to respond to the report with recommendations to address the WBIP's findings (World Bank 2014). The World Bank's executive board created the WBIP after both external pressure from civil society organizations and internal pressure by member state governments.

The WBIP is meant to hold the World Bank accountable to its own safeguard policies, which ideally should lead to greater protection of human rights. Sabine Schlemmer-Schulte argues that the WBIP will be beneficial for human rights because by its very existence it shows "how seriously the WB takes its commitment to abide by its own standards, which in comparison with general international principles, include model human rights standards" (1999: 20). The WBIP has also pushed the WB to take a stand against certain borrower activities that harm human rights. For example, in the report on the Chad-Cameroon Petroleum and Pipeline Project the WBIP encouraged the bank to study the consequences of human rights violations and how they contribute to the failure of World Bank projects (WBIP 2009). The WBIP is not, however, without its detractors, who point out that projects are starting to become "panel-proof" – that is, the social and environmental portions of projects are being written so flexibly as to make it impossible for the WB and its staff to ever be in violation of them (Fujita 2010). Also, as the new findings regarding the World Bank's involuntary resettlement safeguards reveal, simply having safeguard policies on the books is not enough to ensure that those standards are adequate or that the banks are actually following through on those standards.

The accountability mechanisms of the RDBs and the WBIP are similar and they all serve the same main function – to hold the institutions accountable to their safeguard policies. Where the accountability mechanisms of the RDBs and the WBIP differ is that the RDB accountability mechanisms have an additional function – problem solving. The Asian Development Bank was the first RDB to develop an accountability mechanism with both a problem-solving and accountability function. Specifically, the ADB accountability mechanism is comprised of two components. First is the Problem Solving

Function run by the Office of the Special Project Facilitator (SPF). This component is tasked with helping people adversely affected by an ADB project to find a solution to their problem. Resolution of the problem may entail dialogue, information sharing, fact-finding, or mediation (ADB 2012). Second is the Compliance Review Function that is run by the independent Compliance Review Panel (CRP) and tasked with determining whether alleged harm to individuals from an ADB projects is the result of the institution not following its own operations and procedures (ADB 2012). The rest of the RDBs – the AfDB, EBRD, and IADB – all have a similar two-pronged accountability mechanism. The problem-solving components of each accountability mechanism basically work the same way in that they revolve around dialogue between the complainants and other stakeholders in the project and try to resolve the issue without assigning blame.

There is some variation across the accountability mechanisms in how they process complaints, who is allowed to bring a complaint forward, and how the executive board of each institution responds to complaints. Broadly speaking, however, the accountability mechanisms of the MDBs are similar, except for the WBIP's. All of them allow people to register complaints if they believe the bank in question is in violation of one of its operational policies, including its social and environmental safeguards. These mechanisms are meant to hold the MDBs accountable to their own standards of operations and provide some measure of redress for people who are harmed by poorly designed or implemented projects (Nanwani 2014). These mechanisms are greatly limited in their means of providing redress for victims in that it is ultimately up to the board of directors in each institution to decide whether they want to address the problems identified by the inspection mechanism. The approach might be a political necessity since member countries ultimately maintain control over the mechanisms, but an independent mechanism empowered to actually provide redress would be more protective of human rights and indicate the MDBs viewed protecting human rights as a fundamental part of their operation.

Conclusion

Sarfaty (2009) describes human rights in the World Bank as "marginal." What she means is that despite the sometimes strong rhetoric made by some World Bank officials with regard to human rights, the institution "maintains no comprehensive or consistent approach on the policy and operational levels" (648). Sarfaty (2009) pinpoints the World Bank's particular organizational culture as the culprit in the institution's relative lack of incorporation of human rights into its operations. The conclusion of this study on human rights in all the MDBs echoes Sarfaty's study of the World Bank.

The MDBs have an ambivalent engagement with human rights and this makes them marginal to the overall operations of each institution. Rhetorically, the MDBs acknowledge the importance of human rights for economic growth and development, but this support is generally limited to economic and social rights. In other words, the MDBs do not seek to promote and protect all human rights for their own sake but only those rights that are directly connected to economic development. Sarfaty (2009) refers to this as "economizing human rights" – that is, promoting and protecting human rights only so far as they promote economic growth and development.

Aside from the rhetoric, the MDBs have made some actual changes that have led to the protection and promotion of some human rights, although these changes have generally been ad hoc and fragmentary. This can most easily be seen in the safeguard policies of each institution. The MDBs have a variety of safeguard policies that address some human rights issues such as involuntary resettlement and indigenous peoples' rights. However, even the specific safeguards are not generally considered to be on a par with international human rights standards and thus indicate the marginal status that human rights have in the MDBs (Human Rights Watch 2013). The recent revelations regarding the World Bank's poor implementation of its involuntary resettlement safeguards only re-enforces the notion that the safeguard policies of the MDBs need to be more robust if they are to adequately promote and protect human rights.

All of the MDBs hold firm to their original mandates as institutions focused on promoting economic development. All the institutions have made attempts to both safeguard against human rights abuses that may stem from their lending activities and promote human rights through specific types of lending (social development). However, these attempts have been subsumed by the goal of economic development and more glibly by the notion that "human rights abuses are bad for business." Ultimately, this ambivalent approach to human rights might have a positive impact on human rights, or at least a neutral impact, but if the development banks were ever to get serious about human rights it would require changes to their mandates to allow more explicit engagement. This may or may not be preferable for a variety of reasons, but within their current incarnations this is probably all we can expect from the development banks.

Notes

1 The author would like to thank Susan Park and Jonathan Strand for their very valuable feedback. Any errors or omissions are the sole responsibility of the author.
2 In 2006, the Senior Vice-President and General Council Roberto Dañino issued a document titled "Legal Opinion on Human Rights and the Work of the World Bank." This document argued that human rights are legitimate concerns for the institution if they have economic impacts.

References

Abouhard, M. R. and D. Cingranelli. 2008. *Human Rights and Structural Adjustment.* Cambridge: Cambridge University Press.

Abouhard, M. R. and D. Cingranelli. 2006. "The Human Rights Effects of World Bank Structural Adjustment, 1981–2000." *International Studies Quarterly* 50: 233–262.

African Development Bank (AfDB). 2014a. "An Instrument for Consolidating Peace." Tunis, Tunisia: African Development Bank. Available at: www.afdb.org/en/topics-and-sectors/initiatives-partnerships/fragile-states-facility/an-instrument-for-consolidating-peace/ (accessed 30 June 2014).

African Development Bank (AfDB). 2014b. "Investing in Gender Equality For Africa's Transformation." Tunis, Tunisia: African Development Bank. Available at: www.afdb.org/fileadmin/uploads/afdb/Documents/Policy-Documents/2014-2018_Bank_Group_Gender_Strategy.pdf (accessed 30 August 2014).

African Development Bank. (AfDB). 2014c. "New Partnership for Africa's Development."Tunis, Tunisia: African Development Bank. Available at: www.afdb.org/en/topics-and-sectors/initiatives-partnerships/nepad/ (accessed 30 June 2014).

African Development Bank. (AfDB). 2013. "Integrated Safeguard System: Policy Statement and Operational Safeguards." *Safeguards and Sustainability Series* 1(1). Tunis, Tunisia: African Development Bank. Available at: www.afdb.org/fileadmin/uploads/afdb/Documents/Policy-Documents/December_2013_-_AfDB'S_Integrated_Safeguards_System__-_Policy_Statement_and_Operational_Safeguards.pdf (accessed 30 June 2014).

African Development Bank (AfDB). 2001. "The Gender Policy." Tunis, Tunisia: African Development Bank. Available at: www.afdb.org/en/search/?tx_solr%5Bq%5D=The+gender+policy (accessed 30 June 2014).

Asian Development Bank (ADB). 2014a. "Closing the Gender Gap." Manila, Philippines: Asian Development Bank. Available at: www.adb.org/themes/gender/overview (accessed 30 June 2014).

Asian Development Bank (ADB). 2014b. "Education Issues in Asia and the Pacific." Manila, Philippines: Asian Development Bank. www.adb.org/sectors/education/issues (accessed 30 June 2014)

Asian Development Bank (ADB). 2014c. "Health Issues in Asia and the Pacific." Manila, Philippines: Asian Development Bank. Available at: www.adb.org/sectors/health/issues (accessed 30 June 2014).

Asian Development Bank (ADB). 2014d. "Poverty Reduction: Overview." Manila, Philippines: Asian Development Bank. Available at: www.adb.org/themes/poverty/overview (accessed 30 June 2014).

Asian Development Bank (ADB). 2014e. "Social Development: Overview." Manila, Philippines: Asian Development Bank. Available at: www.adb.org/themes/social-development/overview (accessed 30 June 2014).

Asian Development Bank (ADB). 2014f. "Social Protection: Overview." Manila, Philippines: Asian Development Bank. Available at: www.adb.org/sectors/social-protection/overview (accessed 30 June 2014).

Asian Development Bank (ADB). 2012. "Accountability Mechanism Policy." Manila, Philippines: Asian Development Bank. Available at: www.adb.org/documents/accountability-mechanism-policy-2012?ref=site/accountability-mechanism/publications (accessed 31 May 2014).

Asian Development Bank (ADB). 2009. "Safeguard Policy Statement." ADB Policy Paper. Manila, Philippines: Asian Development Bank. Available at: www.adb.org/documents/safeguard-policy-statement (accessed 31 May 2014).

Babb, S. 2009. *Behind the Development Banks*. Chicago, IL: University of Chicago Press.

Bank Information Center (BIC). 2014. "World Bank Breaks its Promise Not to Weaken Protections for the Poor and Planet." Available at: www.bicusa.org/the-world-bank-moves-to-weaken-its-protection-for-the-poor/ (accessed 22 July 2014).

Bissell, R. E. and S. Nanwani. 2009. "Multilateral Development Bank Accountability Mechanisms: Developments and Challenges." *Manchester Journal of International Economic Law* 6(1): 2–55.

CCE Bankwatch Network. 2011. "Are We Nearly There Yet? Dilemmas of Transition After 20 Years of the EBRD's Operations." Available at: http://bankwatch.org/publications/are-we-nearly-there-yet-dilemmas-transition-after-20-years-ebrds-operations (accessed 31 May 2015).

Clark, D. L. 2002. "The World Bank and Human Rights: The Need for Greater Accountability." *Harvard Human Rights Journal* 15: 205–226.

Crippa, L. A. 2010. "Multilateral Development Banks and Human Rights Responsibility." *American University International Law Review* 25(3): 531–577.

Culpeper, R. 1997. *The Multilateral Development Banks: Volume 5, Titans or Behemoths?* Boulder, CO: Lynne Rienner Publishers.

Darrow, M. 2003. *Between Light and Shadow, The World Bank, The International Monetary Fund and International Human Rights Law.* Oxford: Hart Publishing.

De Feyter, K. 2004. "The International Financial Institutions and Human Rights: Law and Practice." *Human Rights Review* 6(1): 56–90.

Eriksen, S. and I. de Soysa. 2009. "A Fate Worse Than Debt? International Financial Institutions and Human Rights, 1981–2003." *Journal of Peace Research* 46: 485–503.

European Bank for Reconstruction and Development (EBRD). 2013. "Political Aspects of the Mandate of the European Bank for Reconstruction and Development." London: European Bank for Reconstruction and Development. Available at: www.ebrd.com/news/publications/instituational-documents/political-aspects-of-the-mandate-of-the-ebrd.html (accessed 31 May 2015).

European Bank for Reconstruction and Development (EBRD). 2008. "Environmental and Social Policy." London: European Bank for Reconstruction and Development. Available at: www.ebrd.com/downloads/research/policies/2008policy.pdf (accessed 31 May 2015).

European Bank for Reconstruction and Development (EBRD). 1991. "Agreement Establishing the European Bank for Reconstruction and Development." London: European Bank for Reconstruction and Development. Available at: www.ebrd.com/news/publications/institutional-documents/basic-documents-of-the-ebrd.html%20 (accessed 31 May 2015)

Forest Peoples Programme. 2013. "African Development Bank set to introduce Indigenous Peoples standards for the first time." *FPP E-Newsletter*, Special Edition on Safeguards, 29 April. Available at: www.forestpeoples.org/enewsletters/fpp-e-newsletter-special-edition-safeguards-april-2013 (accessed 31 May 2015).

Fujita, S. 2013. *The World Bank, Asian Development Bank and Human Rights.* Cheltenham: Edward Elgar Publishing Limited.

Fujita, S. 2010. "The Challenges of Mainstreaming Human Rights in the World Bank." *International Journal of Human Rights* 15(3): 374–396.

Handayani, S. W. 2014. "Poverty Dimension of the Social Protection Index: Assessing Results for Asia and the Pacific." *ADB Briefs* 22 (May): 1–7.

Howard-Hassmann, R. E. 2005. "The Second Great Transformation: Human Rights Leapfrogging in the Era of Globalization." *Human Rights Quarterly* 27(1): 1–40.

Human Rights Watch. 2013. "Abuse-Free Development: How the World Bank Should Safeguard Against Human Rights Violations." New York: Human Rights Watch. Available at: www.hrw.org/reports/2013/07/22/abuse-free-development-0 (accessed 31 May 2015).
Independent Evaluation Group. 2010. "Safeguards and Sustainability Policies in a Changing World." IEG Study Series. Washington, DC: World Bank. Available at: http://go.worldbank.org/ZA4YFV9OL0 (accessed 31 May 2015).
Inter-American Development Bank (IADB). 2014a. "Our Objective, Goals and Sector Priorities." Washington, DC: Inter-American Development Bank. Available at: www.iadb.org/en/about-us/our-objectives-goals-and-sector-priorities,7914.html (accessed 31 May 2015).
Inter-American Development Bank (IADB). 2014b. "Gender and Diversity Fund." Washington, DC: Inter-American Development Bank. Available at: www.iadb.org/aboutus/trustfunds/Fund.cfm?Fund=MGD&Lang=en (accessed 31 May 2015).
Inter-American Development Bank (IADB). 2006. "Operational Policy on Indigenous Peoples and Strategy for Indigenous Development." Sustainable Development Department Sector Strategy and Policy Paper Series, IND-111. Washington, DC: Inter-American Development Bank.
International Bank for Reconstruction and Development (IBRD). 1945. *Articles of Agreement*. 27 December. Washington, DC: Inter-American Development Bank.
Lyne, M. M., D. L. Nielson and M. J. Tierney. 2009. "Controlling Coalitions: Social Lending at the Multilateral Development Banks." *Review of International Organization* 4(4): 407–433.
Martin, D. C. 2011. "Development's Collateral Damage: The World Bank, Involuntary Resettlement, and Human Rights." Masters Thesis, University of Oslo. Available at: www.duo.uio.no/handle/10852/22711 (accessed 31 May 2015).
Nanwani, S. 2014. "Directions in Reshaping Accountability Mechanisms in Multilateral Development Banks and Other Organizations." *Global Policy* 5(2): 242–252.
Rosien, J. 2010. "Understanding the Asian Development Bank's Safeguard Policy." Oxfam Australia. Available at: www.oxfam.org.au/explore/infrastructure-people-and-environment/those-behind-infrastructure-development/the-asian-development-banks-safeguard-policies/ (accessed 31 May 2015).
Sarfaty, G. 2009. "Why Culture Matters in International Institutions: The Marginality of Human Rights at the World Bank." *American Journal of International Law* 103(4): 647–683.
Schlemmer-Schulte, S. 1999. "The World Bank Inspection Panel: A Record of the First International Accountability Mechanism and Its Role for Human Rights." *Human Rights Brief* 6(2): 1, 6–7, 20.
Skogly, S. 2001. *The Human Rights Obligations of the World Bank and the International Monetary Fund*. London: Cavendish Publishing Limited.
Vetterlein, A. 2007. "Economic Growth, Poverty Reduction, and the Role of Social Policies: The Evolution of the World Bank's Social Development Approach." *Global Governance* 13(4): 513–533.
World Bank. 2015. "Action Plan: Improving the Management of Safeguards and Resettlement Practices and Outcomes." Washington, DC: World Bank. Available at: http://pubdocs.worldbank.org/pubdocs/publicdoc/2015/3/71481425483119932 (accessed 25 May 2015).

World Bank. 2014. "Panel Mandate and Bank Policies." Washington, DC: World Bank. Available at: http://ewebapps.worldbank.org/apps/ip/Pages/Panel-Mandate.aspx (accessed 29 June 2014).

World Bank. 2013a. "Social Development: Sector Results Profile." Washington, DC: World Bank. Available at: www.worldbank.org/en/results/2013/04/14/social-development-results-profile (accessed 31 May 2015).

World Bank. 2013b. "Operational Policies." Washington, DC: World Bank. Available at: http://go.worldbank.org/3GLI3EECP0 (accessed 31 May 2015).

World Bank Inspection Panel (WBIP). 2009. "Accountability at the World Bank: The Inspection Panel at 15 Years." Washington, DC: World Bank. Available at: http://go.worldbank.org/PM5924EWE0 (accessed 31 May 2015).

Yukhananov, A. 2015. "World Bank admits botched resettlement policy." *Reuters*, 4 March. Available at: www.reuters.com/article/2015/03/04/us-worldbank-safeguards-idUSKBN0M01ZZ20150304 (accessed 31 May 2015).

Part 2
The role of the MDBs in the international political economy

7 Implications of accommodating rising powers for the regional development banks

Jonathan R. Strand and Michael W. Trevathan

International organizations (IOs) have varied in their reactions to changes in real world power relations as well as the advent of new, influential norms and ideas. Most of the scholarly attention to questions of institutional change has focused on the largest and most conspicuous IOs, especially the United Nations, International Monetary Fund, and World Bank. For instance, there has been a long-running debate over restructuring the UN Security Council to better reflect the world order in 2015 instead of 1945. Change within an IO is often the result of efforts by members that have risen in importance (real or perceived) in global politics. In the late 1980s, for example, Japan found itself the world's second largest economy yet ranked well below smaller economies in its share of votes in the IMF and the World Bank. Through a series of protracted debates, reforms were adopted to increase the voice of Japan in the Bretton Woods Institutions. Another opportunity for change occurs when there are significant shifts in membership, such as the People's Republic of China (PRC) supplanting the Republic of China (Taiwan) in the IMF and World Bank. Other countries have also received institutional accommodation of their newfound importance in world politics, especially during periods of systemic change and crisis such as the end of the Cold War. To reflect its dramatic increase in contributions to the IMF as it recycled petrodollars, Saudi Arabia received an individual seat on the Fund's executive board. Institutional accommodations are often the result of intense political discord and major reforms are usually slow in being negotiated and implemented.

Institutional adjustments can be viewed as changes resulting from concerns for resources and maintaining or increasing the legitimacy of an IO. If current members of an IO are frustrated by their voice within an IO and there are inadequate modifications to satisfy powerful members then the legitimacy of the IO is undermined. Moreover, IOs like the regional development banks (RDBs) are dependent on member states for capital and other resources and attenuation in legitimacy may constrain access to resources as well as weaken compliance by member states. Alternatively, dissatisfied members have the opportunity to create new, competing bilateral or multilateral mechanisms. Partly in response to its frustration with the IMF's response to the Asian Financial Crisis, for instance, Japan proposed an Asia-only alternative monetary fund (Lipscy 2003; Rapkin 2001). While the Asian Monetary Fund was never institutionalized, Japan's proposal was a potential threat to the centrality of the IMF in the global economy. In the wake of the Great Recession, in Europe, the EU responded, in part, by institutionalizing the European Stability Mechanism (ESM) in 2012 to provide support for economies facing specific types of financial and liquidity shortfalls (Rittberger 2014; Miller and Thomas 2013). Meanwhile, the so-called BRICS group (Brazil, Russia, India, China, and South Africa) caused much speculation surrounding the announcement that it will create new IOs in the same policy space as the IMF, World Bank, and the RDBs. Many observers have rushed to conclude that the IOs initiated by the BRICS are in response to frustration and dissatisfaction of these key rising powers with the Bretton Woods Institutions, the G20, and global economic governance more generally.

As is often the case, RDBs are overlooked in much of the discussion of institutional adjustments. Given their regional orientations, however, the RDBs may be more sensitive to the concerns of rising powers. In this chapter we examine institutional change in the RDBs to identify to what extent RDBs have accommodated rising powers. The next section briefly reviews the question of which rising powers can be expected to seek change to global institutions. We then present the types of institutional changes we expect in the RDBs. Next, we identify whether rising powers have gained increased voice in the governance of the RDBs. Has the rising material influence of these governments been met with concomitant increased influence within the RDBs? To answer this question we examine changes in voting shares over the past decade as well as briefly discussing changes to the structure of boards of directors, staffing and leadership of the RDBs, and the use of special financing windows. Our underlying perspective considers recent institutional adjustments as largely due to a mix of both resource dependence and concerns about the legitimacy of the RDBs. We find that accommodation and adjustment by the RDBs has not tracked the increased standing of rising powers and their elevated prestige in world politics. Our conclusion considers the recent moves by rising powers to create institutional alternatives to existing global and regional institutions.

Rising powers and the changing environment for RDBs

Understanding changes to the environment IOs operate within can help explain institutional adjustments to the inner governance structures of IOs. Much has been made of the fast rates of growth experienced by many developing countries over the past 20 years and these economies are often grouped together as potential counterweights to American and, more generally, OECD, dominance in extant global governance. Before examining institutional adjustments made by the RDBs, we first must ask which economies – individually, as a formal group, or as an informal group – are likely to be the sources of change to the environment the RDBs find themselves in. By extension, we expect rising powers will seek influence commensurate with their increased importance in the world economy.

In the past decade there has been a growth industry around competing concepts regarding how to categorize emerging markets. The most widely used grouping is the BRICS group (Brazil, Russia, India, China, and, since 2011, South Africa).[1] What started as an investment banker's idea became an informal grouping of the five countries and recently the BRICS group has taken steps to create new IOs. There are other candidate groups that some have suggested are more useful categorizations of rising powers. One alternative is BASIC, which excludes Russia (which does not have a high rate of economic growth). Another grouping is BRICSAM, which adds Mexico and members of the Association of Southeast Asian Nations (ASEAN) to BRICS (Cooper and Antkiewicz 2010). Another proposed group is CIVETS (Colombia, Indonesia, Vietnam, Egypt, Turkey, and South Africa), a grouping used by the international bank HSBC; another is a more recent grouping proposed by the investment banker who first suggested BRICS, MINT (Mexico, Indonesia, Nigeria, and Turkey). These other groups, however, have not progressed conceptually or in terms of formalizing their relationship as the BRICS (i.e. the BRICS countries) have. In our review of institutional adjustments in the RDBs we focus on the BRICS and other countries that have been noted as potentially part of an important, new group in world politics.

As rising powers, the BRICS are likely to desire greater representation and influence in the international organizations that have historically been under the purview of the more economically developed states (Kahler 2013, 714; Roberts 2010a, 3). The motivation for choosing integration into existing IOs and international institutions versus the creation of new institutions and organizations is less clear. Are the BRICS better served by current global institutions or are there incentives for the BRICS to bypass these IOs and create alternatives? Evidence from voting in the United Nations General Assembly suggests the BRICS are very cohesive on South–South issues and vote very differently to the United States (Ferdinand 2014; Brütsch and Papa 2013).[2]

Historically, the BRICS have generally shown only tepid signs that they seek to upset the current international architecture. One salient reason for the BRICS seeking to maintain the current international framework is the prodigious economic gains that the BRICS have attained while working within the system (Lieber 2014: 141). Even with the advent of the most recent global financial crisis, the BRICS have indicated a desire to participate at the decision-making table and not to overturn it (Kahler 2013: 713, 716; Roberts 2010a: 8–9; Roberts 2010b: 70). Additionally, the BRICS seek greater levels of representation in IOs (Abdenur 2014: 87; Roberts 2010b: 69; Sotiris 2013: 45). Greater representation in IOs may attenuate concerns about the reliance on the U.S. dollar and its international economic policies as a framework for the global economy (Roberts 2010b: 66, 69–71). Together, increasing levels of participation and representation may allow the BRICS to fulfill another important goal in global governance, the ability of the BRICS to maintain maximum policy discretion while navigating the domestic turbulence associated with increasing levels of economic integration (Kahler 2013: 715; Lieber 2014: 143). Additionally, it has been posited that BRICS participation in the current international institutional framework is driven by a desire to coordinate the economic policies of major economic powers to forestall another global financial crisis (Sotiris 2013: 42, 44).

The notion of distributive justice is another important motivation for BRICS integration into the current international institutional framework. As exemplars of the developing world, the BRICS stand poised to represent the interests, both economic and political, of the Global South. From this perspective the BRICS offer the developing world a voice in global governance institutions that have not always been perceived as operating equitably for developing states (Vieira 2012: 322–326). For some, efforts by the BRICS to increase their influence in global economic governance represent a continuation of ideas behind the NIEO and G77 to provide poorer economies more agenda-setting and policy influence.[3]

The case of China depicts the trend of the BRICS seeking greater levels of participation in international bodies. Since the early 1970s China has greatly increased its participation in IOs. However, these numbers are not the only indicator of the goal of greater inclusiveness desired by the BRICS. China's degree of participation within international institutions has also increased. For instance, China traditionally played a reluctant role in IOs like the United Nations, but current trends indicate that China has become a more assertive member of international organizations and has actively engaged in multiple policy areas (Abdenur 2014: 94–95).

If the BRICS do not seek the wholesale overthrow of the current order of global governance, what are their motivations for seeking increasing influence in the current order? In the case of China, influence in the current global system appears to be mainly driven by political and ideational factors, such as the bolstering of state legitimacy, input within the norm-setting process of international development policy, and the ability to incorporate best practices and policies that have been adopted by other South–South leaders (Abdenur 2014: 86). The BRICS (and other emerging powers) face a difficult dilemma: should they continue seeking more influence in extant IOs *or* create competing IOs and institutions. Very likely these countries will pursue both strategies: push for more influence *and*, when stymied, create new forums for global governance. In other words, if the status quo in the World Bank, IMF, RDBs, and other institutional settings remains, China and other governments may seek to bypass extant IOs. Looming large is the question of whether new IOs will compliment or compete with existing global institutions.

Concerns over the voice of developing countries and criticisms of IO policies are not new. There has been a great deal of attention to questions of reforming the IMF and World Bank. One of the first to gain widespread attention was the "50 years is enough" project (Danaher 1994). More recently, several proposals have been explored as part of an ongoing discourse on reforming the Bretton Woods Institutions (Vestergaard and Wade 2013; Rapkin and Strand 2006; Dervis and Ozer 2005; Kelkar, et al. 2004). One focus on the reform debate has been to increase the voice of developing countries (Woods 2006; Rapkin and Strand 2005). Recently, the World Bank implemented its largest set of reforms to its internal governance in decades (Zappile 2014). The Bank's "voice reforms" include a variety of changes meant to improve its internal governance, including adjusting voting weights for developing countries (World Bank 2010). The increase in voting shares, however, has not significantly increased the share of votes held by developing countries or their voting power (Strand and Retzl 2014; Vestergaard and Wade 2013). In short, despite recent institutional adjustments in the World Bank, the influence of China, Brazil, and other rising powers remains small compared to that of the United States, Japan, and (collectively) European Union members.[4]

Even if the recent voice reforms have not dramatically altered voting shares over the past decade, there have been notable changes in some World Bank members' voting shares. Table 7.1 displays members with the largest increases and decreases in relative vote share. Perhaps not surprisingly, China's share of votes has nearly doubled since 2004. Turkey, South Korea, India, and Japan also experienced significant gains in shares. Since these are shares of all votes, increases for some members necessitate decreases for others. The greatest loss of voting share was experienced by the United States. Interestingly, South Africa, Russia, and Brazil saw their relative shares of votes *decrease*. The

Table 7.1 Change in World Bank (IBRD) voting shares, 2004–2014

Member	2004 (%)	2014 (%)	Difference
China*	2.78	5.25	2.46
Turkey	0.53	1.28	0.75
Korea	0.99	1.54	0.55
India*	2.78	3.06	0.28
Japan	7.86	8.13	0.27
South Africa*	0.85	0.82	−0.03
UK	4.30	4.06	−0.25
France	4.30	4.06	−0.25
Italy	2.78	2.52	−0.26
Brazil*	2.07	1.69	−0.38
Russia*	2.78	2.27	−0.51
United States	16.39	15.02	−1.37

Source: World Bank annual reports.

Note: *BRICS member.

United States maintained a greater than 15 percent share of the total votes and thereby retains its de facto veto over decisions requiring an 85 percent qualified majority. As noted by Vestergaard and Wade (2013), the changes in the World Bank relied on some members, including the United States, volunteering to not fully exercise their possible contributions and thereby receive a lower vote share than they are entitled. Put differently, changes to the voting shares of the BRICS countries were mixed and the outcome of the voice reforms temporary.

Identifying institutional change in the RDBs

In this section we detail the types of institutional change we expect if accommodation of rising powers has occurred in the RDBs. Specifically, we are focused on the African Development Bank (AfDB), Asian Development Bank (ADB), and the Inter-American Development Bank (IADB). The European Bank for Reconstruction and Development (EBRD) is not considered here because its membership only includes one emerging market (Russia).[5] Moreover, the EBRD was created in a very different historical context to the other three and its operations are managed more like a private corporation than an IO (see Shields, this volume). The three RDBs examined here were created during the Cold War and have experienced many changes in membership, operations, and development practices. Unlike the World Bank with its nearly universal membership, the RDBs are designed to be regional organizations that give regional governments a substantial voice in policymaking (Strand 2014). This role for regional powers does not preclude ample influence by non-regional countries. Nevertheless, the RDBs are not merely "lesser World Banks." The RDBs have their own identities and institutional cultures and while they exist in a world where the World Bank is the paragon IO in development policy, the RDBs are autonomous and do not automatically or wholly parrot World Bank governance, policies, and norms (Park and Strand, this volume).

What are the possible parameters of institutional adjustments to changing power relations among sovereign states? To organize our examination of institutional accommodation of rising powers, we first identify the aspects of the RDBs where we expect changes to manifest. Rising powers may be expected to seek greater influence over RDB policies, staffing, and leadership. Indications of internal accommodations include adjustments to voting shares, representation on boards of directors, the selection of key officers, as well as the creation of ad hoc arrangements such as special financing windows.

There are four institutional features where we expect institutional adjustments to be most pronounced. The first is in the relative shares of votes allocated to members. Governments have long been sensitive to the perceived and real influence their share of votes in the weighted voting systems used by many IOs (McKeown 2009; Schoultz 1982). In the World Bank and IMF, for instance, the United States has sought to maintain at least 15 percent of the votes in order to hold a veto over important constitutional changes. When China was negotiating membership in the World Bank and IMF it signaled that merely assuming Taiwan's voting share would not satisfy the PRC. In the 1980s and 1990s Japan engaged in a protracted effort to increase its voting shares in the IMF and World Bank (Rapkin and Strand 1997). In short, voting shares matter to member governments.

A second area where rising powers may experience increased influence is with regard to their representation on the boards of directors of the RDBs. In the World Bank, one expectation by China when it negotiated membership in the 1970s was the creation of its own seat on the World Bank Executive Board (Jacobson and Oksenberg 1990). At the end of the Cold War, the Russian Federation continued negotiations to join the IMF begun by the Soviet Union. A condition for Russian membership was the creation of a single seat on the IMF's executive board for Russia (Momani 2007; Gould-Davies and Woods 1999; Assetto 1988). More recently, observers have noted that European members of the Bretton Woods Institutions may need to consolidate their representation on the executive boards (Bini Smaghi 2004). If the RDBs have accommodated China and other emerging powers we expect the number of seats and nature of the seats (individual or voting group) to have changed.

The third material way accommodation is expected to occur is in the selection of key RDB officers, especially the presidents and vice presidents. Leadership selection is an important feature of institutional operations in all IOs (Kahler 2001). In addition, the nationality of the staff can indicate greater attention to one member government or another.

Lastly, rising powers may seek influence outside of traditional lending windows in the RDBs through the creation of ad hoc arrangements such as special financing windows. The MDBs and the IMF have long relied on special funds and most of these assistance windows do not require board approval. For governments that create and finance special funds, they may receive greater control over how the RDB allocates funds for projects. At the same time, however, contributions to special funds are not considered in the determination of votes. Due to the practices used by the IADB in allocating voting shares to regional and non-regional members, non-regional members are limited to only about 16 percent of all votes. In the 1980s Japan sought to increase its contributions to the IADB but faced the restrictions on increasing its relative share of normal contributions. In 1988, Japan created a special fund which allowed it to increase its assistance to the IADB without upsetting the balance of voting shares. If China and other rising powers are facing limits on increasing their contributions (and influence) through regular capital increases, we expect these governments to create special funds in the RDBs.

Changes to institutional design do not capture all aspects of the rising influence of emerging market governments. Ideational or structural power related to ideas and norms also change, although the link to material change is not always as clear or direct as some theories of international politics suggest (Lieber 2014). As the RDBs provide more influence for rising powers, crucial policies and ideas about development are being altered. Nevertheless, the four parameters outlined above point to the need for multivariate explanations of change in the RDBs. The RDBs have formal sets of rules which designate how decisions are made on loans and important policy matters. Observers should not point to one aspect of RDB governance and behavior. The RDBs exist in an international environment where they are subject pressures and ideational conflicts from global society as well as from within their own institutional contexts.[6]

Assessing institutional change in the RDBs

In this section we review the four parameters of institutional change in each of the three RDBs. We start with an examination of the past decade or so of voting shares and then turn to a discussion of other changes, including the structure of the boards of directors, leadership of the RDBs, and the use of special funds.

Voting shares

While it is often noted that formal voting rarely occurs in the RDBs (as with the IMF and World Bank), the voting weights assigned to countries denote their material importance to the institutions and a quantifiable symbol of formal influence and, by extension, legitimacy. The weighting of votes in the RDBs is defined through both formal agreements and informal practices. The number of votes held by a member of a RDB is a function of its contributions to the RDB as well as a common component known as basic votes. Contributions are in part designed to reflect the relative positions of members in the world economy. Members with larger economies are expected to contribute more capital and their voting shares will reflect their higher contributions. The RDBs have rules regarding the distribution of weighted votes in order to maintain the control – or at least the perception of control – of regional members.

In order to assess changes in material influence within the RDBs, we examine changes to voting shares during each bank's most recent capital increase. The relative share of votes held by members captures one dimension of formal influence. However, voting shares do not reflect other avenues of influence, such as the various forms of informal influence members may have over RDB policies (Kilby 2009). There are also formal actions by major shareholders, especially the United States, to link approval of contribution increases (real or callable) to policy changes (Lavelle 2011). Included among these Congressional efforts is the Pelosi Amendment which requires the U.S. representative to the MDBs to follow a strict policy of supporting projects that have undergone environmental impact assessments. Additionally, there have been numerous executive orders by American presidents directing how U.S. representatives vote (Sherk 2007/2008: 284).

In the AfDB, a capital increase was implemented in 2011, with members receiving increases in their votes reflecting the increase in their subscriptions. China's total number of votes increased from 24,925 to 71,545; a 187 percent increase. Brazil saw its votes increase from 10,299 to 28,856 or 180 percent. Most other members also experienced increases of at least 150 percent. The United States' votes increased from 144,678 to 419,162 (190 percent), while Japan's votes increased 192 percent (from 120,025 to 350,895). The AfDB's largest vote holder, Nigeria, experienced a 206 percent increase. When looking at absolute increases in individual members' votes it may appear that the recent capital increase greatly altered the formal influence of members. Consideration of relative voting shares of members, however, demonstrates a very different outcome of the capital increase. Figure 7.1 displays voting shares in the AfDB since 2004 for the top shareholders as well as Brazil, India, and China. The AfDB's most recent capital increase went into full effect in 2011/12. Note the drastic movement in shares in 2011; this is due to the delay in the U.S. and others completing their capital increases. Other than for that one year, the relative shares of emerging markets and the largest shareholders are stagnant. China's relative share before the capital increase was about 1.11 percent and after the increase its share was 1.13 percent. Brazil and India experienced slight decreases in their relative shares of votes. In sum, the capital increase did not adjust the formal influence of members other than the ephemeral effect of delayed contributions.

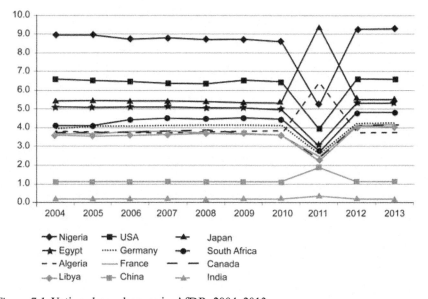

Figure 7.1 Voting share changes in AfDB, 2004–2013

130 Jonathan R. Strand and Michael W. Trevathan

Table 7.2 displays the change in voting shares from 2004 to 2013. Note that even though China became more involved in the AfDB, and in Africa more generally, its share of votes has not changed. The same is true for other BRICS members as well as the United States, South Korea, and Japan. The only BRICS member to see a significant increase over the time period is South Africa. Several regional members of the AfDB experienced notable increases while Botswana saw its voting share halved.

The ADB's recent capital increase was implemented over the 2009/10 period. Most members experienced roughly a threefold increase to their total votes. China, for example, saw its votes increase from 241,323 to 723,490 while Japan's increased from 565,442 to 1,691,507. India's votes increased from 237,242 to over 700,000. Prima facie, these values appear to reflect significant increases in the formal voices of ADB members. Like the AfDB, however, the relative effect of the capital increase was minimal. Figure 7.2 displays voting shares in the ADB from 2004 to 2013, during which time there was one significant capital increase. Clearly there has been little significant change in relative shares. Moreover, as shown in Table 7.3, between 2004 and 2013 there has been almost no shift in voting shares. The only countries to experience an increase in shares are those that joined the ADB during the time period (Armenia, Ireland, Georgia, and Brunei). In fact China (PRC) has a lower share of votes in 2013 (5.47 percent) than it was allocated during the first year of its membership (6.15 percent).

Table 7.2 Change in AfDB voting shares, 2004–2013

Member	2004 (%)	2013 (%)	Difference
South Africa*	4.03	4.81	0.79
Algeria	3.80	4.21	0.41
Libya	3.65	4.04	0.39
Nigeria	8.99	9.28	0.29
Japan	5.42	5.49	0.08
UK	1.68	1.69	0.01
Brazil*	0.44	0.45	0.01
China*	1.13	1.13	0.00
United States	6.57	6.56	−0.01
Korea	0.47	0.46	−0.01
India	0.25	0.23	−0.01
Argentina	0.29	0.10	−0.19
Swaziland	0.36	0.12	−0.23
Kuwait	0.47	0.16	−0.31
Botswana	2.14	1.09	−1.05

Source: AfDB annual reports.

Note: *BRICS member.

Rising powers and regional development banks 131

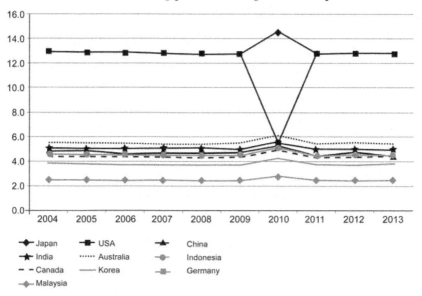

Figure 7.2 Voting share changes in the ADB, 2004–2013

Table 7.3 Change in ADB voting shares, 2004–2013

Member	2004 (%)	2013 (%)	Difference
Taipei, China	1.20	1.17	−0.02
United Kingdom	1.97	1.94	−0.03
Korea	4.39	4.34	−0.05
China*	5.53	5.47	−0.05
India*	5.44	5.38	−0.05
Sweden	0.59	0.12	−0.47
Indonesia	4.72	4.44	−0.29
Portugal	0.59	0.39	−0.20
United States	12.94	12.75	−0.19
Japan	12.94	12.83	−0.11

Source: ADB annual reports.
Note: *BRICS member.

In the IADB, a capital increase was implemented over the 2011–2013 period. The percentage increase in contributions was not as dramatic as in the AfDB and ADB. China, which only joined the IADB in 2009, saw a 24 percent increase in its votes yet remained the lowest vote holder (along with South Korea). Brazil's number of votes increased about 27 percent and the United States experienced a 24 percent increase. In relative terms, however, the percentage of votes held by members did not result in any significant shifts in rank order, as displayed in Figure 7.3. Put differently, the capital increase maintained the status quo of formal influence, with the United States holding by far the largest voting share, followed by regional members Argentina, Brazil, and Mexico. The IADB has special provisions that result in at least 50.05 percent of the votes being held by regional members, 4 percent by Canada, and 30 percent by the United States. Non-regional members from Europe as well as Japan, China, and South Korea are left with only 16 percent of the votes. Without institutional adjustments to change the guaranteed minimum voting shares there is little room for a non-regional member like China to increase its relative share. Table 7.4 reveals that except for

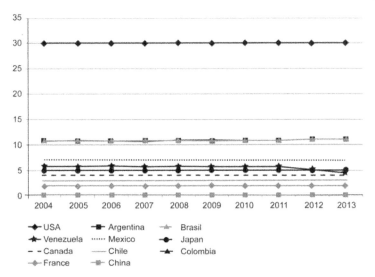

Figure 7.3 Voting share changes in the IADB, 2004–2013

Table 7.4 Change in IADB voting shares, 2004–2013

Member	2004 (%)	2013 (%)	Difference
Argentina	10.76	11.03	0.27
Brazil*	10.76	11.03	0.27
Mexico	6.92	7.09	0.17
United States	30.03	30.05	0.02
China*	<0.01	<0.01	0.00
Korea	<0.01	<0.01	0.00
Japan	5.01	5.01	0.00
United Kingdom	0.96	0.96	0.00
Netherlands	0.34	0.27	−0.07
Venezuela	5.77	4.65	−1.12

Source: IDB annual reports.
Note: *BRICS member.

Venezuela, which experienced a large decrease in its voting share, little change has occurred in the IADB.[7]

Overall, when considering the relative share of votes in the RDBs, it is clear that over the past decade or so there has been almost no adjustment that reflects the increasing importance of China, Brazil, India, South Africa, and other emerging markets in the world economy. This is despite the fact that the RDBs take into account the relative size of a member's economy when determining relative shares. Even with the rapid economic growth of the BRICS – as well as their increasing policy coordination – the RDBs have not adjusted voting shares to reflect the changing reality of the world political economy. There are several possible explanations for why the weighted voting systems have not responded to the rising influence of the BRICS. One reason for a lack of any significant shift in relative voting shares may be resistance by long-time large vote holders to see their influence attenuated. It is unlikely that the United States and European governments are going to readily cede influence. Another explanation may be that the rising economies may not have exerted diplomatic efforts to increase their shares in the RDBs and instead sought influence through other types of governance changes.

Other governance changes

If voting shares have not changed to reflect the new standing of rising powers, perhaps other aspects of the RDBs' governance systems have undergone adjustment? In this section we look briefly at representation on boards of directors/executive boards, leadership selection and staffing, and the creation of special financing windows.

In general, the largest contributors to the MDBs hold single-country seats on executive boards. Most members of the MDBs and the IMF are aggregated into constituencies for the sake of selecting executive directors. Selective representation as it is implemented in the RDBs often results in constituencies with very different numbers of members. In the World Bank there are eight single-country seats and 16 constituencies. Holding a single-country seat can impart greater influence since an executive director does not need to speak for multiple governments. Less tangibly, single-country seats convey a sense of prestige.

The AfDB requires that a majority of the representatives on the board of directors be from African countries. All members of the AfDB except one are aggregated into constituencies. The United States is the only member with a single-country seat. China has been a member of the constituency which includes OECD countries, such as Canada. As of 2014 China is the director for its constituency.[8] During 2008 and 2009 China held the alternate director position for its group. India is currently in a constituency that includes several Scandinavian countries and the directorship is held by Finland; India has never held its group's directorship. Brazil's constituency has almost always been represented by Japan and as of 2014 Brazil holds the alternate director seat. Not surprisingly, South Africa has been a key member of the board and usually holds the director's seat for its constituency. During the last capital increase the number of seats on the board of directors was not changed.

In the ADB historically only the United States and Japan held single-country seats. China joined the ADB in 1986 and assumed an individual seat on the board of directors in 1987 with about a 6.1 percent share of the votes and has maintained its individual seat. Unlike in the World Bank, IMF, and United Nations, China's membership in the ADB was not predicated on supplanting Taiwan and the two governments remain full members. India has often held the director position for its voting group. In the IADB, of the BRICS countries only Brazil has held a director position. In sum, regarding seats on the boards of directors, there is little indication of major shifts to accommodate rising powers. China received its individual seat in the ADB long before concerns about rising powers became salient. India and Brazil have had more success in the RDBs in their own region but not in others. Only China in the AfDB can be seen as having increasing influence on the board of directors, albeit as an alternate director for two years and most recently the director.

In regards to staffing, the RDBs employ a "very loose quota system" in hiring of staff (Sherk 1994: 49). Not surprisingly, large portions of the staff are citizens of the countries that are home to the headquarters of the RDBs. Many of these are employees who carry out routine activities. The nationalities of higher-ranking staff, such as country directors, management positions, and legal advisors, are a better indicator of the informal quota system. While much attention is paid to presidents and vice-presidents, other leadership positions are also crucial in the operations of the RDBs. The leadership in each RDB reflects the interests of member governments as well as the importance of certain policy ideas.

The ADB has over 2500 employees, most of which (about 1,400) are from the Philippines. The majority of the Philippine staff is made up of lower-ranking workers and only a handful fills senior-level positions. Approximately 1,000 members of the ADB bureaucracy are not from the Philippines. Of these, Japan and the United States have the largest number, about 150 each. In 2013 the number of Chinese nationals working for the ADB was 117, up from 100 in 2009, and the number of Indian nationals working for the ADB was 141, up from 113 in 2009 (ADB 2013, 2009). In regard to key leadership positions, the ADB has seven high-level management positions, currently held by nationals of Australia, China, India, Japan, Nepal, France, and the United States. The presidency of the ADB has always been held by a Japanese citizen, often a high-ranking bureaucrat in the Ministry of Finance. Reflecting the practice of Japan selecting the ADB president, the current president is Takehiko Nakao from Japan. Nakao became ADB president after then ADB president Haruhiko Kuroda announced he was named to the position of governor of the Bank of Japan in 2013. Given the rising importance of China, India, and other countries, it was somewhat surprising that there was little effort to name a replacement from China, India, or even South Korea. In other words, Japan's monopoly on the ADB presidency was not challenged by rising powers.

The IADB has about 1,900 staff members and most are stationed in Washington, DC. The IADB's president is selected from regional members. The current president is Luis Alberto Moreno from Colombia. There are several key leadership positions including the executive vice president; a position always held by American citizens. The AfDB has about 2,000 employees and its key management positions are with few exceptions always held by people from borrowing, regional member countries. In reviewing recent annual reports for the three RDBs we find little indication of significant increases in leadership or staffing from the BRICS countries.

One area where BRICS members have engaged in increased support of RDB activities is in collaborative financing agreements and funds for special operations. Use of these alternative facilities may reflect their inability to alter structural aspects of the boards of directors as special funds may allow more direct control and, more importantly, do not factor into the determination of capital subscriptions and voting shares. In the AfDB, most special funds include a variety of donors, including private civil society groups. In 2014, however, China and the AfDB announced the creation of a new investment fund, Africa China Growing Together (AFCT), with a $2 billion commitment by China. The new investment window will be managed by the AfDB and projects will be subject to the same policies as regular AfDB projects (Stevis 2014). Brazil has been active in financing efforts within the AfDB to enhance South–South cooperation, including the funding of a small trust fund. In the ADB China partnered with several Southeast Asian governments, Japan, and Korea to create the Credit Guarantee and Investment Facility in 2010. Individually, China was the first developing country to create a special fund – the PRC Regional Cooperation and Poverty Reduction Fund (PRC RCPRF) in 2005. Decisions on funding projects are made by China's Ministry of Finance, although several ADB departments are involved in implementing and assessing the funded projects. Lastly, in the IADB China has contributed to two special trust funds. The first is the China-IIC SME Equity Investment Trust Fund and the second is the Institutional Capacity Strengthening Thematic Fund (ICSF). The former is administered by a part of the IADB while the latter has a separate secretariat and oversight board to ensure the ICSF adheres to IADB policies on projects. In looking at special financing arrangements it is clear that China and Brazil have made an effort to increase their funding of RDB activities. Whether this is in reaction to the lack of accommodation is difficult to conclude, especially since some of these efforts are very recent. Nevertheless, there is some indication of increased involvement by at least these two rising powers in special financing activities of the RDBs.

Conclusion: bypassing the status quo?

Frustration over internal governance of the RDBs may be just one source of dissatisfaction for BRICS governments. During recent years, the United States, for example, has not been universally supportive of RDB and World Bank projects for the BRICS. Table 7.5 displays the percentage of projects in the RDBs and World Bank (all lending windows) that the U.S. supported 2004–2011. Projects for China have not been supported nearly as often as projects for Brazil, India, and Russia. In the AfDB the U.S. has supported less than 60 percent of all projects for South Africa.[9] Thus, the inadequacy of institutional adjustments examined above is coupled with mixed support for projects for China, and others.

In this chapter we have looked at four parameters of potential institutional adjustments in three major RDBs. We also briefly considered adjustments made by the World Bank. Our primary conclusion is that there has been very little change in the allocation of formal influence in the RDBs over the past decade. The World Bank, by contrast, has engaged in significant voice reforms that saw the bank create new seats on its executive board as well as shift relative voting shares. We did not observe similar changes in the RDBs. Moreover, the changes at the World Bank have not resulted in major shifts in influence and the long-term impact of the reforms have been called into question (Vestergaard and Wade 2013). If the World Bank's institutional adjustments have been limited, the RDBs have been meager. We close with consideration of two implications of the failure of the RDBs to adjust to reflect real world power relations.

First, the RDBs are likely to remain reliant on established powers, especially the United States, for resources. This will allow the U.S. and others to continue to link new allocations of resources to policy and governance changes. Put differently, despite the conspicuous changes to the world political economy, the RDBs remain dependent on traditional capital sources. We may also expect the policy preferences of OECD countries to remain dominant. The RDBs are likely to continue to reflect neoliberal economic policies favored by the United States and global capital (which rising powers respond to as borrowers not as lenders – see Humphrey, this volume). This may change in the

Table 7.5 American support for BRICS projects, 2004–2011 (percentage)

Country	ADB	AfDB	IDB	World Bank
Brazil			96.54	95.96
China	51.85			40.39
India	95.10			92.63
Russia				87.90
South Africa		57.14		77.78

Source: U.S. Treasury Department, compiled by authors.

near future, however, as there is likely to be continued discord over World Bank governance in addition to the United States' failure to accept IMF reform proposals; such discord may spill over to the RDBs.

Second, the primary implication of not accommodating rising powers in the RDBs is the move by China and other BRICS members to create new multilateral development organizations. Recent developments concerning the BRICS challenge to the existing Bretton Woods international financial structure are instructive. The BRICS development fund, the New Development Bank (NDB), is ostensibly built around providing infrastructural development, with some additional degree of focus on social sector projects (African Banker 2013; Guillen and Ontiveros 2013). Another feature of the NDB includes the creation of a pool of foreign currency reserves that can be utilized to attenuate future financial crises (Business Monitor International 2013).

Internal governance of the NDB was a matter of much debate amongst BRICS governments. Major sticking points among the BRICS members include how leadership positions will be filled; the location of the NDB's headquarters; and the conditions that will be attached to the loans provided by the NDB (Business Monitor International 2013). There is agreement among the BRICS that the management and board of governors of the NDB will be composed from member countries (Business Monitor International 2013). Recently, Shanghai was selected as the location of the NDB's headquarters and the first chairperson of the NDB's board will be from India. The governance of the NDB has revealed tensions among the NDB's members. One prominent flashpoint revolves around the NDB's president. China, as the largest economy of the BRICS, desires a permanent role as the bank's president; however, India has pressed for a rotating presidency (Choudhury 2012). China's desire for a fixed presidency was based on the proposition that China would provide nearly half of the NDB's initial capital. India fought this proposal and insisted that each member of the NDB contribute $10 billion to the initial capital fund (Kasturi 2013). However, as of now, the NDB will have an initial Contingent Reserve Arrangement (CRA) of $100 billion, with China contributing 41 billion, South Africa contributing $5 billion, and Brazil, Russia, and India each contributing $18 billion (Business News Americas 2014). The tensions over contributions and the NDB's presidency reveal, as one Indian official intimated, that the NDB risks becoming another institution dominated by one country, in this case China (Kasturi 2013).

However, before we can consider the salience of a BRICS-led development fund it is important to observe that there are multiple tensions that threaten to undermine the putative rival to the World Bank and the IMF. While the members of the BRICS share the characteristics of rising economic powers, they do not share an economic or a political ideology. Furthermore, the BRICS contend not only with the U.S. but also with one another in terms of geopolitical concerns and diverse economic interests (Business Monitor International 2013).

A more direct challenge to the RDBs, especially the ADB, comes in the form of the proposed Asian Infrastructure Investment Bank (AIIB). In addition to supporting the BRICS-led NDB, China has fostered the development of the AIIB. The claimed goal of the AIIB is to attenuate the shortfalls for funding infrastructure projects and increase competition for infrastructure financing. To that end, China has agreed to fund the majority of the 50 billion in start-up capital for the AIIB (Perlez 2014a). AIIB governance proposals include shareholding by both member states and private investors (Drysdale 2014). The development of the AIIB has already included three rounds of talks with putative Asian member states (China Daily Africa 2014).

Support from Asian governments for the AIIB appears to be robust. Two close allies of the United States, South Korea and Australia, initially adopted favorable positions on the AIIB, and despite intense pressure from the United States appear on the cusp of signing up to the new IO (Reuters 2014; Crowe 2014; Earl 2014). Furthermore, fellow BRICS member India has voiced support for the AIIB, bolstering the number of states supporting its creation (The Economic Times 2014). Other organizations also appear to be in favor of the AIIB, including the head of the EBRD, Suma Chakrabarti, who in reference to both the NBD and the AIIB said:

> The creation of these new bodies is also an implicit criticism of the existing multilateral system as being too slow to adapt to the shifting geopolitical power structures and to the development needs of emerging economies.
>
> (EBRD 2014)

The United States has been less than supportive of the AIIB and some signs suggest the U.S. has worked to convince some countries not to join (Perlez 2014b). American efforts, however, have not stopped major OECD countries, such as France and Germany, from committing to the AIIB and by our count at least four-dozen governments have indicated interest in the Chinese-led IO.

Based on the lack of significant accommodation of rising powers, especially China, in the RDBs we expect challenges to the status quo to continue, although this will be a function of the negotiation tactics used by BRICS governments reflecting whether they are willing to conform or challenge extant global governance institutions (Narlikar 2013, 2010). Rising powers will continue to press for more adjustment in existing IOs while pursuing alternative governance arrangements through the creation of new formal and informal organizations and institutions. A major policy and theoretical concern in need of further exploration is why, given the increases in the material wealth of rising powers, are we not seeing substantial changes in the multilateral institutions. The legimacy of IOs that do not accommodate the increasing real world influence of the BRICS countries (and others) may be weakened, at least in the eyes of these increasingly important global powers.

Given the rapid deployment of two new IOs by the BRICS and China, the landscape of global governance appears to be on the cusp of a major restructuring, with rising powers assuming a greater leadership role in the management of development institutions. It remains to be seen whether the NDB and AIIB will complement or compete with the World Bank and RDBs over development policy.

Notes

1. For consideration of regional voting blocs, see Strand and Rapkin (2005).
2. Ferdinand's (2014) results for the UNGA differ from Vreeland and Dreher's (2014) argument regarding the UN Security Council where they find there is a systematic tie between developing countries elected to serve as non-permanent members that vote with the United States and the flow of bilateral and multilateral aid.
3. Of course, there are many policy and ideological cleavages in South–South relations that work against increased solidarity.
4. In the IMF, recapitalization of Fund resources and voice reforms has been stymied by domestic politics in the United States.
5. Note, however, that while Russia's voting share has not been increased its access to EBRD resources has increased in recent years.
6. This chapter focuses on governance changes but there are several areas of development practice where rising powers may disagree with the United States, World Bank, and RDBs and ideational discord may also contribute to a desire to bypass existing IOs.
7. The values for China and Korea are based on their first year of membership.
8. Note that in 2007 China hosted the first meeting of the AfDB in Asia (Deng 2008: 231).
9. For detailed analysis of United States support of MDB loans, see Strand and Zappile (2015)

References

Abdenur, Adriana Erthal. 2014. "China and the BRICS Development Bank: Legitimacy and multilateralism in South–South cooperation." *IDS Bulletin* 45(4): 85–101.
Asian Development Bank (ADB). 2009. *Annual Report*, Vol. 1. Manila: Asian Development Bank.
Asian Development Bank (ADB). 2013. *Annual Report*. Manila: Asian Development Bank.
African Banker. 2013. "Will BRICS bank break IMF, World Bank monopoly?" 14 February.
Assetto, V. J. 1988. *The Soviet Bloc in the IMF and the IBRD*. Boulder, CO: Westview Press.
Bini Smaghi, L. 2004. "A single EU seat in the IMF?" *Journal of Common Market Studies* 42(2): 229–248.
Brütsch, C. and M. Papa. 2013. "Deconstructing the BRICS: Bargaining coalition, imagined community, or geopolitical fad?" *Chinese Journal of International Politics*. 6(3): 299–327.
Business Monitor International. 2013. "BRICS Bank: Opportunities and limitations." 26 March.

China Daily Africa Weekly. 2014. "Asian Infrastructure Investment Bank to bridge financing gap." 30 June.
Choudhury, D. R. 2012. "China eyes top job at BRICS Bank." *Mail Today*, 2 March.
Cooper, A. and A. Antkiewicz (eds). 2010. *Emerging Powers in Global Governance: Lessons from the Heiligendamm Process.* Waterloo, ON: Wilfrid Laurier University Press.
Crowe, D. 2014. "Canberra set to sign for China-led bank." *The Australian*, 13 October.
Danaher, K. (ed.). 1994. *50 Years Is Enough: The Case Against the World Bank and the International Monetary Fund.* Boston, MA: South End Press.
Deng, Y. 2008. *China's Struggle for Status: The Realignment of International Relations.* Cambridge: Cambridge University Press.
Dervis, K. and C. Ozer. 2005. *A Better Globalization: Legitimacy, Governance, and Reform.* Washington, DC: Center for Global Development.
Drysdale, P. 2014. "China's new bank will help close funding gap." *Australian Financial Review*, 22 September: 47.
Earl, G. 2014. "China steps up bank pressure." *Australian Financial Review*, 22 September: 6.
EBRD. 2014. "The new multilateralism: The role of regional development banks: A personal reflection from three decades of development experience." Speech by Suma Chakrabarti. 9 October.
The Economic Times. 2014. "India to support China's Asian Infrastructure Investment Bank idea." 7 October.
Ferdinand, Peter. 2014. "Rising powers at the UN: an analysis of the voting behaviour of BRICS in the General Assembly." *Third World Quarterly* 35(3): 376–391.
Gould-Davies, N. and N. Woods. 1999. "Russia and the IMF." *International Affairs* 75(1): 1–22.
Guillen, M. and E. Ontiveros. 2013. "The BRICS and their bank." *Korea Times*, 21 April.
Jacobson, H. K. and M. Oksenberg. 1990. *China's Participation in the IMF, the World Bank, and GATT: Toward a Global Economic Order.* Ann Arbor: University of Michigan Press.
Kahler, M. 2001. *Leadership Selection in the Major Multilaterals.* Washington, DC: Institute for International Economics.
Kahler, M. 2013. "Rising powers and global governance: Negotiating change in a resilient status quo." *International Affairs* 89(3): 711–729.
Kasturi, C. S. 2013. "Rival to World Bank, with India equal role." *The Telegraph* (India), 7 September.
Kasturi, C. S. 2014. "Delhi foils China bid to control new bank." *The Telegraph* (India), 6 July.
Kelkar, V., V. Yadav, and P. Chaudhry. 2004 "Reforming the Governance of the International Monetary Fund," *The World Economy* 27(5): 727–743.
Kilby, C. 2009. "Donor influence in multilateral development banks: The case of the Asian Development Bank." *Review of International Organizations* 1(2):173–195.
Lavelle, K. C. 2011. *Legislating International Organization: The US Congress, the IMF, and the World Bank.* New York: Oxford University Press.
Lieber, R. J. 2014. "The rise of the BRICS and American primacy." *International Politics* 51(2): 137–154.
Lipscy, P. Y. 2003. "Japan's Asian Monetary Fund Proposal." *Stanford Journal of East Asian Affairs* 3(1): 93–104.

McKeown, T. J. 2009. "How U.S. decision-makers assessed their control of multilateral organizations, 1957–1982." *Review of International Organizations* 4(3): 269–291.
Miller, M. and D. Thomas. 2013. "Eurozone Sovereign Debt Restructuring: Keeping the Vultures at Bay." *Oxford Review of Economic Policy* 29(4): 745–763.
Momani, B. 2007. "Another seat at the board: Russia's IMF executive director." *International Journal* 62(4): 916–939.
Narlikar, A. 2013. "Introduction: Negotiating the rise of new powers." *International Affairs*, 89(3): 561–576.
Narlikar, A. 2010. *New Powers: How to Become One and How to Manage Them*. New York: Columbia University Press.
Perlez, J. 2014a. "U.S. opposing China's answer to World Bank." *New York Times*, 10 October: 1.
Perlez, J. 2014b. "U.S. balks at Beijing's development bank plans: Americans lobby against project seen as a Chinese tool for buying influence." *New York Times*, 10 October: 16.
Rapkin, D. P. 2001. "The United States, Japan, and the power to block: The APEC and AMF cases." *The Pacific Review* 14(3): 373–410.
Rapkin, D. P. and J. R. Strand. 2006. "Reforming the IMF's weighted voting system." *The World Economy* 29(3): 305–324.
Rapkin, D. P. and J. R. Strand. 2005. "Developing country representation and governance of the International Monetary Fund." *World Development* 33(12): 1993–2011.
Rapkin, D. P. and J. R. Strand. 1997. "The United States and Japan in the Bretton Woods institutions: Sharing or contesting leadership?" *International Journal* 52(2): 265–296.
Reuters. 2014. "Three major nations absent as China launches World Bank rival in Asia." 24 October.
Rittberger, B. 2014. "Integration without representation? The European Parliament and the reform of economic governance in the EU." *Journal of Common Market Studies* 52(6): 1174–1183.
Roberts, C. 2010a. "Polity Forum: Challengers or stakeholders? BRICs and the Liberal World Order." *Polity* 42 (January): 1–13.
Roberts, C. 2010b. "Russia's BRICs diplomacy: Rising outsider with dreams of an insider." *Polity* 42 (January): 38–73.
Schoultz, L. 1982. "Politics, economics, and U.S. participation in multilateral development banks." *International Organization* 36(3): 537–574.
Sherk, D. 2007/2008. "Multilateralism and United States foreign economic policy." *Kansas Journal of Law and Public Policy* 17(2): 273–284.
Sherk, D. 1994. "Emerging markets and the multilateral development banks." *Columbia Journal of World Business* 29(2): 44–52.
Sotiris, P. 2013. "The emergence of the BRICS: Implications for global governance." *Journal of International and Global Studies* 4(2): 37–51.
Stevis, M. 2014. "China launches $2 billion African Development Fund." *The Wall Street Journal*, 22 May.
Strand, J. R. 2014. "Global Economic Governance and the Regional Development Banks." In *Handbook of Global Economic Governance*, edited by M. Moschella and C. Weaver. London: Routledge, pp. 290–303.

Strand, J. R. and D. P. Rapkin. 2005. "Regionalizing multilateralism: Estimating the power of potential regional voting blocs in the IMF." *International Interactions* 31(1): 15–54.

Strand, J. R. and K. J. Retzl. 2014. "Institutional design and good governance in the World Bank." Paper presented at the 2014 annual meeting of the International Studies Association, Toronto, ON.

Strand, J. R. and T. M. Zappile. 2015. "Always vote for principle, though you may vote alone: United States political support for multilateral development loans, 2004–2011." *World Development* 72: 224–239.

Vestergaard, J. and R. H. Wade. 2013. "Protecting power: How western states retain the dominant voice in the World Bank's governance." *World Development* 46: 153–164.

Vieira, M. 2012. "Rising states and distributive justice: Reforming international order in the twenty-first century." *Global Society* 26(3): 311–329.

Vreeland, J. R. and A. Dreher. 2014. *The Political Economy of the United Nations Security Council: Money and Influence*. New York: Cambridge University Press.

World Bank. 2010. *World Bank Group Voice Reform: Enhancing Voice and Participation of Developing and Transition Countries in 2010 and Beyond*. Washington, DC: World Bank.

Woods, N. 2006. *The Globalizers: The IMF, the World Bank and their Borrowers*. Ithaca, NY: Cornell University Press.

Zappile, T. M. 2014. "World Bank." In *Democratization of International Institutions*, edited by L. Levi, G. Finizio and N. Vallinoto. New York and London: Routledge, pp. 80–93.

8 The "hassle factor" of MDB lending and borrower demand in Latin America

Chris Humphrey

As any observer of the world economy is well aware, many developing countries are in a much stronger economic position than in past decades. Commodity price booms have stocked government coffers, macroeconomic and fiscal management is much improved, and global capital flows have risen immensely. For example, public debt among emerging and developing countries represented on average only 40 percent of GDP in 2010 and was expected to decline to 30 percent by 2015 (IMF 2011), while the non-OECD share of total global foreign exchange reserves rose from below 30 percent in 1990 to about 65 percent in 2010 (Reisen 2013). These trends are particularly pronounced in Latin America, which is now a largely "middle-income" region. Public debt is declining overall in Latin America, and the share of it supplied by MDBs and the IMF is also declining in relative terms (Figure 8.1).

Despite these major shifts in the global economy, academic research has as yet paid relatively little attention to how this may be impacting the operations of multilateral development banks (MDBs). The great majority of MDB studies from the main theoretical traditions – realist considerations of power

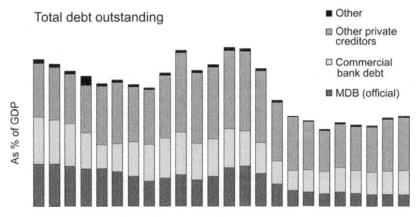

Figure 8.1 Outstanding public debt by source in Latin America
Note: "MDB" includes IMF.
Source: IADB Strategic Policy and Development Effectiveness Office 2014.

144 *Chris Humphrey*

politics (Harrigan et al. 2006; Dreher et al. 2009; Kilby 2011; Kilby and Bland 2012), rationalist focus on incentives among main actors in MDB activities (for example, Gutner 2005; Woods 2006), or more sociology-based constructivist approaches (for example, Barnett and Finnemore 1999, 2004; Weaver 2008) – focus on the decision-making process of MDBs themselves. For these researchers, the important question to be asked is what factors might lead an MDB to award a loan to a country, not whether a country may want to borrow or not, or why.

This scenario of constant demand by borrowers is unlikely to be realistic now, especially in the larger middle-income countries. Countries such as Mexico, Brazil, Indonesia, Turkey, China, and others are now in a much different position, with generally reduced need for external resources (due to stronger external account and fiscal balances) and a myriad of financing sources (multilaterals, traditional and new bilaterals as well as capital markets). In such a context it would be surprising indeed if borrower countries did not carefully consider the different attributes of an external lender before agreeing to a loan. Such a calculus would balance various factors such as loan pricing, bureaucratic hassle factor, technical assistance and knowledge, as well as political factors and even individual relationships.

The present study compares a sub-set of operational characteristics that influence loan demand in three MDBs operating in Latin America: the World Bank, the Inter-American Development Bank (IADB), and the Andean Development Corporation (CAF).[1] These three banks were selected because i) they operate in the same region and can hence be directly compared from the point of view of the borrower, and ii) they vary in governance arrangements, with the World Bank controlled by non-borrowing countries, the CAF by borrowing countries and the IADB more balanced between borrowers and non-borrowers (Figure 8.2). The hypothesis to be tested is that the balance of power between these two groups is a key explanatory factor in determining MDB operational characteristics.

The theoretical argument underpinning this approach is that the balance of governance power between borrowers and non-borrowers shapes MDB operational characteristics in fundamental ways. This builds on and refines previous theoretical approaches to understanding international organizations (IOs). Numerous researchers in the realist tradition and/or employing rationalist-oriented principal–agent frameworks seek to understand how IOs further (or not) the interests of their main state backers, usually the United States or the U.S. in conjunction with other G7 countries.

Clearly the U.S. and G7 wield extensive formal and informal power at numerous IOs, and in particular the World Bank and major regional MDBs, as numerous studies have convincingly shown (Babb 2009; Stone 2011; Kilby and Bland 2012). However, as Lyne et al. (2009), Gutner (2002) and Copelovitch (2010) all point out, the U.S. is far from being the only shareholder able to influence the major IOs. This chapter builds on the "complex principal" concept developed by Lyne et al., which takes into account formal

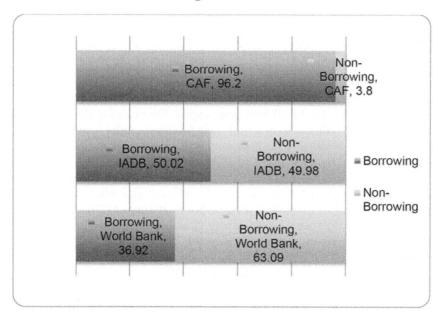

Figure 8.2 MDB shareholder voting power, 2012
Source: Annual reports, World Bank, IADB, and CAF 2012.

voting rules and the interests of numerous principals in seeking to understand social lending patterns at the World Bank. Powerful shareholder countries cannot possibly be involved in the myriad different projects taken on by the World Bank or other MDBs – they do not have the time or the interest. As well, other MDBs exist that are structured in a similar way to the major MDBs but have less or no involvement by the US or G7 shareholders (see Zappile, this volume).

To better understand the totality of MDBs and compare them to one another, a more refined approach is required. At the same time, following the lead of Lyne et al. (2009) would be extraordinarily difficult to operationalize, considering the high number of shareholders in each MDB. Thus, this study aggregates shareholders into two groups: borrowers and non-borrowers, following on similar approaches used by Humphrey and Michaelowa (2013) and Humphrey (2014a). While this simplifies a more complex reality of differing viewpoints within these two groupings on many issues, evidence suggests that within the context of MDB governance borrower shareholders tend to have similar interests as a group, as do non-borrower shareholders. The balance of power between these two groups, in turn, to a significant degree defines many MDB operational characteristics.

The focus here is on three non-financial "hassle factors" required to process a loan: overall loan-processing time, environmental/social safeguards, and procurement rules. The bureaucratic loan requirements analyzed are, for the most part, uniformly negative "hassle factors" from the point of view of borrowers, and thus reduce loan demand, all else being equal.[2] Other non-financial characteristics that could influence lending demand, such as policy conditionality or technical expertise, are much more dependent on the circumstances of individual countries, and are not analyzed here (loan pricing – another key factor impacting demand for loans – is examined in Humphrey 2014a).

The hassle factor for MDB loans can impact the overall viability of MDBs as institutions. MDBs are banks, and their financial model is predicated on a steady supply of borrowers[3] to generate the revenues needed to cover administrative costs and the generation of global public goods such as development knowledge. Particularly important are middle-income borrowers, who have the largest loan portfolios at the MDBs and are also most likely to have alternative sources of finance at their disposal. If some MDB characteristics are limiting borrower demand, and these characteristics are directly traceable to MDB governance arrangements, then this could indicate that the prevailing governance pattern of MDBs of the last several decades may no longer be suitable for the current global economic realities.

The chapter compares overall loan processing time, environmental and social safeguards, and procurement procedures in the three MDBs, and traces causal links between the interests of borrowing and non-borrowing countries in establishing the relative positioning of these characteristics along a continuum. Lastly, the chapter presents preliminary evidence linking the characteristics to the evolution of loan demand from borrowers. Evidence is derived from interviews with country representatives[4] and staff at the three MDBs undertaken 2009–2013, as well as a review of MDB documents and secondary material. It should be emphasized that the data and policies analyzed here were current as of 2013 – reforms to business procedures are being contemplated by all of the MDBs, in large part because of the impact they have on borrower demand.[5]

Loan approval procedures and processing times

The time MDBs take to design, review, negotiate, and approve loans is a significant burden to borrowing country governments. Loan preparation requires a considerable commitment of time by top-level ministerial officials to discuss project details with MDB staff – time taken away from normal government business. As well, many projects have potentially important economic impacts, and delays represent a significant opportunity cost. Procedures and times vary considerably among the three MDBs analyzed here (Table 8.1).

World Bank[6]

Estimates of time required to process a World Bank loan from identification to board approval vary according to the type of loan, with investment loans

Table 8.1 Loan approval procedures and times

	World Bank	IADB	CAF
Approval time	14–16 months	6–10 months	3–6 months; 1.5 if urgent
# of missions	• Identification • Pre-appraisal • Appraisal • Negotiation	• Identification • Appraisal • Negotiations (often VC*)	• Identification • Negotiations (often VC)
# of review phases	• Concept • Quality enhance • Decision • Board	• Eligibility (often virtual) • Quality/risk (often virtual) • Operations • Board	• Business committee • Loan and invest committee • Board (for larger loans)
Caveats	• Decision meeting can be skipped for low-risk invest loans since 2009 (but rare due to risk-averse staff)	• Missions faster than WB (example: negotiations ½ day vs. 2–3 days) • Shorter project documents and reading time before meetings than WB	• Missions faster than either IADB or WB • Loans below US$75 mln approved by president • Non-resident board meets 3–4 times/year; can approve loans by email

Source: Development Effectiveness Overview reports (2009–2012) for IADB, Corporate Scorecard for World Bank (2008 and 2012), borrower and staff interviews for CAF.

Note: * VC = video conference.

typically taking longer due to more stringent safeguard and procurement procedures than with budget support (adjustment) lending. The World Bank's Corporate Scorecard reports an average of 14 months for approving all types of loans on average in 2012, down from 16 months in 2008 (World Bank 2008, 2012). Most investment loans involve four separate country missions (identification, pre-appraisal, appraisal, and negotiations) as well as four full formal internal reviews (concept, quality enhancement, decision to appraise, and board approval) (World Bank, 2012a). Low-risk, repeater investment loans are sometimes allowed to skip the decision meeting as part of the recent investment loan reform, but few loans actually qualify for this procedure (World Bank interview, 7 September 2011).

Most of the obstacles slowing down the review process were instigated at the behest of non-borrowing countries, against borrower wishes, according to multiple interviews. A staffer in the Latin America region said, "The World Bank is majority-owned by Part 1 countries like the US, Japan, France, Netherlands, and the Nordics. So every time there's a screw up, another rule gets written and process gets added, formal or informal … These ideas come from the Part 1 countries, they're certainly not the borrowers' ideas – they didn't come to the Board asking for tighter restrictions on how we do things" (ibid.).

This formalistic, risk-averse, and lengthy set of procedures for loan approval also pertains to any modification to a loan that has already been approved. Staff must prepare a restructuring paper to be approved by the relevant country director and signed off on by the regional vice-president (World Bank 2012b). This process is required even for something as simple as extending the closing date of a loan – a common problem, particularly with investment projects (World Bank interview, 7 September 2011). Any restructuring involving safeguard re-categorization or changes to a project's development objectives must be submitted to the board for approval.

IADB

The processing time required for loans at the IADB is faster and less onerous to borrowers than at the World Bank. The average time required for full project preparation and approval averaged 6–9 months, 2009–2012 (IADB 2009, 2012c) – slightly faster than the World Bank, and improving in recent years. The number and type of formal steps for sovereign loan approval seem comparable on paper to the World Bank.[7] However, required documents are considerably shorter, the reading period prior to review meetings is shorter, and two of the review meetings are "virtual" rather than physical, all of which speed up the process. As well, most projects require only two formal missions, compared to four for the World Bank, and final loan negotiations usually take place via video conference rather than an in-country mission (IADB interview, 24 January 2012).

Staffers and shareholders agreed that the approval times at the IADB, while better than the World Bank, are still disincentives for borrowers, and also that the bureaucratic obstacles overwhelmingly derive from the interests of non-borrowing shareholders. The Brazilian ED stated that "It's difficult to reduce the speed, because the internal process and all the different committees. This comes from the non-borrowers ... they created a lot of steps in the process, and this means the project takes a year instead of six months" (IADB ED interview, 10 January 2012). Non-borrowers agreed that they were the cause of much bureaucratic overhead. A European G7 AED said, "We have really strengthened internal oversight and environmental and social safeguards and this might perceived by borrowing members as making doing business more complicated with the IADB" (IADB AED interview, 13 January 2012).

IADB's procedures are more streamlined due to the greater influence of borrowing country shareholders to approve slightly less onerous review requirements, according to interviews. Although major non-borrowers would prefer stricter oversight processes, one top operations staffer said that they – especially the U.S. – limit using their power to issues of strong concern, in the interests of more consensual governance in light of the nearly 50–50 split on the board (IADB operations staff interview, January 24, 2012). As well, the

IADB's "Latin" character is seen as smoothing procedural requirements. Of the IADB's nearly 2,000 employees, 68 percent were from regional borrowing countries at the end of 2009 (IADB, 2012b). The Chilean ED noted that "there is more cultural proximity with the IADB, it's perceived as more of our bank than the World Bank. I mean, the World Bank's regional vice-president[8] doesn't even speak Spanish" (IADB ED interview, 24 January 2012).

CAF

CAF's loan approval procedure is far faster and less formal than that of the other two MDBs. Major loans routinely move from conception to final approval within three months, or even faster if the country needs it, according to several CAF operations and policy staffers interviewed. All concurred that the reason for the reduced bureaucracy is directly linked to the fact that borrowing country shareholders control the institution. "We have definite advantages in terms of flexibility and reaction time compared to the other multilaterals," said one operations staffer. "We are much less rigid than the other multilaterals, which have certain impositions from donating countries that we do not" (CAF interview, 25 May 2009).

CAF loans face only two review levels, according to staffers in operations and high-level managers.[9] The *Comité de Negocios Corporatives* (Corporate Business Committee) considers whether the proposed project conforms to CAF policies and business strategy and is the only review that considers a project's concept and development impact. The project is then presented to the *Comité de Préstamos e Inversiones* (Loan and Investment Committee) to analyze the loan's implications for CAF's finances. CAF review meetings are much less lengthy, according to a former CAF staffer who has worked at all three MDBs. "Projects are discussed and have to get approved, but the meetings are really fast and not nearly as serious as the IADB and the World Bank" (CAF interview, June 1, 2009).

Final approval is also radically different at CAF. Sovereign loans below $20 million can be approved directly by operations vice-presidents and sovereign loans below $75 million can be approved directly by the president, with no further review, according to a top-level CAF manager (CAF interview, 24 August 2011) – a delegation unimaginable at the other two MDBs. As well, the executive board itself is a group of finance ministers and central bank governors who meet only three to four times a year, rather than a permanent sitting board. Because they are top-level officials, they take major decisions quickly without having to consult with their capitals, as executive directors at the World Bank and IADB (generally mid-level bureaucrats) do.

Environmental and social safeguards

Environmental and social safeguards consist of procedures on different types of lending operations meant to "safeguard" the project from having negative impacts on the environment and on vulnerable social groups. This section compares the current environmental and social (E&S) safeguard framework, and then shows how shareholder interest has shaped their design.

Safeguard framework

The World Bank currently has 10 operational policy E&S safeguards (six related to the environment, two on social issues and two on legal issues) while the IADB has four (two on the environment and two on social issues). CAF has a list of 14 safeguards (six related to the environment, seven on social issues, and one overarching safeguard), which are not codified into formal policy (CAF 2007). The most controversial of the safeguard issues relate to environmental impact and involuntary resettlement. According to a recent review of safeguard policies by the World Bank's IEG, these are also the most commonly triggered – 72 percent of investment loans globally between 1999 and 2008 trigger environmental assessments and 30 percent involuntary resettlements (World Bank 2010a).[10] As such, the analysis below focuses on these two safeguards.

Environmental protection

The environmental safeguard policies of the World Bank (OP 4.01) and the IADB (OP 703) are in many respects quite similar. All project teams are to perform an initial screening to determine which "category" a project falls into – A, B, or C – depending on similar criteria for expected environmental impacts. Category A projects are considered to imply the greatest environmental risk, Category B only local impacts that can be mitigated, and Category C minimal or no environmental impacts.[11] On the basis of the categorization, the project team and borrower are then required to follow a number of other steps during the loan approval and implementation process, with more rigorous procedures for Category A projects.

In a number of key areas, however, World Bank and IADB environmental safeguards differ, with the latter being more flexible. Both mandate an EA done by the borrower, but the World Bank requires Category A project EAs to be undertaken by "independent EA experts not affiliated with the project" (World Bank 1999a: para. 4). The IADB's policy makes no mention of who should undertake the EA, meaning it could acceptably be done by an environmental unit within the relevant ministry or by the government's environmental oversight body (IADB 2007). As well, the World Bank requires Category A project borrowers to "engage independent, internationally recognized environmental specialists to advise on all aspects of the project relevant to the EA" (World Bank 1999a: para. 4). The IADB *"may* ask the borrowers to establish an advisory panel of experts" (IADB 2007: 24, emphasis added) for Category A projects, but the guidelines explicitly state that "not all category A projects will a priori require an advisory panel" (ibid.: 25), leaving a considerable degree of leeway depending on the circumstances.

The IADB's stipulations are also more relaxed regarding consultations with affected people – a considerable burden for governments. While both MDBs require consultations for both Category A and B projects, the World Bank specifies that "the borrower consults project affected groups and local non-governmental organizations (NGOs) about the project's environmental aspects and take their views into account" (World Bank 1999a: para. 14). The IADB requires only that borrowers consult with "affected parties", with no mention of NGOs (IADB 2006: 10). The World Bank states that the EA review will give "special attention to, among other things, the nature of the consultations with affected groups and local NGOs and the extent to which the views of such groups were considered" (World Bank 1999b: para. 12), while the IADB guidelines make no similar statement. During implementation, the World Bank requires borrowers to continue consultations, while the IADB does not (IADB 2006: 10).

The institutional arrangements for EA approval within each MDB also vary, with the IADB project teams afforded considerably more independence compared to World Bank teams. In the World Bank, the project team is required to work with the Regional Safeguards Advisor (RSA) – a separate office pertaining to the Operations Vice-Presidency, and not to the country teams – at all stages of the process beginning with the initial screening and categorization, and the RSA can shut the project down at any point (World Bank 1999b). For the IADB, the team makes its own decision on categorization, and only Category A projects require approval from the Committee on Environmental and Social Impact (CESI) (IADB 2007). For Category B projects, the CESI will review "only those operations that the Committee considers necessary" (ibid.: 25). The EAs produced by borrowers are reviewed only by the project team (ibid.: 30–31).

While the general environmental directives of the IADB and World Bank are quite similar, implementation is less rigorous at the IADB. One safeguard specialist formerly at the IADB and now at the World Bank noted that at the IADB:

> there's really no consequence for administration and timing of categorizing A or B, absolutely no consequence, the process is exactly the same. For us [at the World Bank], there are a lot of processes to go through, there is a difference in level of scrutiny that projects go through here.
> (World Bank interview, 6 September 2011)

Similarly, an independent panel reviewing IADB safeguards stated that safeguard requirements "were often uneven or too general to provide explicit, legally binding guidance to countries and ultimately, to Bank staff charged with supervising compliance" (IADB, 2011a: 25–6). A top environmental staffer at the IADB noted that actions required by the EA for project completion are frequently not followed up on and "kind of disappear" (IADB interview, 7 December 2011).

At CAF, environmental safeguards are contained in a few short paragraphs with no formal obligations put on project teams or borrowers – a far cry from the detailed policies and guidelines at the World Bank and IADB. The overriding principle, as emphasized by CAF's first safeguard, is that "all projects financed by CAF conform to the environmental legislation of the country where the project is executed, as well as the international agreements and commitments by shareholding countries" (CAF 2007: 13, author's translation). That is to say, CAF simply ensures that the country follows its own E&S laws, and places no other external obligation on the borrower. Regarding environmental evaluation, the policy states that CAF undertakes its own evaluation as part of the normal project cycle, that "when it is considered necessary, [CAF] requests the presentation of complementary environmental evaluations, studies and analysis," with no specifics given (ibid.). CAF clearly absolves itself of any responsibility, stating that "It is the responsibility of the client to adopt measures necessary to avoid, control, mitigate and compensate environmental and social impacts and risks" (ibid.).

As should be evident, while the IADB and World Bank differ to a degree in the rigor of their environmental safeguards, CAF is several orders of magnitude more lax, leaving almost complete flexibility to assess each project as it chooses. This assessment is supported by an independent study of CAF, which points out that the CAF's policies only call for departing from national laws on consulting affected populations or taking measures to safeguard the environment "when it is considered necessary," and "the policies give no orientation to indicate under what conditions the bank could consider it 'necessary' to do so" (Bank Information Center 2008: 14, author's translation). Environmental assessments are not formally stipulated in CAF's policies, and according to the NGO not a single assessment had been undertaken up to 2008 (ibid.: 17). Further, while CAF's environmental strategy refers to numerous documents involved in the approval process, none of those documents are publicly available.

Involuntary resettlement

When a project has a significant land use component – such as transport infrastructure, hydropower facilities, or slum upgrading – resettlement safeguards may be triggered. The resettlement policies of the IADB (OP 710) and World Bank (OP 4.12) are similar in most respects, and as with environmental oversight, differ in a few specific but potentially important details. Project teams in both MDBs are mandated to seek alternative designs that do not involve resettlement, and broadly require compensation and assistance to those who are resettled to achieve a standard of living equal to or better than pre-project levels.

In designing a resettlement plan, the World Bank requires "meaningful consultations with affected persons and communities, local authorities, and, as appropriate, nongovernmental organizations" (World Bank 2001a: para. 14), and that displaced people should be "meaningfully consulted and should have opportunities to participate in planning and implementing resettlement programs" (ibid.: para. 2b). By contrast, the first sentence of the consultations section of the IADB's implementation guidelines for resettlement states that, "*Where possible*, the affected population should be involved in the design of the resettlement plan" (IADB, 1999: 18, emphasis added). The guidelines then go on at great length to detail why consultations with community authorities and local NGOs can lead to conflicts and might be best avoided, and offer a variety of flexible options for the borrower to take affected people's views into account when designing the resettlement plan depending on local conditions. The World Bank further requires the creation of a third-party dispute resolution mechanism to address grievances related to the resettlement plan (World Bank 2001a: Annex A, para. 17), which is discussed but not mandated in the IADB's guidelines (IADB 1999).

On the issue of compensation to affected individuals, both MDBs clearly state the principle of re-establishing or exceeding prior levels of livelihood. However, the World Bank policy states that individuals be "provided prompt and effective compensation at full replacement cost for losses of assets" (World Bank 2001a: para. 6), while the IADB specifies "fair and adequate compensation and rehabilitation" (IADB 1998: 1), providing greater leeway for project teams and governments. Further, the World Bank emphasizes that "Preference should be given to land-based resettlement strategies for displaced persons whose livelihoods are land-based" (World Bank 2001a: para. 11), while the IADB policy states only that "The options that are offered should be appropriate for the people affected, and should reflect their capabilities and realistic aspirations" (IADB 1998: 4), again providing considerably more flexibility (especially as resettling land-based people is often extremely difficult).

The World Bank team must work with the regional Social Development unit, the Legal Vice-Presidency and a special Resettlement Committee, all of which must review and approve borrower actions (World Bank 2001b). Once under implementation, the project is "not considered complete – and Bank supervision continues – until the resettlement measures set out in the relevant resettlement instrument have been implemented" (ibid.: para. 16). For the IADB, the project team essentially has to pass one hurdle – the submission and approval of an Environmental and Social Impact Report by the Committee on Environmental and Social Impact (CESI), after which it moves into the regular project channels of the Loan Committee and the board for final approval (IADB 1999). While the resettlement commitments of the borrower are incorporated into the loan agreement, they are not in the legal agreement, unlike the World Bank (ibid.). Under the IADB's policy guidelines, project completion does not depend on resettlement completion (ibid.).

Evidence from internal World Bank studies supports the conclusion that its resettlement policies are more stringent than other MDBs, including the IADB. A World Bank Internal Evaluation Group study from 2010 concluded that World Bank resettlement safeguards were at times stricter than in industrialized countries. The report quoted one World Bank country director as saying, "There is a serious disconnect between what countries are doing and our social safeguards. The resettlement policy is way out of line with what our clients have" (World Bank 2010: 93). The IEG compared the World Bank's policies with the IADB's, and concluded that the latter was more flexible and project-specific (ibid.). The same study reported that 73 percent of surveyed government officials found World Bank safeguards significantly stronger than those of other institutions (ibid.).

CAF's safeguard regarding resettlement states the same over-arching principles as the other two MDBs' but contains absolutely no specific requirements. The policy states simply that in the case of projects requiring resettlement, CAF "requests the formulation of plans that compensate or offer similar or better conditions of life to affected groups, and that receiving communities are taken into account" (CAF 2007: 15, author's translation). The policy further says that CAF "supports developing skills and options for local community development, especially for indigenous people who, due to their vulnerable condition, could be directly affected by an operation" (ibid.).[12] This is obviously much less of a burden to governments than the requirements of the World Bank and IADB.

Linking to shareholder interest

Policies related to E&S protection falls on a continuum, with the World Bank generally at one end, the IADB in the middle, and the CAF at the other extreme (Table 8.2). The evidence clearly indicates that this is a function of shareholder interest and balance of power in each MDB's governance.

World Bank

Numerous sources indicate that the force behind the World Bank's drive for strict E&S safeguards is the interests and voting power of non-borrowing shareholders. The two most comprehensive reviews of the creation of safeguards at the World Bank both document how activist NGOs brought pressure to bear on the World Bank via the U.S. Congress and political parties in western Europe (mainly Germany and the U.K.), which led to the implementation and continual tightening of safeguards in the 1980s and 1990s against the vocal opposition of borrowing countries.[13]

This view is substantiated by current executive directors. One Latin American alternate ED stated that "It all comes from developed countries – the Nordic chair generally pushes a lot about performance standards, France and Germany also push, and the United States too depending on the project"

Table 8.2 Comparison of two safeguards

	World Bank	IADB	CAF
Environment			
Experts	Independent experts for EA and Category A advisory panel	No stipulation; advisory panel not required	National systems
Consultations	Includes NGOs	Only "affected parties"	National systems
Bureaucracy	Separate regional safeguard team (often conflicts with project team)	No separate safeguard specialists— project team makes decisions	Ad hoc review as part of regular loan approval
Resettlement			
Trigger	Caused by or related to project	Directly caused by project only	National systems
Consultations	Required	"Where possible"	National systems
Dispute resolution	3rd party mechanism required	Not required	National systems
Type of resettlement	Land-based preferred for those with land-based livelihoods	"Appropriate" resettlement	National systems
Bureaucracy	Social Development Unit, Resettlement Committee, Legal	Only project team	Ad hoc review as part of regular loan approval
Project completion	Not until resettlement completed	No requirement	No requirement

(World Bank AED interview, 14 December 2011). An advisor to a European G7 ED said, "We get a lot of lobbying about environmental and social human rights safeguards," and added that tighter safeguards are resisted by many borrowers. "Some MICs [middle-income countries] definitely say this isn't the way we should be going about our business" (World Bank ED staff interview, 30 January 2012).

IADB

The IADB's safeguard policies are in most respects very similar to the World Bank, although they have tightened at a slower pace. E&S safeguards were thoroughly revamped starting in 2003, bringing them much more in line with World Bank (IADB 2006), driven by the non-borrowing shareholders. "It was the U.S. and the other donors, no question about it," according to the environmental staffer (IADB interview, 7 December 2011). As a result of the new policies, the number of policies going through safeguard compliance review jumped from 480 in 2007 to 775 in 2009 (IADB 2011b). The AED of a European G7 non-borrower commented, "I can't see any non-borrowing country wanting to weaken safeguard procedures. That's the basis on which the Americans can support a capital increase" (IADB AED interview, 31 January 2012). Indeed, the U.S. Treasury's report to Congress in 2011 justified its agreement to the most recent capital increase in part by noting that its requirement for the IADB to revise E&S safeguards had been complied with (U.S. Department of Treasury 2011).

Despite the many similarities with World Bank safeguard policies, the IADB's rules are less formalistic in a way that offers more flexibility to both staff and borrowing countries. A researcher examining World Bank and IADB policies on civil society influence concluded that compared to the World Bank, the IADB's "loosely framed policy reduces opposition and leaves broad discretion with the IDB's country offices and borrowing government officials" (Nelson 2000: 419–420). Staffers and EDs agree with this overall assessment. One European G7 AED said, "We are probably less legalistic than the World Bank" in safeguard implementation (IADB AED interview, 31 January 2012), while a top environmental staffer added, "Compared to the World Bank, we are less procedural – it's more about the outcome. We wanted some flexibility; it fits the institutional culture better" (IADB interview, 7 December 2011).

CAF

In contrast to the other two MDBs, the fact that borrower shareholders control CAF ensures that it imposes no binding external constraints on environmental and social aspects of project lending, beyond respect for national laws. By the accounts of former CAF officials as well as an independent NGO report (Bank Information Center 2008), CAF had essentially no safeguards at all until a 2007 policy statement. A top CAF environmental specialist who left in the early 2000s to work at other development institutions said flatly, "When I was there, CAF didn't have any environmental policy" (World Bank interview, 6 September 2011). Staffers at the CAF defend the environmental policies as respectful of local laws. "We feel that if you are respecting local laws and doing your work, you don't have to go further than that," said one CAF operations staffer, explicitly linking the issue with hassle factors for borrowers. "We don't go to the extremes as others in ways that would make CAF more expensive and complicated" (CAF interview, 23 August 2011).

CAF staffers point to the difference in shareholder composition as the fundamental reason for the variance in policies. "The reason is fundamentally from the composition of the board. If for example we had Nordic and European countries on our board, environmental issues are very important to them, the bar is a lot higher," according to an operations staffer (ibid.). An IADB environmental official agreed that governance played the fundamental role in shaping the different policies. "There's no European, North American or Japanese shareholders in CAF, which are the countries that tend to raise these concerns" (IADB interview, 7 December 2011).

Procurement safeguards

Procurement rules – the procedures by which the government spends the proceeds of loans to acquire goods and services – are very similar at the World Bank and the IADB. A World Bank procurement specialist, who previously worked at the IADB in harmonizing procurement policy among MDBs, said, "We are 98 percent similar in every aspect" (World Bank interview, 24 April 2012). An examination of procurement guidelines for the World Bank and the IADB reveals that they are almost word-for-word copies of one another (World Bank 2011; IADB 2011b). Rules on which type of expenditures must be bid, which type of loans require using procurement guidelines, and cut-off values requiring international competitive bidding are the same for both banks.

According to the World Bank procurement specialist, borrowing government officials are constantly demanding to know why they must follow these rules instead of their own national systems. "They say, 'We have our own laws, why should we follow your procedures?'" (World Bank interview, 24 April 2012). A long-time staffer in the World Bank's Operations Policy division said he hears similar complaints in Latin America. "A country like Mexico has their own procurement laws, which they think are quite good. To a large extent the Bank thinks they are good too, but the Board has resisted country systems for procurement" (World Bank interview, 7 September 2011).

The over-riding importance of procurement policy to the U.S. and its veto power over capital increases, coupled with the support of other non-borrower shareholders, has meant that the greater influence of borrower countries at the IADB has not translated into less stringent procedures faced by borrowers. The IADB was forced by non-borrowers to adopt the World Bank's procurement guidelines wholesale in the mid-2000. "The U.S. said, 'If you don't take the World Bank's policy on this, we won't agree to the next capital replenishment.' And the Europeans backed the Americans, so we did it," according to a former IADB procurement specialist currently at the World Bank (World Bank interview, 24 April 2012). A European G7 shareholder AED at the IADB concurred that the overwhelming pressure came from the U.S. "This is an action taken by the U.S. across the board in all MDBs to say, 'That's a red line for Congress.' I think the issue is that as part of the pitch to sell multilateralism to Congress, the U.S. has to say, 'For every dollar we put in to these multilaterals, we get seven back for U.S. Inc.'" (IADB AED interview, 31 January 2012).

Nonetheless, the IADB is able to make procurement compliance more flexible than it is at the World Bank. A procurement specialist who has worked at both MDBs said, "It's the same set of rules, but World Bank implementation is more rigid, and the IADB is more flexible in how to implement those rules. That's why there's a clear preference with the IADB for the countries in the region" (World Bank interview, 24 April 2012). An IADB procurement official agreed, saying that their application of the rules was less legalistic than the World Bank, and that as a result countries preferred to work with the IADB (IADB interview, 27 April 2012).

The contrast between the World Bank and IADB at one end of the continuum and CAF at the other is stark regarding procurement. CAF has no procurement or financial policies whatsoever – once the country is granted a loan, it is free to spend the resources as it sees fit. A top CAF policy manager stated:

> The only procurement rule we have is that countries follow their own legislation. We don't have any of the types of procurement policies that cause problems with the IADB and the World Bank, which come from the interests of donor countries ... they have an interest that their companies can bid on projects, but in the CAF we don't have that.
> (CAF interview, 24 August 2011)

Impact of non-financial policies on borrowing

The above analysis of non-financial lending policies in all three MDBs suggests a relatively clear continuum from the point of view of borrowing countries: the World Bank's policies are the most onerous, the IADB's similar but with a greater degree of flexibility, and CAF's rely entirely on the laws and procedures used by each country, with no external imposition. This section makes the causal link between MDB characteristics and lending patterns based on evidence from interviews and reports by the MDBs themselves.[14]

The clearest evidence of the impact of World Bank safeguard and bureaucratic impositions on lending comes from concerns of World Bank management itself. The *Cost of Doing Business Task Force* report from 2001 states that:

> The Bank has more favorable lending terms than the five Multilateral Development Banks (MDBs). At the same time, Bank safeguard and financial requirements and other business practices tend to be more comprehensive, more stringent and more consistently enforced and are perceived by clients to add costs.
> (World Bank 2001c: 10)

A 2010 study by the World Bank's IEG found little improvement, noting that environmental, social, and financial safeguards clearly limited lending. "The impact of this chilling effect was reported by a majority of team leaders from Latin America and the Caribbean and over 40 percent from East Asia and Pacific and South Asia" (World Bank 2010: 46).

The impact is particularly strong on major infrastructure projects such as road building, urban transit, and energy plants, which are more likely to trigger safeguards and cause procurement problems. The 2001 *Cost of Doing Business* study found: "Given other opportunities for financing, IBRD borrowers articulated an explicit hierarchy of preference for official borrowing in these infrastructure sub-sectors: domestic resources, bilateral donors, Regional Banks and lastly, the World Bank" (World Bank 2001c: vii). A top IADB environmental staffer related a recent story about Brazilian plans for two major hydroelectric plants. "There was a point when some folks at the IADB were trying to court Brazil to finance that project, and the immediate response from the Brazilians was, 'Not on our life, you'll come running in here with your safeguards,'" the staffer said (IADB interview, 7 December 2011).

While the IADB's safeguards and procedures are somewhat less onerous to borrowers than the World Bank's, both MDBs are considered much more difficult to work with than the CAF. "This is definitely an advantage for the CAF," said the Argentina IADB ED (IADB ED interview, 13 January 2012). A top CAF policy staffer stated, "I think the agility and rapidity of the CAF vis-à-vis the other banks is a competitive advantage and it does partially compensate for the higher cost of our loans … . The fact that the CAF can react so much faster than the others is a major advantage" (CAF interview, 24 August 2011). A top IADB Treasury official, discussing the reasons behind the CAF's sharp increase in lending, agreed that non-financial characteristics are key, despite CAF's higher loan costs. "For some countries, it's definitely worth paying extra to avoid those hassles" (IADB interview, 15 November 2010).

Conclusion

The evidence reviewed here supports the hypothesis that the non-financial characteristics of each of the three MDBs vary as a direct function of the balance of power between non-borrowing and borrowing shareholders. Further, these characteristics in turn act as an important determinant of demand for loans by borrowing countries. Hence, the research presented here suggests that governance arrangements have a direct impact on the desire of countries to borrow from one MDB rather than another. In light of the fact that borrower revenue is an essential resource for MDBs to be financially sustainable, this in turn indicates that governance arrangements play a key role in shaping the viability of MDBs as financial concerns, through their influence on borrower demand.[15]

In all three of the characteristics analyzed – overall loan processing procedures, environmental and social safeguards, and procurement rules – the World Bank is unquestionably the most willing to impose strict rules above and beyond any national procedures and to enforce those rules in a rigid, legalistic way. The IADB generally follows the lead of the World Bank in the "letter of the law", but offers borrowing countries more flexibility in implementation, with the end result being somewhat faster and more fluid loan approval procedures. The CAF, by contrast, has few layers of bureaucracy and review and essentially no safeguards beyond following national law, meaning its loans are approved much more quickly and with minimal bureaucratic requirements. As a top level IADB policy staffer put it succinctly, "Countries feel that the IADB is more their bank than the World Bank. But of course they perceive the CAF as even more their bank then the IADB. We are in the middle between the two in these different governance dimensions" (IADB interview, 18 January 2012).

Interviews with country shareholder representatives and MDB staffers, as well as a review of available MDB reports, all point to the balance of power between non-borrowing and borrowing shareholders as the key variable defining this continuum. The dominance of non-borrower countries in the governance of the World Bank means that their priorities – environmental and social protection (driven by NGO lobbying), procurement rules (driven by a combination of corporate interests and mistrust of borrower government institutions), and multiple layers of internal review (driven by shareholders' desire to exert strong control over the MDB staff) – take precedence over the desire of borrowers to get loans with minimum hassle.

The fact that the IADB is more evenly divided between borrowers and non-borrowers translates into different characteristics. The slight majority of borrowers relating to day-to-day decision-making such as loan approval, coupled with the "trump card" of U.S. veto power over any changes to the capital structure, means borrowers and non-borrowers tend to seek consensus and avoid open conflict on most issues, according to both borrower and non-borrower shareholders interviewed for this research. The main exception is the U.S. threat of withholding a capital increase if it does not get its way on policy issues it considers critical, for example environmental safeguards or procurement procedures. But even here, the fewer layers of staff oversight and majority vote on loan approvals means that borrowers can influence the way those policies are implemented in a way more amenable to their interests.

In the CAF, by contrast, the shareholding dominance of borrowing countries has led to a very different set of operational characteristics. With the shareholders unified in their goals for the MDB, the staff is given very clear objectives (unlike the mixed and at times conflicting messages at the other two banks) and has considerably less incentive to develop or pursue interests that do not coincide with those shareholder goals.[16] Hence, the administration is much more vertical with far fewer bureaucratic layers, and management is given much greater freedom and trust by the shareholders. In addition, borrowing shareholders have no incentive to impose extra rules or procedures that go beyond their own national laws – such as the environmental, social, and financial safeguards at the other two MDBs. A high-level CAF executive summed the situation up neatly: "Here there's no difference between donor and creditor countries that causes problems and slows things down in the other banks" (CAF interview, 24 August 2011).

The rapidity and low-hassle factor of the CAF appears to act at least in part to offset its higher interest rates, particularly in relation to major infrastructure projects, where environmental, social, and procurement rules would be more problematic at the IADB and World Bank. In some ways the IADB appears to have the best of both worlds, with financial terms similar to the World Bank by virtue of the economic might of its non-borrowing members but slightly less onerous non-financial characteristics due to the stronger influence of borrowers. The World Bank, by contrast, appears to be relying on low price and some expertise advantage to attract borrowers: possibly a dangerous model in light of improved know-how and market access by many middle-income countries that are the World Bank's largest clients.

While the World Bank and IADB have made some efforts to reduce their hassle factor, resistance by non-borrowers has limited progress, especially at the World Bank.[17] The CAF, by contrast, continues growing very rapidly, to the point where it lends almost as much as the other two MDBs in Latin America, and now has 18 members (up from five originally). It may be that governance arrangements dominated by borrower countries are more appropriate for the emerging global economic and political context, while older-style dominance of a few wealthy western countries – the dominant model for the past 70 years – may have been surpassed by history. Certainly CAF's very rapid growth, as well as the recent creation of a new MDB by the BRICS nations,[18] suggests that a tectonic shift in the governance of international development is well underway.

Notes

1 CAF recently changed its official English name to "Development Bank of Latin America".
2 It should be noted that interviews for related research found that in some cases countries do find some value in the technical assistance that comes along with these three factors to improve project quality or strengthen domestic systems.
3 Also essential is strong access to capital markets for MDBs to fund themselves. The importance of this issue is analyzed in Humphrey 2014b.
4 This includes both executive directors (EDs) and alternate EDs (AEDs). All are formal representatives selected by member countries. The former are designated to sit at board meetings and vote in the first instance, while the latter substitute if the ED is not available.
5 For example, the World Bank is currently undergoing a two-year review of safeguard procedures, and is likely to launch reforms in 2015. See World Bank 2014.
6 The information in this chapter on World Bank loan requirements relates to all borrower countries, not just Latin America. Although there could conceivably be small differences between countries, all policies and processing requirements are the same for every borrower country.
7 The IADB 2012 lists the major steps as: Develop Project Profile, Eligibility Review, Proposal for Operation Development, Quality and Risk Review,

Operations Policy Committee Review, and finally approval by Executive Board (IADB 2012a).
8 U.S. national Pamela Cox, at the time of the interview.
9 The CAF's formal loan approval process is not publicly available (CAF interviews 25 May 2009; 23 August 2011; 24 August 2011).
10 The remaining safeguards are triggered on between 1% and 12% of projects.
11 The World Bank also has a Category FI for projects supported by financial intermediaries with some Bank financing, which the IADB does not include.
12 "Support" is the author's translation of the Spanish word "*propende*", which has no good translation to English, but suggests a tendency or propensity toward a certain action, and is hence actually even weaker than "support."
13 Wade 1997; Shihata, 1991, 1995, 2000.
14 Multivariate statistical tests were undertaken to address similar questions (though not limited to hassle factors) in Humphrey and Michaelowa 2013.
15 The capital contributions and reputation in financial markets of non-borrowers were critical for both the World Bank and IADB to begin operations. However, this is much less relevant today, as the example of the CAF as well as the desire of many borrowers to increase their capital contributions (and hence governance power) at the IADB and World Bank demonstrate. Non-borrowers do help keep funding (and hence loan) costs down at the two larger MDBs compared to the CAF, but even here the influence is less than one might expect (see Humphrey 2014a). In other regions such as sub-Saharan Africa, the contributions of non-borrowers to concessional lending windows generate a different dynamic than in Latin America.
16 The example of the CAF, in fact, makes one question whether the principal-agent dynamics much utilized to analyze MDBs are not misguided. The real tension may not be between principals and agents, but rather between different sets of principals. On this issue, see Hawkins et al., 2006, in particular Chapters 1, 8 and 9.
17 The ongoing safeguard reform (World Bank 2014) is likely to be a case in point, similar to the investment loan reform, country systems initiative and the Program for Results lending instrument. In all cases, the direction of reform is broadly supported by management and borrowers but restricted so severely by non-borrower shareholders as to undermine the effort.
18 See *Financial Times*, 2014.

References

Babb, S. 2009. *Behind the Development Banks: Washington Politics, World Poverty, and the Wealth of Nations*. Chicago, IL: University of Chicago Press.
Bank Information Center. 2008. Corporación Andina de Fomento, Guión Básico para la Sociedad Civil. June. Available at: www.bicusa.org/en/Institution.19.aspx (accessed 5 February 2012).
Barnett, M. and M. Finnemore. 1999. "The Politics, Power and Pathologies of International Organizations." *International Organization* 53(4): 699–732.
Barnett, M. and M. Finnemore. 2004. *Rules for the World: International Organizations in Global Politics*. Ithaca, NY: Cornell University Press.
Copelovitch, M. 2010. "Master or Servant? Common Agency and the Political Economy of IMF Lending." *International Studies Quarterly* 54(1): 49–77.
Corporación Andina de Fomento (CAF). 2007. Estrategia Ambiental del CAF. April. Caracas: CAF.

Dreher, A., J. Sturm and J. Vreeland. 2009. "Development Aid and International Politics: Does Membership on the UN Security Council Influence World Bank Decisions?" *Journal of Development Economics* 88(1): 1–18.

Gutner, T. 2002. *Banking on the Environment: Multilateral Development Banks and Their Environmental Performance in Central and Eastern Europe.* Cambridge, MA: MIT Press.

Gutner, T. 2005. "Explaining the Gaps Between Mandate and Performance: Agency Theory and World Bank Environmental Reform." *Global Environmental Politics* 5(2): 10–37.

Financial Times. 2014. "Shanghai Wins Race to Host New Brics Bank." 15 July.

Harrigan, J., C. Wang and H. El-Said. 2006. "The Economic and Political Determinants of IMF and World Bank Lending in the Middle East and North Africa." *World Development* 34(2): 247–270.

Hawkins, D., D. Lake, D. Nielson and M. Tierney. 2006. *Delegation and Agency in International Organizations.* Cambridge: Cambridge University Press.

Humphrey, C. 2014a. "The Politics of Loan Pricing in Multilateral Development Banks." *Review of International Political Economy* 21(3): 611–639.

Humphrey, C. 2014b. The Invisible Hand: Financial Pressure and Organizational Convergence in Multilateral Development Banks. Paper presented at the European Political Science Association Conference, Edinburgh, Scotland, 20 June 2014.

Humphrey, C. and K. Michaelowa. 2013. "Shopping for Development: Multilateral Lending, Shareholder Composition and Borrower Preferences." *World Development* 44: 142–155.

Inter-American Development Bank (IADB). 1998. Involuntary Resettlement Operational Policy and Background Paper. Washington, DC: IADB.

Inter-American Development Bank (IADB). 1999. Involuntary Resettlement in IDB Projects, Principles and Guidelines. Washington, DC: IADB.

Inter-American Development Bank (IADB). 2006. Environment and Safeguards Compliance Policy. OP-501, 19 January. Available at: http://idbdocs.iadb.org/wsdocs/getdocument.aspx?docnum=665902 (accessed 25 April 2012).

Inter-American Development Bank (IADB). 2007. Implementation Guidelines for Environment and Safeguards Compliance Policy. Available at: http://idbdocs.iadb.org/wsdocs/getdocument.aspx?docnum=35597106 (accessed 25 April 2012).

Inter-American Development Bank (IADB). 2009. Development Effectiveness Overview. Washington, DC: IADB.

Inter-American Development Bank (IADB). 2011a. Final Report to the Inter-American Development Bank. Independent Advisory Group on Sustainability, January. Washington, DC: IADB.

Inter-American Development Bank (IADB). 2011b. Policies for the Procurement of Goods and Works Financed by the Inter-American Development Bank. March, GN-2349-2349, IADB. Available at: http://idbdocs.iadb.org/wsdocs/getdocument.aspx?docnum=774392 (accessed 2 March 2012).

Inter-American Development Bank (IADB). 2012a. Project Cycle. Available at: www.iadb.org/en/projects/project-cycle,1243.html (accessed 16 March 2012.

Inter-American Development Bank. 2012b. Bank Staff. Available at: www.iadb.org/en/about-us/bank-staff,6126.html (accessed 24 March 2012).

Inter-American Development Bank (IADB). 2012c. Development Effectiveness Overview. Washington, DC: IADB.

International Monetary Fund (IADB). 2011. World Economic Outlook. Washington, DC: IMF.

Kilby, C. 2011. "Informal Influence in the Asian Development Bank." *Review of International Organizations* 6(3–4): 223–257.

Kilby, C. and E. Bland. 2012. Informal Influence in the Inter-American Development Bank. Villanova School of Business Economics Working Paper no. 22. Available at: http://wp.peio.me/wp-content/uploads/2014/04/Conf5_Kilby-01.10.11.pdf (accessed 25 May 2015).

Lyne, M., D. Nielson and M. Tierney. (2009). "Controlling Coalitions: Social Lending at the Multilateral Development Banks." *Review of International Organizations* 4(4): 407–433.

Nelson, P. 2000. "Whose Civil Society? Whose Governance? Decisionmaking and Practice in the New Agenda at the Inter-American Development Bank and the World Bank." *Global Governance* 6: 405–431.

Reisen, H. 2013. *Economic Policy and Social Affairs in the BRICS*. Gütersloh: Bertelsmann Stiftung.

Shihata, I. 1991. *The World Bank in a Changing World*, Vol. 1. New York: Springer.

Shihata, I. 1995. *The World Bank in a Changing World*, Vol. 2. New York: Springer.

Shihata, I. 2000. *The World Bank in a Changing World*, Vol. 3. New York: Springer.

Stone, R. 2011. *Controlling Institutions: International Organizations and the Global Economy*. Cambridge: Cambridge University Press.

U.S. Department of Treasury. 2011. 2011 NAC Report. 10 June. Available at: www.treasury.gov/resource-center/international/development-banks/Pages/congress-index.aspx (accessed 18 February 2012).

Wade, R. 1997. "Greening the Bank: The Struggle Over the Environment, 1970–1995." In *The World Bank: Its First Half-Century*, Vol. II, edited by D. Kapur, et al. Washington, DC: The Brookings Institution, pp. 611–734.

Weaver, C. 2008. *Hypocrisy Trap: The World Bank and the Poverty of Reform*. Princeton, NJ: Princeton University Press.

Woods, N. 2006. *The Globalizers: The IMF, the World Bank, and Their Borrowers*. Ithaca, NY: Cornell University.

World Bank. 1999a. OP 4.01 – Environmental Assessment. Available at: http://web.worldbank.org/WBSITE/EXTERNAL/PROJECTS/EXTPOLICIES/EXTOPMANUAL/0,contentMDK:20064724~menuPK:64701637~pagePK:64709096~piPK:64709108~theSitePK:502184,00.html (accessed 2 March 2012).

World Bank. 1999b. BP 4.01 – Environmental Assessment. Available at:http://web.worldbank.org/WBSITE/EXTERNAL/PROJECTS/EXTPOLICIES/EXTOPMANUAL/0,contentMDK:20064614~menuPK:4564187~pagePK:64709096~piPK:64709108~theSitePK:502184,00.html (accessed 2 March 2012).

World Bank. 2001a. OP 4.12 – Involuntary Resettlement. Available at: http://web.worldbank.org/WBSITE/EXTERNAL/PROJECTS/EXTPOLICIES/EXTOPMANUAL/0,contentMDK:20064610~menuPK:4564185~pagePK:64709096~piPK:64709108~theSitePK:502184,00.html (accessed 2 March 2012).

World Bank. 2001b. BP 4.12 – Involuntary Resettlement. Available at: http://web.worldbank.org/WBSITE/EXTERNAL/PROJECTS/EXTPOLICIES/EXTOPMANUAL/0,contentMDK:22941226~menuPK:4564187~pagePK:64709096~piPK:64709108~theSitePK:502184,00.html (accessed 2 March 2012).

World Bank. 2001c. *Cost of Doing Business: Fiduciary and Safeguard Policies and Compliance*, 16 July. Washington, DC: World Bank.

World Bank. 2008–2012. Corporate Scorecard. Available at: http://corporatescorecard.worldbank.org/ (accessed 22 June 2013).
World Bank. 2010. Safeguards and Sustainability Policies in a Changing World. Independent Evaluation Group. Washington, DC: World Bank.
World Bank. 2011. OP 11.00 – Procurement. Available at: http://web.worldbank.org/WBSITE/EXTERNAL/PROJECTS/EXTPOLICIES/EXTOPMANUAL/0,contentMDK:20064773~menuPK:64701633~pagePK:64709096~piPK:64709108~theSitePK:502184~isCURL:Y,00.html (accessed 25 April 2012).
World Bank. 2012a. Project Cycle. Avaiable at: http://web.worldbank.org/WBSITE/EXTERNAL/PROJECTS/0,contentMDK:20120731~menuPK:41390~pagePK:41367~piPK:51533~theSitePK:40941,00.html (accessed 23 February 2012).
World Bank. 2012b. OpMemo – Project Restructuring: New Procedures (Revised). Available at: http://web.worldbank.org/WBSITE/EXTERNAL/PROJECTS/EXTPOLICIES/EXTOPMANUAL/0,contentMDK:22394249~menuPK:4564193~pagePK:64709096~piPK:64709108~theSitePK:502184,00.html (Accessed 23 February 2012).
World Bank. 2014. Review and Update of the World Bank Safeguard Policies: Objectives and Scope. Available at: http://consultations.worldbank.org/review-and-update-world-bank-safeguard-policies-objectives-and-scope (accessed 17 July 2014).

Interviews

CAF

CAF former staff, at time of interview working as World Bank staff, 1 June 2009. Personal interview.
CAF management, 23 August 2011. Personal interview.
CAF operations staff, 25 May 2009. Personal interview.
CAF top management, 24 August 2011. Personal interview.

IIADB

IADB (Argentina) Executive Director Eugenio Díaz-Bonilla, 13 January 2012. Personal interview.
IADB (Brazil) Executive Director Sérgio Portugal, 10 January 2012. Personal interview.
IADB (Chile) Executive Director Alejandro Foxley, 24 January 2012, Personal views. personal interview.
IADB environment operations staff, 7 December 2011. Personal interview.
IADB European G7 Alternate Executive Director, 13 January 2012, anonymity requested. Personal interview.
IADB European G7 Alternate Executive Director, 31 January 2012, anonymity requested. Personal interview.
IADB Latin American Executive Director staff, 24 January 2012, anonymity requested. Personal interview.
IADB operations staff, 24 January 2012. Personal interview.
IADB operations strategy staff, 18 January 2012. Personal interview.
IADB operations strategy staff, 24 January 2012. Personal interview.
IADB procurement specialist, 27 April 2012. Personal interview.
IADB Treasury staff, 15 November 2010. Personal interview.

World Bank

World Bank (Brazil) Executive Director Rogério Studart, 12 December 2011 (previously served as IADB ED). Personal interview.

World Bank environment staff, formerly with CAF and IADB, 6 September 2011. Personal interview.

World Bank European Executive Director staff, 30 January 2012, anonymity requested. Personal interview.

World Bank Latin American Alternate Executive Director, 14 December 2011, anonymity requested. Personal interview.

World Bank OPCS staff, 7 September 2011. Personal interview.

World Bank procurement specialist, 24 April 2012. Personal interview.

9 The European Bank for Reconstruction and Development as organic intellectual of neoliberal common sense in post-communist transition

Stuart Shields[1]

This chapter sets out to explore the role played by the European Bank for Reconstruction and Development (EBRD) as an 'organic intellectual' in the Gramscian sense, providing intellectual ballast for the hegemony of neoliberal reformers in post-communist transition. The EBRD was founded in 1991 as part of the response to the collapse of the Soviet Union. Its activities, predominantly private sector investment, have been focused on Eastern Central Europe (ECE), but since the Arab Spring the EBRD is increasingly active in the Middle East and North Africa (MENA). With its headquarters in London, the EBRD's membership includes 64 countries, the European Commission and the European Investment Bank.[2] The management of EBRD activities is primarily organised by its president and board of governors. Since its inception all but one president (the current incumbent, Suma Chakrabarti) have been Europeans. The EBRD Board of Governors is comprised of the finance ministers of the membership. The EBRD is responsible for providing project financing for private sector investments in banking, industrial and business sectors. Where it invests in the public sector it supports privatisation and restructuring of the state sector (Linarelli 1995).

The chapter's starting point is to note the *explicit political orientation* of the EBRD, an orientation in contrast to that of other regional development banks (RDBs) investigated in this collection. Unlike the other RDBs, the EBRD has a palpable political mandate to not only facilitate economic reform:

> The purpose of the Bank shall be to foster the transition towards open-market economies and to promote private and entrepreneurial initiative in the Central and Eastern European countries committed to and applying the principles of multiparty democracy, pluralism and market economies.
>
> (EBRD 1990: Art. 1)

The EBRD works as a 'permanent persuader' (Gramsci 1971: 10), whose social function is to aid the passage of common sense into hegemony through their specialisation in the elaboration of ideas (ibid.: 8–9, 347).

In ECE this manifests as mobilising and perpetuating neoliberal development 'common sense' among aspirational members of the working class with the allure of becoming middle class, in return for supporting reforms of which they are not the principle beneficiaries (Gramsci 1971: 129; on ECE see Shields 2012b). This conception of the organic intellectual is useful in displaying the subordinate position intellectuals occupy in relation to the leading class in the historic bloc.

The organic intellectual offers a 'trench system that sustains' neoliberal hegemony 'through its complexity and interlocking levels' (Jones 2006: 86). This is a starting point for conceptualising the organic intellectual as the collective intellectual, extending the term to include RDBs akin to Cox's discussion of internationalisation (Cox 1981), Taylor's (2004) work on the World Bank, and Murphy's historical appraisal of global governance as a form of world order (Murphy 1994). Various fractions of capital utilise these institutional frameworks in an attempt to forge their interests and ideologies into common sense (Bruff 2008: 54). The EBRD acts as collective organic intellectual to formulate common interests and assert them externally (Macartney 2010). Organic intellectuals aid in organising hegemony by converting a plethora of diverse issues into a common vision; this is the hegemonic project and the EBRD is a vital bastion of neoliberal hegemony in ECE.

The chapter illustrates the developing intellectual commitment of the EBRD to neoliberalism while interrogating the role of the EBRD in refining its strategies to maintain the disciplining power of neoliberalism.[3] The argument is laid out in three substantive steps. In the first section I explore how Gramsci's notion of the organic intellectual provides useful traction in explaining the activities of the EBRD. The second section periodises three waves of the EBRD's activities as organic intellectual of neoliberal 'common sense' in post-communist transition: 1) the initial post-communist construction of the market; 2) the configuration of the 'correct' socio-economic institutions; and 3) the promotion of neoliberal formulations of competitiveness. In the third and final section the chapter outlines the latest articulation of neoliberalism by the EBRD acting as organic intellectual in the aftermath of the 'global financial crisis'.

Situating the EBRD as organic intellectual of post-communist transition

In this section I want to outline how thinking of the EBRD as an organic intellectual might help us to gain traction in analysing the construction of neoliberal hegemony in post-communist transition. The production of 'common sense' in transition encourages us to reflect on the politics of ideas. Similar concerns are raised by constructivist scholarship on ECE. Epstein, for example, notes the importance of international institutions in providing direction for disorientated local elites through their expert knowledge and the consistency of their policy prescription (Epstein 2008).[4] While this is a crucial and convincing account in unveiling the causal power of ideas in framing the way transition is perceived by actors, it is less convincing on why it is these neoliberal development ideas that triumph over alternatives. The Gramscian focus on hegemony as a form of class relations locates the pervasive power of ideas in reproducing class relations and concealing contradictions. Social content as well as form matters when ideas are presented as adrift from the social structure, i.e. independent of the class relations that produce them. The section traces these social relations by reflecting on the role of the organic intellectual in Gramsci's often fragmentary writings and then indicating how this has been utilised in the assessment of multilateral institutions.

For others in this collection the question of hegemony is more often framed as a discussion of legitimacy (see Chapter 1). The IPE literature has tended to treat this issue as empirical knowledge informing the decisions of principle actors. Put differently, ideas are part of the background of agent behaviour. In terms of ECE I question explanations for why certain ideas are acceptable and 'succeed' where others diminish. The production of ideas is central to the condensation of strategies of accumulation (Bruff 2011; Macartney 2010). Social change is enacted by social agents and elements shaping their 'common sense' are open to contestation.[5] Consent is never absolute but ideational coherence enables hegemonic social forces to resist challenges (Carroll 2010: 174). What this begins to unravel is the way that hegemonic social forces come to articulate their particular interests as political projects (Wood 1995: 20), indicating that some ideas become dominant in shaping popular perceptions of more general possibilities for action.

For analysis of post-communist transition a Gramscian perspective challenges orthodox 'transitologists' to unravel the specific institutional forms in which capital has been structured and consent organised in the transition.[6] Doing so enables a more cohesive integration of domestic, international and transnational levels of analysis in attempting to theorise the simultaneously complimentary and contradictory relationship between state and capital (see Shields 2012a, esp. Ch. 2). For the EBRD this encourages the exploration of the ongoing practical transformations in the forms of consent and an appraisal of the opportunities and dangers that these changes represent. Such a perspective offers significant reorientation from the orthodox toolkit transitology.

Social change is produced by historically situated agents whose actions are enabled and constrained by their social self-understandings (Gramsci 1971: 164–5, 326, 375–7, 420). Popular 'common sense', then, becomes a terrain of political struggle (Gramsci 1971: 323–4, 419–25). The theorisation of a politics of common sense is an attempt to de-reify capitalist social relations, including state-based conceptions of politics, and construct an alternative social order out of the historical conditions of capitalism (Gramsci 1971: 329–39, 242–3).

This is not an esoteric or abstract discourse but a reality 'formed in specific historical relations, with specific feelings, outlooks, [and] fragmentary conceptions of the world' (Gramsci 1971: 198). This does not necessarily correspond to good sense but to a dominant view of the world where 'every social stratum has its own 'common sense' and its own 'good sense', which are basically the most widespread conception of life and man [sic]', (Gramsci 1971: 326) constituted by a variety of different and contradictory positions that span an entirety of beliefs and ways of seeing the world. Accordingly, there is no predisposition to coherence; however, common sense fuses the diversity of understandings of the world into an unproblematic and 'natural' worldview that provides the foundation for hegemonic order, a combination of consent and coercion through ideological legitimisation.

The strategic vocabulary that Gramsci furnishes provides a set of concepts that, unlike orthodox theories of transition, mediate between the abstract structures of capital and concrete instances of agency. In doing so, this reveals the practical context of social relations. In brief, this occurs through particular concessions by dominant forces to subordinate groups mediating between objective class conflict and the construction of a general will, as do the efforts of organic intellectuals. Civil society mediates between the mode of production and the means of coercion. Historic blocs mediate between social being and social consciousness. These concepts enable the theorisation of practice in post-communist transition within a dialectic of agency and structure while also supporting the possibility of formulating strategies for social transformation. Gramsci's notion of hegemony, in contrast to the Weberian concept of 'power over', reveals the organisation of consent to capitalist leadership and the possibility of constructing an alternative hegemonic bloc. This enables the empirical exploration of the practical content of hegemony organised by the EBRD around neoliberal strategies of accumulation as the common sense option for post-communist reform.[7]

Perhaps the most important element in a Gramscian perspective is the shift in discourse from the language of capital-logic and class struggle to a language of politics and strategy. For Gramsci, the analytical imperative to transcend economism was fuelled by a practical need for subordinate groups to move beyond a defensive understanding of their own immediate interests, to create their own hegemonic conception of the 'general interest'. In place of the abstract base-superstructure model, Gramsci developed the concrete-practical concept of 'historic bloc' 'to indicate the way in which a hegemonic class combines the leadership of a bloc of social forces in civil society with its leadership in the sphere of production' (Simon 1982: 86). Such a broad and durable alliance requires a relationship of compromises, through which the class (or fraction thereof) is able to represent the 'universal' interests of the whole of society while uniting to itself a group of allies (Sassoon 2000: 111). Organic intellectuals play a crucial role in this process. Gramsci argues that:

> Every social group, coming into existence on the original terrain of an essential function in the world of economic production, creates together with itself, organically, one or more strata of intellectuals which give it

homogeneity and an awareness of its own function not only in the economic but also in the social and political fields.

(Gramsci 1971: 5)

Given my point above that organic intellectuals can be not just individuals but also organic-collective intellectuals, they do not simply produce ideas, they help to affirm and articulate ideas and strategies in complex and often contradictory ways due to their class position and proximity to the leading groups in production and the state.

While this reinforces the importance of production (Murphy 1994), it also reveals the 'organising' function of intellectuals. For Gramsci, 'human mass does not "distinguish" itself, does not become independent in its own right without, in the widest sense, organising itself; and there is no organisation without intellectuals' (Gramsci 1971: 334). The knowledge produced by institutions like the EBRD serves to inform and organise. It organises the social forces it belongs to and contributes to the development of the hegemonic project. If the hegemonic project stems from the economic sphere it also transcends this into the political and social spheres incorporating broader issues that harmonise the interest of the leading and subordinate classes. Thus a specific ideology is expressed in universal terms by institutions like the EBRD.

More directly then, how might a RDB offer the 'intellectual and moral leadership' that has the 'same energy as a material force' (Gramsci 1971: 377)? As Cox's seminal work claims, it is in the naturalisation of particular interests as world order: 'The rules and practices and ideologies of a hegemonic order conform to the interests of the dominant power while having the appearance of a universal natural order' (Cox and Sinclair 1996: 243). Hegemony then, is about the limits of the possible of what constitutes legitimate policy. RDBs as multilateral institutions aggregate material and ideological processes, facilitating the co-option of state elites and assimilating counter hegemonic impulses (Taylor 2004: 126). This then is not crude dominance but nuanced hegemony as multilateral institutions regulate international organisation. Neoliberal social forces export the common sense of their preferred model of political economy through multilateral institutions such as the RDBs alongside the World Bank and its annual *World Development Report* or their *Doing Business* reports that articulate a set of appropriate economic indicators and policy prescriptions for development. The EBRD's annual *Transition Report* provides similar prescriptions but is focused on ECE and MENA. Consensus formation among the 'managers' of the global economy is transmitted into national policy formation, as Taylor clarifies in his discussion of the IMF and World Bank commitment to 'good governance': 'It is via interventions, negotiations, conditionality is, the making of concessions and the arrival at 'consensus' that paramount sectional interests are able to be displayed as the common interest' (Taylor 2004: 127). This is not some shadowy conspiratorial cabal but illustration of the success of neoliberal social forces and their hegemonic project. Similar examples can be found in the emergence of the European competitiveness discourse (van Apeldoorn 2002), the Cold War role of the Congress for Cultural Freedom (Scott-Smith 2002), and the response of global leaders to the financial crisis with neoliberal austerity measures in recent years (Gill 2012).

It is in this sense that the EBRD can be understood as a historically constructed organisation of consent, resting upon a practical material base. Gramsci provided some suggestive remarks on the dialectical relation between the two in capitalist formations. In the exercise of the cultural leadership through which the economy and the people are organised, a decisive role is played by organic intellectuals, whose own existence is grounded in the technical aspects of the fundamental productive functions of the modern bourgeoisie. As the later sections will illustrate, one of the EBRD's central roles is to extend such technical aspects into parts of the world where the bourgeois class has been absent. For Gramsci this process was clear: 'the capitalist entrepreneur creates alongside himself the industrial technician, the specialist in political economy, the organisers of a new culture, of a new legal system, etc.' (Gramsci 1971: 16).

There is, then, an openness to the problematic of the RDB. The organisation of consent is not deduced as a functional necessity; it arises as a contingent accomplishment, incorporating a mixture of strategic interventions and unintended consequences. It expresses no more than a balance of class and popular forces that has achieved a certain degree of durability across successive conjunctures. In like measure, an organic crisis in which the reigning historic bloc begins to dissolve inspires innovations and interventions at various sites in economy, state and civil society, which may have the effect of reorganising consent around a restructured economic nucleus and a different pattern of class and popular alliances. It follows from this analysis that a Gramscian perspective on the EBRD places considerable importance on the autonomous influence of ideas and institutions in the development of the post-communist transition order. It is a historical question to be answered by an empirical study of the particular case. In the next section I discuss the historical question of the ideas configured by the EBRD as it attempts to enhance the prospects for neoliberal hegemony in ECE.

Periodising the EBRD's activities as organic intellectual in post-communist transition

Having laid out the chapter's terms of engagement with the EBRD as Gramscian organic intellectual in the preceding section, I want to now turn to the historical emergence of three tropes of common sense in the EBRD's discourse. Remember that organic intellectuals provide ideological coherence, legitimacy and technical solutions to the perceived 'problems' of a social order, in this case the antediluvian of communist system. In this sense organic intellectuals like the EBRD are the midwife of neoliberalisation.[8] The second section of the chapter accordingly periodises these tropes of EBRD activity as neoliberal 'common sense' in post-communist transition: 1) the initial post-communist construction of the market, 2) the configuration of the 'correct' socio-economic institutions, and 3) the promotion of neoliberal formulations of competitiveness. More directly in relation to the EBRD, a first phase of transition in ECE was based on making the market (i.e. privatisation, liberalisation, and deregulation). The immediate result of these changes was a massive fall in output with a concomitant rise in unemployment. This period is known as the transition recession. Having witnessed the 'failure' of initial moves towards completion of the market economy in ECE, the EBRD recognised the necessity of complementing the first phase with the development of appropriate institutions and behaviour that support the functioning of markets and private enterprise. Reminiscent of the post-Washington Consensus, a second phase aimed to complete the transition and open up oligarchic and exclusive political-economic institutional frameworks and practices to competition. When that also 'failed' the EBRD turned to reinvigorate the common sense of transition with a new commitment to competitiveness.

From economic shock therapy ...

As noted above, in contrast to the other RDBs the EBRD is not coy about its commitment to facilitating not only economic but also political reform. Just after its establishment the EBRD acknowledged its role as permanent persuader, accepting that:

> this poses a major challenge: to create a new economic framework, while simultaneously changing the political system, behaviour, and even the attitudes of the people involved, without creating intolerable social conditions which could seriously endanger their societies and threaten those nearby.
> (EBRD, 1991: 23)

The priority areas for the EBRD in the early 1990s were developing the financial sector through technical assistance to governments and bank officials; supporting the creation of new financial actors; developing infrastructure in telecommunications, transport, energy and environment; conversion of the military industry sector; general privatisation and restructuring; and supporting small and medium-sized enterprises overlapped considerably with IMF and World Bank tasks (EBRD, 1990: Art. 1). The EBRD had three distinct undertakings: 1) an explicit commitment to political transformation; 2) a clearly defined emphasis on private sector development;[9] and 3) a strategic role as the first pan-European institution linking the ECE states to the West (Smith, 2002).[10] Yet this was to be no equivalent of the Marshall Plan (Ivanova 2007). According to Bronstone (1999), the zeal of the US, with British support, masterminded a transition driven by private foreign capital.[11]

The initial formation of the EBRD was an opportunity for neoliberal social forces to reassert their common sense and configure transition in a particular way. The EBRD represents both a consolidation of neoliberal thinking about the appropriate route for the transition to take and closure around what constituted legitimate intervention in ECE.[12] This constituted a stylised form of transition treating it as an axiomatically linear process and offering a pragmatic, one-dimensional 'toolkit' to solve the problems of ECE. It should be clear from comments earlier on the role played by organic intellectuals in framing transition that this is not a spontaneous process, as neoliberalism necessitates a constant stream of ideological and material forces to synthesise a long-term framework for political and economic interests (Shields 2012a: 78). Neoliberal social relations did not just fall fully formed from the sky as the Berlin Wall collapsed. The launch of the first wave of neoliberal transition, economic Shock Therapy, mapped out the parameters of the reform debate for the first half of the 1990s. Furthermore, it reveals the degree to which the neoliberal context, already configured by organic intellectuals, *was the only rational course of action*. Second, by embedding transition within an uncompromising anti-communist and pro-Western normative framework, the first-wave neoliberal blueprint for transition supplies a clear set of definitions and a then uncontroversial set of goals, while simultaneously offering expertise as a means of implementation (Shields 2012a: 24). The outcome was that it was considered better to undertake all the changes concurrently and as rapidly as possible because of the threat that the 'losers' would feel the social costs and uncertainties pushed through by the shocks of change a lot quicker than the 'winners' would experience success – a message that persists to this day (on ECE compare World Bank 2000; and EBRD 2007; and for contemporary developments in MENA see EBRD 2013).

To institutional shock therapy ...

This second wave aimed to complete the transition process and open up oligarchic and exclusive political economic institutional frameworks and practices to competition. Even in 1991 the EBRD considered such concerns vital:

> The countries of [ECE] have shown themselves determined to create new democratic market economies. The linkage between the political, economic and social components of the changes have become increasingly clear. A market economy requires an adequate legal and democratic political framework to foster the spirit of enterprise, individual rights and institutional stability necessary for sound investment.[13]
>
> (EBRD 1991: 26)

In the second wave of neoliberalisation the EBRD pointed to the harm done by vested interests and rent-seeking in preventing the completion of transition. This was illustrated in the 1999 *Transition Report*'s assertion that 'building institutions that support markets and private enterprise remains a fundamental challenge of transition, but establishing the appropriate laws and regulations is not sufficient' (EBRD 1999a: 9).

The need to open up key sectors of the economy to competition (especially the coal, ship building and steel industries), as well as to promote entrepreneurship and remove existing distortions in the ECE labour market that impeded the supply and development of quality human capital resonates with Gramsci's idea of the organic intellectual's 'scientific' knowledge informing and organising consent. Having witnessed the failure of initial moves towards completion of the market economy, the necessity of complementing liberalisation and privatisation with the development of institutions and behaviour that support the functioning of markets and private enterprise was recognised.

In effect this abandons economic shock therapy and in its place proposes institutional shock therapy. As the EBRD noted in 1995:

> the next period of the transition must be led by high-quality investment ... *with the right kind of institutions, leadership and partnership*, the private markets in these countries can deliver the quality investment which is necessary for successful economic growth.
> (EBRD 1995: 8, emphasis added)

Despite the shift in strategy, progress was protracted with 'little further progress ... achieved during the past three years to improve the investment climate, the competitiveness of the economy and the level of administrative capacity' (EBRD 2004: 1; also World Bank 2004). Market-oriented reforms advanced with the lion's share of responsibility in actively 'improving the investment climate and enhancing competitiveness' ceded to the EU *and the EBRD* (World Bank 2004).

And the promotion of competitiveness

While competitiveness is on the whole largely ignored in the field of IPE, this is not the case in institutions like the EBRD.[14] The 1999 *Transition Report* identifies the first two waves of transition common sense noted above and foreshadows the third's emphasis on the centrality of competitiveness to transition. It avers that change must be:

> embodied in the social norms, practices and behaviours of both government and the private sector – institutions need social capital and social foundations. The experiences of the first ten years of transition point to the ways in which both formal institutions can be built on firm foundations and social capital accumulated. Of particular importance are: (i) the experiences of liberalisation and privatisation, (ii) the demands for good governance from entrepreneurs and civil society, and (iii) the forces of competition.
> (EBRD 1999a: 9)

If building the market and getting the correct institutions in place was insufficient for the successful completion of transition then the alternative was to turn to the region's population and improve their entrepreneurial capabilities. Elsewhere among the organic intellectuals of neoliberalism change was similarly afoot. At the World Bank, Chief Economist Joseph Stiglitz (1998) was emphasising the need for greater flexibility rather than the dogmatic application of a priori models and a greater sensitivity to national and regional conditions. As Fine notes, the Stiglitz approach 'builds up from the micro to the macro from notions of civil, as opposed to market imperfections and with the potential for non-market improvements with impact upon the market' (1999: 10).

This form of micro-level social engineering, internalising shock therapy, is directly reflected in the key challenge confronted in ECE: changing attitudes. Thinking of this in a Gramscian way, the aim of the EBRD was 'to raise theoretically great mass of the population to a particular cultural and moral level, a level (or type) which corresponds to the needs of the productive forces for development, and hence to the interests of the ruling class' (Gramsci 1971: 258). The solution identified was a set of policies and ideas that guided a commitment to the discursive construction of a neoliberal agenda for competitiveness. Labour market reform was an essential component of this strategy, and its principal objective, as elsewhere, was the creation of a 'flexible' labour force.[15] It is not surprising that the EBRD promoted competitiveness; recall that the 1990 agreement establishing the EBRD declared that its purpose was 'to promote private and entrepreneurial initiative' in ECE (EBRD, 1990).[16]

In 1999 the bank adopted an operational strategy, *Moving Transition Forward*, which reflects early formulations of the key aspects of the competitiveness agenda. The EBRD argued that the:

> primary responsibility for shaping the response to the transition challenges' lies with the countries of the region themselves, and they are urged to foster investment, entrepreneurial and market skills and build popular support for them, while the [IFIs] and the international community will play a crucial supporting role.
>
> (EBRD 1999b)

Since the emergence of the competitiveness agenda, the EBRD has acted as a vehicle for what Carroll terms 'market-building', a programme of an 'all-encompassing technocratic agenda being operationalised in the name of development' (Carroll 2012: 351) at the intersection of the financial sector and civil society.

These three shifts in the EBRD discourse around transition have played a central role in the emergence of neoliberal common sense since 1989. This consolidated earlier phases of neoliberalism when the state's withdrawal from the economy was emphasised during 'roll-back' neoliberalism. This was followed by increasing the role of the state as regulatory overseer for the economy: a period of 'roll-out' neoliberalism (Peck 2010: 30). This latter process drew on an increasingly wide range of co-opted social forces. In the next section the chapter turns to the most recent formulation of what constitutes common sense as the EBRD responds to the so-called global financial crisis.

The EBRD and common sense after the 'global financial crisis'

In the preceding sections, the chapter outlined three waves of the EBRD's neoliberal 'common sense' in post-communist transition: the construction of the market, configuring the 'correct' socio-economic institutions, and the promotion of neoliberal formulations of competitiveness. In the final section the paper suggests that a new articulation of common sense can be found in the EBRD's work since the 'global financial crisis'. The latest evolution of post-crisis common sense emphasises a drive to actively build markets within the resultant economic space. As the then chief economist of the EBRD, Erik Berglof, noted in the 2010 *Transition Report*, the crisis was not a moment for ECE to lose its collective nerve: 'complacency would threaten not only recovery, but also long-term economic growth. There can be no return to the region's pre-crisis dynamism without new reform' (EBRD 2010: iv). For the EBRD, ECE remains perilously close to becoming becalmed in transition without further reform.[17]

However, the debate has moved beyond the promotion of competitiveness at national and global levels and the current crisis is viewed as an opportunity to press ahead with a revised version of the neoliberal project. The EBRD recognised the crisis as a moment of opportunity to more aggressively push reform: 'Most countries are demonstrating continuing commitment to market reforms and democratic processes. A crisis can lead to reversals but it can also create new opportunities in healthier and stronger systems. *The EBRD is committed to being the catalyst in this process*' (EBRD 2008: 21, emphasis added). For the EBRD the message is clear: reform must not slow, 'we must not allow the crisis to lead to reversals of the huge progress which has been achieved over the last two decades' (EBRD 2008: 1).

Just as the shift in the 1990s to the second wave emphasis on institutions reflected a refusal to change overall direction, since the mid-2000s and further exacerbated since 2007/8 we have witnessed the renewal of the neoliberal model. Rather than providing impetus for an alternative, the crisis has reinforced a continued commitment to neoliberalism. Rather, the trend in the EBRD since 2008 has been to engender a revised neoliberal common sense that reinforces the interests of dominant fractions of transitional capital, portrayed as essential in order to protect consumers and borrowers. The response to the crisis has been increased dialogue and cooperation with other IFIs, joining forces in investments and policy dialogue.[18] Discussions culminated in an emergency response to crisis that set out to minimise systemic risks in ECE and refocusing on domestic production and finance. This was subsequently formalised and made permanent in 2011 with the EBRD tasked to 'help via surveillance, data collection, policy advice and financial support'

(EBRD 2012a) .The joint IFI Action Plan, the Vienna Initiative, created by the EBRD, EIB and World Bank in February 2009 brought €25 billion of investment to the financial sectors of ECE from 2010 (EBRD 2009: 12).

The EBRD as collective organic intellectual is resuming and expanding neoliberal common sense since the 'crisis'. This is a crucial move in organising and reinforcing a key social force in transition societies – the *petit bourgeoisie*. It will be the *petit bourgeoisie* who stabilise democratic norms. Gramsci was careful to link the *petit bourgeoisie* with organic intellectuals, arguing for the largely unacknowledged role of those 'intellectual' activities associated with continually reproducing the socio-economic order in terms that are 'commonsensical'. More recently the EBRD has identified six transitional challenges: 1) reducing barriers to market entry; 2) privatisation of state-owned enterprises (SOEs); 3) lowering state subsidies; 4) financing small and medium-sized enterprises (SMEs); 5) boosting endogenous private sector growth; and 6) government transparency (EBRD, 2011). As the evidence from the previous three waves of neoliberal common sense in ECE illustrates, these may not be short-term 'transitional' change but rather longer-term semi-permanent forms of 'structural adjustment' intertwined in three decades of the EBRD as collective organic intellectual resuming and expanding neoliberal policies.

The EBRD's six points are clearly directed at private sector development. Productive employment, wage levels, and reflections on the social impact of privatisation are ignored. Why might this be the case? SMEs are considered fundamental to job creation, private sector development and distribution of the benefits of development (Dannreuther and Perren 2013). The EBRD identifies that remedying the lack of financing to SMEs is crucial to improving the business environment by reducing red tape, improving efficiency and supporting competitiveness. The ideological dimension of social reproduction has become more pronounced:

> In the modern world the category of intellectuals, understood in this sense, has undergone an unprecedented expansion. The democratic-bureaucratic system has given rise to a great mass of functions which are not all justified by the social necessities of production, though they are justified by the political necessities of the dominant fundamental group.
> (Gramsci 1971: 13)

What this evinces is how the EBRD is beginning to compile a new mode of transition common sense as it reinforces its practices in ECE and extends to MENA during and following the financial crisis. The aftermath of crisis is of course something that ECE has much experience of. The EBRD is cognisant of this, with few stated illusions about the social and political challenges ahead, 'such challenges are not new for us, the EBRD is, indeed, well equipped. It can draw on its two decades of experience supporting often tumultuous transition processes in the post-Soviet bloc' (Gacek 2013).

Strategic intervention is proposed for the financial sector including funding local banks to finance SMEs with a risk-sharing component, as well as offering microfinance. Is this about productivity, or is it more about the transfer of equity? As Carroll has argued, equity 'in stark contrast to state-oriented loans, allows deep marketisation organisations to take stakes in companies, to provide liquidity and promote the transition of companies along the marketisation path' (Carroll 2012: 385). Or put differently, intensifying exploitation implicated in the increased responsibility of the population (especially women) under uncertain labour conditions in the aftermath of neoliberal restructuring (Shields and Wallin 2012). This is more than just business as usual or a slight discursive shift in the post Washington Consensus. Instead, the EBRD is implicated in utilising the crisis as an opportunity for *the fullest imbrication possible of the public and private spheres*.

This is a step on from the creation of the neoliberal market, institutional reforms or promotion of competitiveness. Such forms of state-oriented neoliberal reform are no longer pivotal. Yes, much of the terminology will be recognisable: social impact assessments, consultations, benchmarking, and participation. Yes, many of the policy instruments will be recognisable: loans, technical assistance, monitoring, and evaluation but instead the EBRD is committed to opening up new spaces for accumulation. States in transition, whether in ECE, MENA, or for that matter elsewhere, provide enormous opportunities for profit. The financial intermediaries promoted by the EBRD: micro-finance organisations, private equity funds, commercial banks and other financial entities offer all sorts of possibilities. This is based on the fabrication of what the EBRD's operational response describes as 'reforms will constitute ... an enabling environment' imperative to attracting capital and expanding private sector activity (EBRD 2012b: 30).

Conclusion

This chapter made a modest attempt to uncover the implications of organic intellectuals and their technocratic blueprints. It explored the role of the EBRD as collective organic intellectual in advancing neoliberal reforms to the point of completion in ECE. Their social function is to elaborate a dominant ideology in order to ensure the reproduction of neoliberal social relations as common sense. It should be evident this is a *political* project of agenda setting to prevent the emergence of legitimate alternatives, whereby 'the pressures and limits of what can ultimately be seen as a specific economic, political, and cultural system [i.e. capitalism] seem to most of us the pressures and limits of simple experience and common sense' (Williams 1977: 110). The EBRD has utilised new historical circumstances to necessitate new thinking to commit the embedding and dissemination of the common sense idea surrounding post-communist transition. Any 'project for substantial change ... confronts pre-existing mentalities and structures and practices of power' (Sassoon 2000: 5). The discursive formation of post-communist

180 *Stuart Shields*

transition reifies neoliberal institutions so as to close down the categories of political economy and deny their contradictory social constitution, while neglecting due consideration of the historicity and contingency of reform. Thus neoliberal social forces remain engaged in shoring up the hegemony of common sense amongst powerful transnational epistemic communities of experts, policymakers and capitalists, thereby delimiting the space for counter-hegemonic ideologies and limiting the debate on possible alternatives to neoliberalisation.

The role of the EBRD has therefore been to offer structural coherence in post-communist transition. The EBRD perpetuates a neoliberal 'common sense' among aspirational members of the working class with the allure of becoming middle class in return for supporting neoliberal reforms, despite not being the principle beneficiaries of such reforms. The chapter showed how a threefold series of strategies have been employed by the organic intellectuals of neoliberal social forces, as exemplified by the EBRD case, against resistance or alternatives that subsequently led to the closure of policy flexibility at the national level. First was the initial construction of the market in the first wave of neoliberalism, second was the wave of institutional reforms necessitated by the failures in the first wave, and third was the reliance on the centrality of the promotion of neoliberal competitiveness to complete the reform process. The final move in these strategies in more recent times has been to interpret the 'global financial crisis' as an opportunity for individuals to internalise the reform process and bypass the mendacity of the post-communist state. These waves of neoliberalisation translated how organic intellectuals have invoked new forms of social relations involved in social reproduction across state–society complexes. A new modality of post-crisis reform is emerging that undoubtedly requires further investigation, in particular how private interest is privileged and transformed into the general interest of the broader public of post-crisis ECE or MENA.

Notes

1 An earlier version of this chapter was presented at an International Studies Association Annual Convention Catalytic Workshop on Global Economic Governance and the Development Practices of the 'Other' Multilateral Development Banks in 2014. I am grateful to the participants in that workshop whose constructive comments have resulted in a much-revised chapter and in particular the workshop organisers, Susan Park and Jonathan Strand.
2 The following states receive EBRD investments: Albania, Armenia, Azerbaijan, Belarus, Bosnia and Herzegovina, Bulgaria, Croatia, Cyprus, Estonia, Georgia, Greece, Hungary, Jordan, Kazakhstan, Kosovo, Kyrgyzstan, Latvia, Liechtenstein, Lithuania, Macedonia, Moldova, Mongolia, Montenegro, Poland, Romania, Russia, Serbia, Slovakia, Slovenia, Tajikistan, Turkey, Turkmenistan, Ukraine and Uzbekistan. The following states are EBRD members: Australia, Austria, Belgium, Canada, Cyprus, Czech Republic, Denmark, Egypt, Finland, France, Germany, Greece, Iceland, Ireland, Israel, Italy, Japan, Luxembourg, Malta, Mexico, Morocco, Netherlands, New Zealand, Norway, Portugal, South Korea, Spain,

The EBRD as organic intellectual 181

Sweden, Switzerland, Turkey, the United Kingdom and the US, the European Community and the European Investment Bank. Full details on funding, operations and membership can be seen at the EBRD's website, www.ebrd.com, while discussions concerning the establishment of the institution can be found in Weber (1994).

3 It is perhaps just worth reflecting whether or not a representative position can be ascertained solely from EBRD material. While this has certain limitations, especially in transmitting the notion that the EBRD, or for that matter any institution, is monolithic in its own internal politics. Given my reference to the work of Gramsci, it should be clear that the chapter rejects the assumption that rhetoric (ideology) might be detached from 'real', material interests. What passes for rhetoric is representative of consciously configured hegemonic projects. Where possible I have also noted the parallelism across other related institutions.

4 It is also worth just noting that the EBRD plays only a relatively minor role compared to the other IFIs in Epstein's assessment of the social context of transition common sense. See also Appel (2004) for a similar analysis.

5 This implies a dialectic unity of structure and agency such that structures shape social agents' self-understandings and behaviour whilst social agents re-shape structures through increased awareness of their own social context (Gramsci 1971: 323–30). This is of course similar to social constructivism, though the relationship of the material-economic to the ideational/ideological distinguishes the two. This avoids the reification and constraints apparent in either holistic or individualistic accounts of IPE (see Bruff 2011).

6 I use the term transitologists/transitology with some degree of irony. I am referring to the mix of policy makers and academics (often the same people) that provided the orthodox toolbox for transition. This toolkit comprised the standard Washington Consensus components: the depoliticisation of ownership, the depoliticisation of allocative mechanisms, the marketisation of the economy and the imposition of hard budget constraints (see Shields 2012a: 24), presented to the populations of the region as scientific and axiomatic. The knowledge formulated by the EBRD would be an example of transitology and a quick check of EBRD senior staff biographies illustrates the revolving door between certain political parties, academia, and institutions like the EBRD.

7 A full exploration of this emergent historical bloc is beyond the scope of this short chapter. However, for a more developed example of how this kind of analysis can be deployed to explore the integration of often dissonant interests and ideas into a more coherent set of social forces in the case of ECE, see Shields 2012b.

8 Clearly the EBRD would not have been in a position to offer its solutions without the collapse of communism. However, the EBRD is one of a number of organic intellectuals doing their bit to construct the ideational components of neoliberal hegemony prior to that collapse. I mention a number throughout the chapter (the IMF, the World Bank). For discussion of the role played by *individuals* performing their specific social role e.g. Polish Finance Minister Leszek Balcerowicz, see Shields (2012). Institutions like the EBRD rarely fall fully formed form the sky, but are part of a wider recomposition of common sense.

9 Sixty percent of committed loans, guarantees and equity investments shall be provided to the private sector. A commercial branch of the bank, lending at market interest rates, controls this part of the business. The remaining 40 percent to the state sector is mainly for infrastructure projects and is carried out by a development branch at concessionary rates. See Standard & Poors' (2013) ratings assessment of the EBRD for full details.

10 The EBRD is frequently assumed to be an EU institution. While it is not part of the formal EU institutional architecture the EU, and other EU institutions and

182 *Stuart Shields*

member states are shareholders. For a brief discussion of the possible links between the EIB and the EBRD, see Robinson 2009.

11 Strand's analysis of relative voting power in the EBRD illustrates clearly how such discussions were not left to chance but built into the EBRD fabric, rather like the IMF, the World Bank, and other RDBs: we can assess *whose* political preferences are more likely to be exercised through the EBRD's decision-making rules. Given that the United States has the greatest voting power in the bank perhaps we can expect the political bias of bank decisions to more closely reflect American neo-classical economic principles.... What is also clear, at least in the formal analysis of influence over electoral outcomes, is that smaller, borrowing members have essentially little or no voting power. In sum, the policies implemented by the Bank are likely to reflect the interests of the larger, capital-donating members (Strand, 2003: 350).

12 Between 1991 and 1993, 46% of 95 signed projects were with the Czech Republic, Hungary and Poland (though admittedly these three had the most developed private sectors in which the EBRD could invest). In general, the EBRD funds up to 35% of the total project costs for either a 'greenfield' project or an established company. Processing and dispersal of loans was streamlined in the mid-1990s and greater attention was paid to finding partners in small and medium-sized enterprises (SMEs). The bulk of profitable projects and enterprises were left to private foreign investors and lenders, while state-owned enterprises in greatest need of external funding were denied.

13 As noted elsewhere in this collection, the connection to other organic intellectuals such as the World Bank is evident. James Wolfensohn, then president of the World Bank, described the situation thus: There are a set of 'globally accepted principles' underpinning the global governance consensus which require political, economic and social reform in all states ... the most important obstacles to impartial and transparent justice .... We looked at [ECE] and developing countries, and we discovered that the first and biggest is the takeover of the justice systems by economic interests and the elite. Second, and significantly behind, particularly in Eastern Europe and the former Soviet Union, is political interference (Wolfensohn 2001).

14 For some notable exceptions, compare the different perspectives in Cammack 2006, Cerny 1997, Dostal 2004, Fougner 2006.

15 For example, Agenda 2000 attempted to ready ECE for EU membership, but within the broader context of a hegemonic neoliberalism: "Successive ... governments have made serious attempts to improve competitiveness by framing policy in a comprehensive medium-term context, integrating macroeconomic and structural policies as well as preparations for EU accession ... an ambitious medium-term programme aiming at export- and investment-led growth, continued disinflation and sound public finance.... a comprehensive reform ... which focuses on the requirements of EU accession, and more specifically on the need for greater fiscal discipline and the channelling of national savings into investment" (European Commission 1997: 33).

16 It is worth reiterating the emphasis on competitiveness throughout the chapter. While competition may well drive the emergence of free trade and competitive markets through comparative advantage according to mainstream economics, I am more concerned here with how the *promotion of competitiveness* was part of a wider trend from the late 1990s onwards in the global political economy (e.g. see Cammack 2006). Competitiveness is of course always an imperative of liberalisation in post-communist transition. The three waves of neoliberalisation motif is not a rigid delimitation but rather a way of revealing how certain policies ebb and flow over time and in different places. The chapter shows how EBRD reform strategies are embedded in a particular set of wider reforms and evolving social relations. This discursive shift, in institutions like the RDBs, began to emphasise

competitiveness through the promotion of policies like the country ownership of reforms, the building of 'better' entrepreneurs. On ECE, and how this discursive shift unfolds in the EBRD in particular, see Shields and Wallin (2012).
17 Berglof states a, defining feature of transition over the past 20 years has been the speed of reform. In some cases motivated by the prospect of EU-accession, countries across the Transition region made rapid progress towards creating the institutions required for markets to function. In recent years the reform process has stagnated, despite significant scope for further improvement. While this stagnation predated the global financial crisis in 2008/9, the crisis may have compounded the problem by eroding popular support for market reform (Berglof, 2013).
18 This parallels the IMF's strategic thinking: The crisis has revealed flaws in key dimensions of the current global architecture, but also provides a unique opportunity to fix them. On the flaws, surveillance needs to be reoriented to ensure warnings are clear, successfully connect the dots, and provide practical advice to policy makers. An effective forum for policy makers with the ability and mandate to take leadership in responding to systemic concerns about the international economy is key ... These are all ambitious undertakings. But the damage wrought by the crisis provides an opportunity to make progress on seemingly intractable issues. The moment should not be missed (IMF 2009: 13).

Bibliography

van Apeldoorn, B. 2002. *Transnational Capitalism and the Struggle Over European Integration*. London: Routledge.
Appel, H. 2004. *A New Capitalist Order: Privatization and Ideology in Russia and Eastern Europe*. Pittsburgh, PA: University of Pittsburgh Press.
Berglof, E. 2013. 'Emerging economies are 'stuck in transition'. Speech at the European Central Banks conference, Emerging Market Economies as an Engine of Growth for the Global Economy: Facts and Challenges, Frankfurt, 10 July. Available at: www.ebrd.com/news/2013/emerging-economies-are-stuck-in-transition.html (accessed 31 May 2015).
Bronstone, A. 1999. *The European Bank for Reconstruction and Development: The Building of a Bank for East Central Europe*. Manchester: Manchester University Press.
Bruff, I. 2008. *Culture and Consensus in European Varieties of Capitalism: A' common Sense' Analysis*. Basingstoke: Palgrave Macmillan
Bruff, I. 2011. 'The Case for a Foundational Materialism: Going Beyond Historical Materialist IPE in Order to Strengthen It'. *Journal of International Relations and Development* 14(3): 391–399.
Cammack, P. 2006. 'The Politics of Global Competitiveness'. Papers in the Politics of Global Competitiveness, no. 1, Institute for Global Studies, Manchester Metropolitan University.
Carroll, T. 2012. 'Working On, Through and Around the State: The Deep Marketisation of Development in the Asia-Pacific'. *Journal of Contemporary Asia* 42(3): 378–404.
Carroll, W. K. 2010. 'Crisis, Movements, Counter-hegemony: In Search of the New'. *Interface: A journal for and about social movements* 2(2): 168–198.
Cerny, P. G. 1997. 'Paradoxes of the Competition State: The Dynamics of Political Globalization'. *Government and Opposition* 32(4): 472–496.

Cox, R. W. 1981. 'Social Forces, States and World Orders: Beyond International Relations Theory'. *Millennium: Journal of International Studies* 10(2): 126–155.

Cox, R. W. and T. Sinclair. 1996. *Approaches to World Order*. Cambridge: Cambridge University Press.

Dannreuther C. and L. Perren. 2013. *The Political Economy of the Small Firm*. London: Routledge.

Dostal, J. M. 2004. 'Campaigning on Expertise: How the OECD Framed EU Welfare and Labour Market Policies – and Why Success Could Trigger Failure'. *Journal of European Public Policy* 11(4): 440–460.

Epstein, R. A. 2008. *In Pursuit of Liberalism: International Institutions in Postcommunist Europe*. Baltimore, MD: JHU Press.

European Bank for Reconstruction and Development (EBRD). 1990. *Agreement Establishing the European Bank for Reconstruction and Development*. London: EBRD.

European Bank for Reconstruction and Development (EBRD). 1991. *Annual Report: A Changing Europe*. London: EBRD.

European Bank for Reconstruction and Development (EBRD). 1995. *Transition Report 1995: Investment and Enterprise Development*. London: EBRD.

European Bank for Reconstruction and Development (EBRD). 1999a. *Transition Report 1999: Ten Years of Reform*. London: EBRD.

European Bank for Reconstruction and Development (EBRD). 1999b. *Annual Report*. London: EBRD.

European Bank for Reconstruction and Development (EBRD). 2004. *Transition Report 2004: Infrastructure*. London: EBRD.

European Bank for Reconstruction and Development (EBRD). 2008. *Annual Report*. London: EBRD.

European Bank for Reconstruction and Development (EBRD). 2009. *Annual Report*. London: EBRD.

European Bank for Reconstruction and Development (EBRD). 2010. *Transition Report 2010: Recovery and Reform*. London: EBRD.

European Bank for Reconstruction and Development (EBRD). 2011. 'Transition to Transition (T2T) Initiative'. Office of the Chief Economist paper from the EBRD Stimulating Growth and Investment During Transition meeting, Cairo, 24 October.

European Bank for Reconstruction and Development (EBRD). 2012a. *The Vienna Initiative*. Available at: www.ebrd.com/pages/news/features/vienna-initiative.shtml (accessed 10 September 2012).

European Bank for Reconstruction and Development (EBRD). 2012b. *EBRD Egypt Country Assessment*. London: EBRD.

European Bank for Reconstruction and Development (EBRD). 2013. "European Union and EBRD Officially Launch a Facility for Advisory Support to SMEs in Egypt". EBRD press release, 24 June. Available at: www.ebrd.com/pages/news/press/2013/130624a.shtml (accessed 15 March 2014).

European Commission. 1997. Agenda 2000: Commission Opinion on Poland's Application for Membership of the European Union, DOC/97/16, Brussels, 17 July.

European Commission. 2000. 'The Lisbon European Council: An Agenda of Social and Economic Renewal for Europe'. Contribution of the European Commission to the Special European Council in Lisbon DOC/00/7, Brussels, 28 February.

Fine, B. 1999. 'The Developmental State Is Dead: Long Live Social Capital?', *Development and Change* 30(1): 1–19.

Fougner, T. 2006. 'The State, International Competitiveness and Neoliberal Globalisation: Is There a Future Beyond 'the Competition State'?' *Review of International Studies* 32(2): 165–185.
Gacek, H. 2013. 'Old Lessons Help EBRD Strengthen Future prospects'. *The Banker*, 1 November.
Gill, S. 2012. *Global Crises and the Crisis of Global Leadership.* Cambridge: Cambridge University Press.
Gramsci, A. 1971. *Selections from the Prison Notebooks.* London: Lawrence & Wishart.
IMF. 2009. *World Economic Outlook: Sustaining the Recovery.* Washington, DC: IMF.
Ivanova, M. 2007. 'Why There Was No Marshall Plan for Eastern Europe and Why This Still Matters'. *Journal of Contemporary European Studies* 15(3): 345–376.
Jones, S. 2006. *Antonio Gramsci.* London: Routledge.
Linarelli, J. 1995. 'European Bank for Reconstruction and Development: Legal and Policy Issues'. *Boston College International and Comparative Law Review* 18: 361–400.
Macartney, H. 2010. *Variegated Neoliberalism: Convergent Divergence in EU Varieties of Capitalism.* London: Routledge.
Murphy, C. 1994. *International Organization and Industrial Change.* Oxford: Oxford University Press.
Peck, J. 2010. *Constructions of Neoliberal Reason.* Oxford: Oxford University Press.
Robinson, N. 2009. 'The European Investment Bank: The EU's Neglected Institution'. *Journal of Common Market Studies* 47(3): 651–673.
Sassoon, A. S. 2000. *Gramsci and Contemporary Politics: Beyond Pessimism of the Intellect.* London: Routledge.
Scott-Smith, G. 2002. *The Politics of Apolitical Culture: The Congress for Cultural Freedom, the CIA and Post-War American Hegemony.* London: Routledge.
Shields, S. 2012a. *The International Political Economy of Transition: Transnational Social Forces and Eastern Central Europe's Transformation.* London: Routledge.
Shields, S. 2012b. 'Opposing neoliberalism? Poland's renewed populism and the global political economy'. *Third World Quarterly* 33(2): 383–405.
Shields, S. and Wallin, S. 2012. 'Beyond Eastern Europe: The European Bank for Reconstruction and Development's Gender Action Plan and the Fourth Wave of Neoliberalism'. New Approaches to Building Markets in Asia, Working Paper no. 44. Available at: http://lkyspp.nus.edu.sg/cag/wp-content/uploads/sites/5/2013/05/NATBMA_WP12-44.pdf (accessed 25 May 2015).
Simon, R. 1982. *Gramsci's Political Thought: An Introduction.* London: Electric Books.
Smith, A. 2002. 'Imagining Geographies of the 'New Europe': Geo-Economic Power and the New European Architecture of Integration'. *Political Geography* 21(4): 647–670.
Standard & Poors. 2013. *Ratings Direct.* London: Standard & Poors.
Stiglitz, J. 1998. 'More Instruments and Broader Goals: Moving Toward the Post-Washington Consensus'. Helsinki: UNU World Institute for Development Economics Research (UNU/WIDER).
Strand, J. 2003. 'Power Relations in an Embedded Institution: The European Bank for Reconstruction and Development'. *Journal of European Integration* 25(2): 115–129.
Taylor, I. 2004. 'Hegemony, Neo-Liberal 'Good Governance' and the International Monetary Fund: A Gramscian Perspective.' In *The Role of Ideas in Multinational Institutions*, edited by M. Bøås and B. D. McNeill. New York: Routledge, pp. 124–136.
Weber, S. 1994. 'Origins of the European Bank for Reconstruction and Development'. *International Organization* 48(1):1–38.

Williams, R. 1977. *Marxism and Literature*. Oxford: Oxford University Press.
Wolfensohn, J. D. 2001. *Empowerment, Security and Opportunity Through Law and Justice*. Speech at the World Bank Conference, St. Petersburg, Russia, 9 July.
Wood, E.M. 1995. *Democracy Against Capitalism: Renewing Historical Materialism*. Cambridge: Cambridge University Press.
World Bank. 2000. *The First Ten Years Analysis and Lessons for Eastern Europe and the Former Soviet Union*. Washington, DC: World Bank.
World Bank. 2004. *World Development Report 2005*. Washington, DC: World Bank.

10 Sub-regional development banks
Development as usual?

Tina M. Zappile

Sub-regional development banks (SRDBs) are poised to advance regionalism as a more effective tool for development financing (Birdsall and Rojas-Suarez 2004) given their restricted regional membership and localized expertise, in addition to the opportunity to learn from decades of experience from the World Bank and larger regional development banks (RDBs) operating in their geographical area. However, they also face obstacles such as low levels of capital; an overreliance on capital subscriptions from member states for operations; access to technical expertise; obscurity within their region; and crowding out by larger development institutions. SRDBs are a heterogeneous group of development institutions sometimes operating in partnership with RDBs and the World Bank, as is the case with the Caribbean Development Bank (CDB). They also provide 'non-traditional' forms of assistance that target specific regional needs – a void left by larger development institutions. For example, the Pacific Islands Development Bank (PIDB) makes residential loans alongside more traditional commercial development loans issued by most multilateral development banks (MDBs). Most SRDBs have small portfolios as compared to larger institutions while others, such as the Development Bank of Latin America (CAF) have surpassed World Bank and RDB lending in the region as well as in particular sectors (Beattie 2014; Humphrey 2014). Recently, scholars have turned to identifying how differences in specific dimensions and aspects of legitimacy can manifest themselves in policies and output of SRDBs compared to the MDBs (Humphrey 2014).

Mechanisms for evaluating development institutions have focused primarily on the World Bank, RDBs, U.N. agencies, and state-owned institutions. A loosely organized transnational network serving as a watchdog for MDBs includes: the Multilateral Organisation Performance Assessment Network (MOPAN), various initiatives of the Center for Global Development (CDB), and assessments by independent researchers with deep organizational knowledge (Easterly and Pfutze 2008). This chapter is a mapping exercise designed to identify key SRDBs, analyze whether they have adopted changes in structure or institutional behavior recommended by think tanks, policymakers, and others in this transnational network, and discuss differences in 'organizational legitimacy' and the degree of 'resource dependency' they face as a result. It does so by evaluating key dimensions underpinning organizational legitimacy across several SRDBs to provide a baseline for comparison and to further explore the notion that there are trade-offs in different aspects of legitimacy, as some are inversely related in this analysis. As such, this chapter provides a direction for future research on this sub-category of development institutions that is poised to meet and advance the call for a more regionally focused development agenda.

Development institutions range in scope in terms of their degree of specialization in their lending and aid practices (Easterly and Williamson 2011) and geographical inclusion of donor and borrower states. Ranking institutions according to scope would confer the top spot to the World Bank Group as the major multilateral development institution. However, development institutions range in type from various forms of regional arrangement to single-state-owned or sovereign development bank. RDBs focus their agenda and funding on a specific region, although many have been operating in increasingly larger geographical areas and include a large proportion of non-regional members as key shareholders and decision makers. SRDBs on the other hand remain more locally focused and are defined by the World Bank (2014) as being owned by smaller groups of countries, "typically borrowing members and not donors." While smaller regional arrangements have the potential to be more effective coordination mechanisms in the absence of a global arrangement or where global arrangements are flawed, they are prone to the same criticisms as any other multilateral organization.

Applying a framework of 'organizational legitimacy' that is comprised of 'representative' and 'operational' legitimacy, a select sample of major SRDBs are evaluated along the following five dimensions recognized as important for 'input' and output' legitimacy (Park and Strand, this volume; Scharpf 1999): membership and governance structure, accountability mechanisms, commitment to transparency, internal project evaluation, inclusion of civil society and environmental interests in the planning process and subsequent projects. The following SRDBs are examined: the Caribbean Development Bank (CDB or CariBank), the Central American Bank for Economic Integration (CABEI), the East African Development Bank (EADB); the West African Development Bank (BOAD); the Development Bank of Latin American/the Andean Development Corporation (CAF); the Financial Fund for the Development of the River Plate Basin (FONPLATA); the Eurasian Development Bank (EDB); the Black Sea Trade and Development Bank (BSTDB), the Central African States Development Bank (CASDB or BDEAC); the Eastern and Southern African Trade and Development Bank (PTA Bank of Common Market for Eastern and Southern Africa (COMESA)); the North American Development Bank; and the Pacific Islands Development Bank (PIDB).

This framework of legitimacy advances efforts to determine what elements of democratic principles might be "feasible (for IOs) under 'real-world' circumstances" (Moravcsik 2004, 337) for this subset of multilateral banks. It achieves this by underscoring the dilemma SRDBs face in simultaneously addressing regional interests and satisfying demands from regional members in light of norms to adopt organizational features and 'best practices' recommended for development institutions at the global level. While IGOs such as the International Monetary Fund have sought to balance a high degree of influence and subsequent demands from powerful member states with efforts to address criticisms targeting their deficit in representative legitimacy (through mechanisms of participation and evaluation) there is still room for improvement (Copelovitch 2010, Strand 2014).

To maintain SRBDs' comparative advantage as a driver for development at the regional level they must also maintain a high degree of representative legitimacy, possibly at the cost of technical expertise and other dimensions of operational legitimacy. The absence of external accountability mechanisms and a lack of inclusion of civil society in the planning process decreases input legitimacy and, indirectly, output legitimacy, although it may be the case that this reflects the trade-off for SRDBs in retaining representative legitimacy. In practice, it seems that SRDBs adhere to some of these operational dimensions while ignoring others as they allocate a limited set of resources to achieve their mandate(s). Results from this analysis suggest that while some SRDBs have adopted a structure and policies that mimic the World Bank and RDBs, most have retained organizational features that favor regional member states and retain this comparative advantage in a variety of ways. Representative legitimacy therefore appears to be inversely related to operational legitimacy for SRBDs in this analysis; banks that score high along the former have moderate to extensive deficits in multiple dimensions of operational legitimacy.

The tradeoff between representative legitimacy and operational efficiency is not unique to this category of international organizations. However, SRBDs are under particular pressure to retain a high degree of representative legitimacy. Primarily, SRDBs are created to serve regional interests and they remain poised to do so by: restricting membership or granting a high degree of decision-making power to regional members when non-regional members are permitted; increasing access to technical expertise to the degree possible given their membership and cooperation with other partners; focusing their limited resources on the primary activity of lending or otherwise supporting development projects for regional members that are tailored to their stated needs; and providing channels of access for civil society within regional states to ensure they serve that population through their activities. They must determine the degree to which they incur a legitimacy deficit in order to advance these other institutional goals. To illustrate, by restricting its membership the PIDB retains a high degree of 'representative legitimacy' but at a probable cost of missing out on the technical expertise provided by non-regional members from which other SRDBs like the CBD clearly benefit. Alternatively, the BSTDB has been able to restrict membership to its region while adopting a governance structure and policies similar to those of the World Bank; it has maintained its regional focus while adhering to some

190 *Tina M. Zappile*

norms along the other four operational dimensions included in this study. SRDBs are uniquely positioned to make strategic choices in regards to their structure and policies in terms of balancing representative and operational legitimacy to favor regional development efforts.

The chapter is organized as follows. Section one defines development institutions to recognize institutional heterogeneity and discusses the difficulty in creating a typology to adequately capture institutional variety. Next, the five dimensions along which SRDBs are analyzed are introduced in terms of how they relate to the legitimacy and resource dependence frameworks referenced in this volume (Park and Strand, this volume), followed by analysis of each dimension including how it compares to the World Bank. The chapter ends with a discussion summarizing how SRDBs compare along these dimensions and makes recommendations for future research on this subset of MDBs.

Defining SRDBs

The questions of what an SRDB is and which institutions are part of this category can solicit a range of answers, even from experts in development institutions. For example, should the North American Development Bank comprised of only three states and established as a direct extension of NAFTA be in the same category as the Caribbean Development Bank, which operates across its region in partnership with the Inter-American Development Bank (IDB) and World Bank; consults with borrowing members; and issues numerous publications throughout the year? Or is it similar enough to the Pacific Islands Development Bank, which issues residential loans alongside more traditional development loans to public or private entities and consists of islands and states, or the East African Development Bank with a large set of institutional members who serve on a governing council? The criteria currently used to define development institutions is membership, followed by the scope of operations in terms of whether they have broad mandate to foster development or focus more specifically on certain sectors or types of project. Arguably these criteria should be revisited and augmented to include aspects such as levels of lending activity, total capital or assets, and eligibility for assistance.

The World Bank (2014) identifies three major categories of development institutions based on membership and scope of mandate(s). "Multilateral development banks" are comprised of the World Bank Group and four major regional development banks (RDBs) of the AfDB, ADB, EBRD, and IDB, whereas "multilateral financial institutions" are banks with fewer members and less broad mandate(s) and include the Islamic Development Bank, Nordic Fund, and European Investment Bank, among others. Finally, SRDBs are characterized by being limited to regional members. However, in practice, several have adopted membership structures and policies that blur these demarcations established by the World Bank. Several SRDBs were created as part of broader regional movements and reflect efforts to address development concerns particular to the region, while the origin and motivation of others are unclear. Banks that are extensions of existing regional arrangements include the PTA Bank of COMESA as part of the Central African States Development Bank of the Central Africa Economic and Monetary community (CEMAC), the West African Development Bank (BOAD) as part of the West African Monetary Union (WAMU), and the North American Development Bank that was established alongside the North American Free Trade Agreement (NAFTA). Others, such as the Pacific Islands Development Bank, were established by member states in a similar fashion to the creation of the World Bank institutions. Additionally others, such as the Black Sea Trade and Development Bank, were formed by a single state (Russia) partnering with regional members but maintaining almost complete control in terms of governance.

Further complicating the World Bank's three categories of development institutions is the existence of what can be called a *sovereign development bank (SDB)*. Much like a sovereign wealth fund, a sovereign development bank can be defined as a state-owned bank with development mandate(s). An example is the Development Bank of Southern Africa (DBSA); despite having a sub-regional or regional name it is owned and operated by South Africa.

In terms of function, SRDBs are more regionally specialized than RDBs, providing assistance to a relatively smaller number of regional states, though there is a broad range across SRDBs in terms of the scope of their mandate(s), size, membership, and portfolio. Table 10.1 presents a snapshot of the 2013 lending portfolio for select SRDBs in order from large to small to illustrate the heterogeneity of these institutions based on their activities. Note the range in dollar amounts underscoring that while some SRDBs are mini-RDBs or World Banks in terms of the scope of their activities, others have expanded their activities to include projects, capital injections, and other activities that call for larger financial commitments.

The operational activity of SRDBs presented in Table 10.1 can be compared to select RDBs for the same year: the IADB approved $13.29 billion (IADB 2013) and the AfDB approved $4.39 billion (AfDB 2014).

Historically, there is also a wide range of aggregate lending across SRDBs dependent in part on the year they were formed, changes in involvement in the region over time, or changes in assets. For example, between 1970 and 2010 the Caribbean Bank offered $10.5 billion for 1739 projects to 19 recipients and between 1988 and 2010 the Latin American Bank provided $87.8 billion for 781 projects to 17 recipients (Tierney et al. 2011). While CAF has provided more financial assistance over a shorter period of time, the CDB has provided assistance for more small-size projects. Both these SRDBs are larger than others such as the Black Sea Trade and Development Bank which between 2000 and 2014 approved EUR 2.9 billion for 277 projects (BSTDB 2013) or the North American Bank that provided $2.5 billion for 385 projects to only two recipients between 1996 and 2011 (Tierney et al. 2011).

192 *Tina M. Zappile*

Table 10.1 Portfolio analysis of SRDBs

Bank	Headquarters	Loans and grants approved in 2013
Central American Bank for Economic Integration (CABEI)	Tegucigalpa, Honduras	$1.35 bill[1]
West African Development Bank (BOAD)	Lome, Togo	$1.03 bill 42 operations[2]
Eurasian Development Bank (EDB)	Almaty, Kazakhstan	$750 mill[3]
Eastern and Southern African Trade and Development Bank (PTA Bank of COMESA)	Bujumbura, Burundi	$297.28 mill 22 projects[4]
Caribbean Development Bank (CariBank or CDB)	Bridgetown, Barbados	$167.43 mill: $139.0 in loans for 10 projects; $28.4 in grants[5]
East African Development Bank (EADB)	Kampala, Uganda	$92.3 mill[6]
Development Bank of Latin America (CAF)	Caracas, Venezuela	$18.0 mill[7]
Pacific Islands Development Bank (PIDB)	Hagatna, Guam	$4.83 mill 129 loans[8]
Black Sea Trade and Development Bank (BSTDB)	Thessaloniki, Greece	$3.94 mill[9]

Sources: Tierney et al. (2011), individual annual reports (see footnotes).
Notes: Figures are reported in USD and were converted from reported currencies on August 15, 2014.

While most SRDBs lag behind RDBs in terms of levels of financial assistance, the sections that follow identify dimensions along which they more closely mimic RDBs in terms of their policies, the issuing of annual publications and staff working papers, and the hosting of workshops with partners to provide opportunities for regional access to technical development expertise.

Evaluating SRDBs: a framework for analysis

Dimensions for which to evaluate SRDBs were drawn from previous empirical research on democracy in IOs (Levi, Finizio, and Vallinoto 2013; Zweifel 2006). Dimensions of SRDBs considered and evaluated here represent criteria considered relevant to organizational legitimacy and include:

a   Membership and governance structure
b   Accountability mechanisms
c   Inclusion of civil society and environmental interests
d   Commitment to transparency
e   Evaluation of performance/projects.

These dimensions have been recognized as important, if not critical, for the legitimacy of the World Bank and RDBs, as discussed in other chapters in this volume. Given that SRDBs are both a distinct and heterogeneous group of development institutions outside the major IFIs, this is a starting point for research across different types of development institutions. It is recognized that while banks should be arguably held to higher standards given their capacity to fulfill external demands for greater accountability or transparency, these standards remain useful to evaluate any organization tasked with serving a broad mandate such as development. The primary goal(s) of development institutions remains the same at a meta-level, therefore applying the same standards regardless of variance in size or scope across categories has value. As each dimension is discussed, conditions under which SRDBs should be held to a different standard than the World Bank are identified to account for the comparative advantages they provide in the development community. A normative argument can be made that some of these comparative advantages should exclude them from mainstream criticisms of the World Bank and select RDBs; however, the exercise of comparing across categories is an appropriate method of initial enquiry.

Concepts of 'input' and 'output' legitimacy (Park and Strand, this volume; Scharpf 1999) provide a framework to evaluate representation, governance, and decision-making as a set of organizational features distinct from the ability of an SRDB to meet its mandate(s) as judged by the parties they are intended to benefit. Broadly, input legitimacy is defined here as authority or expertise, autonomy (Barnett and Finnemore 2004), and agreed-upon forms of representation. Input legitimacy is determined by dimensions of membership, governance structure, accountability mechanisms, internal project evaluation, and inclusion of civil society in the planning process. Output legitimacy of the SRDBs in terms of whether they achieve their mandate(s) is considerably more difficult to evaluate. Rather, it is defined here more expansively to include issuing loans or adopting lending policies that reflect the demands of those served. In most cases for SRDBs, the population served by the organization's output or policies and projects is the same: member states. Therefore, commitment to transparency, accountability mechanisms, and inclusion of civil society are indirectly considered important, as they can be conditions to ensure organizational output meets the appropriate set of demands.

Focusing on input legitimacy, 'representative legitimacy' is reflected by dimensions of membership and governance while 'operational legitimacy' is comprised of the other dimensions. These are both considered components of 'organizational legitimacy'. Representative legitimacy for SRDBs is unlike that of other MDBs in that, by definition, they restrict membership within their region. While this allows an SRDB to maintain a high degree of input legitimacy, select SRDBs that allow for non-regional or institutional members must further ensure that their governance structure defers a high degree of power to regional members. Non-member states can detract from the legitimacy of IOs simply from "guilt by association" (Johnson 2011). Alternatively, non-regional and institutional membership can enhance the degree of expertise or authority (Barnett and Finnemore 2004) for SRDBs by providing resources, including technical expertise, which can otherwise be lacking in smaller-scale MDBs.

A rationalist principle-agent (P-A) model is useful for evaluating the SRDBs in that a high degree of representative legitimacy is likely to reflect an organization with a set of principals whose interests are more closely aligned, as compared to banks with clearer divisions between borrowing and non-borrowing members as subsets of principals (Humphrey 2014; Humphrey and Michaelowa 2013). This affects input legitimacy in terms of maintaining adequate representation of borrowers and output legitimacy in terms of whether lending and other policies meet the demands of borrowers.

The effect of representative legitimacy on authority, or whether a trade-off between the two exists, then depends on level of resources and expertise among regional members; 'technical authority' might be low without resource-rich members while 'delegated authority' would remain high (Barnett and Finnemore 2004). A high degree of representational legitimacy might also decrease the autonomy of the organization in favor of greater input legitimacy. Furthermore, as a result of their restricted membership SRDBs are likely to experience a different degree of resource dependence, with potentially limited operational activities in their region and subsequent vulnerability to other sources of influence to counter low levels of resources and expertise among member states. In the case of CAF, EADB, and BOAD, membership is open to private banks, which creates the potential for conflicts of interest when advising member states to fund particular projects or make decisions in other arenas of policy.

In regard to the other operational dimensions considered in this analysis, accountability mechanisms provide SRDBs with opportunities to respond to internal or external complaints. Internal accountability mechanisms may signal a higher level of autonomy, as its presence may be the result of member states checking the behavior of SRDBs. Alternatively, the lack of an internal accountability mechanism might also signal a higher degree of input legitimacy as it relates to representation or governance structure; simply, there may not be a need for one if the SRDB is a direct extension of member states, as is the case of CAF (Humphrey, this volume). Inclusion of civil society directly supports input legitimacy by increasing opportunities for the beneficiaries of SRDB projects to directly participate in planning, while output legitimacy can be supported if projects reflect civil society demands. Transparency arguably supports organizational authority in that it provides opportunities for sub state and transnational actors to review policies, gather data to measure results, and ensure that their interests are adequately represented by member states or the organization itself.[10] The presence of standards and mechanism(s) for project evaluation ideally contributes to its authority or expertise, as it provides the organization an opportunity to identify and learn from their past performance. This may also advance output legitimacy if the SRDB relies on evaluations in making decisions about future policies or lending practices, although at a cost for member states.

Recognizing that SRDBs have both comparative advantages and weaknesses across the five dimensions selected for evaluation, it is expected that their comparative advantages lie in maintaining a high degree of representative legitimacy, possibly at the cost of technical expertise or other dimensions related to operational legitimacy more broadly defined. The absence of external accountability mechanisms and a lack of inclusion of civil society in the planning process decreases input legitimacy and indirectly, output legitimacy, although it may be the case that this reflects the trade-off for SRDBs in retaining representative legitimacy. These points are further addressed in the sections that follow.

Membership and governance structure

The primary comparative advantage of SRDBs is their potential to advance regionalism as a more effective tool for development financing (Birdsall and Rojas-Suarez 2004). While most SRDBs restrict membership to states in their region, a few, notably the CDB, have expanded membership to mimic the organizational structure of larger banks. Furthermore, some also include institutional members, creating a hybrid set of principals made up of states and private entities. In this case, a high level of 'representative legitimacy' can be maintained if the SRDB guarantees a high degree of decision-making authority in its governance structure if it allows non-regional or institutional members.

Regional and non-regional or institutional members for each SRDB are identified in Table 10.2. Sub-regional banks that have expanded membership beyond their region include BOAD, CDB, CABEI, CAF, EADB, and PTA Bank of COMESA. In addition, the governance structure of each SRDB is reported in this table. It is coded as 'traditional' if they mimic the World Bank's model of a board of directors, board of governors, an acting director or president, management divisions, and other similar units. It is coded as 'semi-traditional' if it has at least one component of the traditional model and 'non-traditional' if it departs completely. Additional details regarding the feature(s) that vary from the traditional structure are provided if it does not match to a high degree. 'NA' is used for SRDBs with unclear governance structures, often due to lack of data.

While most SRDBs maintain a high degree of representational legitimacy, there exists a trade-off with authority or technical expertise. Non-regional and/or institutional members may enhance technical expertise but at the cost of lowering representative legitimacy. While the CDB has maintained a high degree of technical legitimacy due to its available resources and partnerships with the IADB and World Bank, it also maintains non-regional membership, another important source of technical expertise. Another consequence of a

Table 10.2 Governance structure and membership of SRDBs

Bank (headquarters)	Regional members	Non-regional and institutional members	Governance structure
Caribbean Development Bank (CDB)	Non-borrowing: Colombia, Mexico, Venezuela Borrowing: Anguilla, Antigua and Barbuda, Barbados, Belize, British Virgin Islands, Cayman Islands, Dominica, Grenada, Guyana, Haiti, Jamaica, Montserrat, St Kitts and Nevis, St Lucia, St Vincent and the Grenadines, Suriname, The Bahamas, Trinidad and Tobago, Turks and Caicos Islands	Canada, China, Germany, Italy, United Kingdom	Traditional
Pacific Islands Development Bank (PIDB)	Chuuk (Federated States of Micronesia), Commonwealth of the Northern Mariana Islands (CNMI), Guam, Kosrae (Micronesia), Marshall Islands, Palau, Pohnpei (Micronesia), Yap (Micronesia)	No	Traditional
Latin American Development Bank (CAF)	Series A: Argentina, Bolivia, Brazil, Colombia, Ecuador, Panama, Paraguay, Peru, Uruguay, Venezuela Series B: Bolivia, Colombia, Ecuador, Peru, Venezuela Series C: Costa Rica, Spain, Mexico, Dominican Republic, Chile, Portugal, rinidad and Tobago	Banca Privida (series B)	Traditional
Eurasian Development Bank (EDB)	Armenia, Belarus, Kazakhstan, Kyrgyz Republic, Russia, Tajikistan	No	Traditional
Black Sea Trade and Development Bank (BSTDB)	Albania, Armenia, Azerbaijan, Bulgaria, Georgia, Greece, Moldova, Romania, Russia, Turkey, and Ukraine	No	Traditional

Bank (headquarters)	Regional members	Non-regional and institutional members	Governance structure
Central American Bank for Economic Integration (CABEI)	Guatemala, El Salvador, Honduras, Nicaragua, Costa Rica, Panama, Dominican Republic	Non-borrowing: Mexico, Spain, Taiwan Borrowing: Argentina, Belize, Colombia	Semi-traditional: Board of Governors only
East African Development Bank (EADB)	Kenya, Rwanda, Tanzania, Uganda (holding 90% of shares)	Non-regional: Netherlands, Germany Institutional: African Development Bank, SBIC-Africa Holdings, Commercial Bank of Africa, Nairobi, Nordea Bank of Sweden, Standard Chartered Bank, and Barclays Bank, UK	Non-traditional or Hybrid: Traditional plus "Governing Council" plus an "Advisory Panel" made up of institutions
West African Development Bank (BOAD)	Benin, Burkina Faso, Ivory Coast, Guinea-Bissau, Mali, Niger, Senegal, Togo (total shares = 93.39%)	Non-regional: France, Germany, European Union, Belgium, India, China, Morocco Institutional: African Development Bank (AfDB); Central Bank of West African States (BCEAO)	Non-traditional: Corporate-like
Financial Fund for the Development of the River Plate Basin (FONPLATA)	Argentina, Bolivia, Brazil, Paraguay, Uruguay	No	NA
Central African States Development Bank (CASDB or BDEAC)	Cameroon, Central Africa, Congo, Gabon, Equatorial Guinea and Chad	No	NA
PTA Bank of (COMESA)	Burundi, Comoros, China, Djibouti, Egypt, Eritrea, Ethiopia, Kenya, Malawi, Mauritius, Rwanda, Seychelles, Somalia, Sudan, Tanzania, Uganda, Zambia, Zimbabwe	Non-regional: China Institutional: AfDB	NA

Source: Individual bank websites.

high level of representative legitimacy is the possibility that it may simultaneously decrease the likelihood that the SRDB can achieve and maintain selectivity, the practice of criteria-based lending. Selectivity in lending, or allocating funds to less corrupt, more democratically free, poor countries, has been recognized as a best practice in order to improve incentives for states to alter behavior in exchange for greater development assistance (Easterly and Pfutze 2008; Easterly and Williamson 2011). Despite their ability to be more selective globally, the exclusivity of their membership remains defined by the geographical borders of their region and as a result, SRDBs may not be in a much better position that larger development institutions that have historically lent without discrimination of the type of government in place or level of borrower corruption.

In terms of output legitimacy, the restricted membership arrangement of SRDBs has been found to lead to differences in lending policies in CAF, specifically increasing their "organizational agility" (Humphrey and Michaelowa 2013: 146) or ability to quickly disburse loans in response to borrower demand. In theory, this arrangement is paradoxical. From a rational P-A perspective, while an SRDB like CAF may be more closely bound to its principals since it serves as a direct extension of its members, this reflects a loss of organizational autonomy. However, it simultaneously maintains high degrees of organizational and output legitimacy as a result of having a set of principals with more closely aligned interests that lead to swift favorable outcomes for member states. A conclusion from this section is that SRDBs are less likely to be susceptible to the dominance of a single or small set of powerful states to the same degree as the World Bank and select RDBs are to the U.S. and other dominant states (e.g. China, Japan, Germany), thereby ensuring a high degree of representative legitimacy as a component of input legitimacy and output legitimacy as defined in this chapter.

The P-A model also applies to resource dependence or the extent to which SRDBs are susceptible to demands from member states in exchange for capital. SRDBs are potentially more susceptible to these demands given their smaller portfolios and high degree of reliance on capital subscriptions for operations. However, their dependence on member resources may lead to different organizational outcomes if as a general rule the members making demands in exchange for capital are also borrowers. In contrast to the World Bank, there is more likely to be an agreement of interests of both donors and borrowers within SRDBs as they are often the same set of actors. Predicting different institutional outcomes for SRDBs assumes that borrower and donor states have divergent interests, which is clear at the World Bank but less so with regional arrangements (Humphrey 2014), especially those reflecting more tightly agreed-upon principles of development policies and acceptable terms of intervention from non-state actors.

Governance structure, specifically in terms of the distribution of voting power among members (Buira 2005; Rapkin and Strand 2006) and the appointment process of key officials (Levi, Finizio, and Vallinoto 2013;

Zweifel 2006), also influences the relationship between representative legitimacy and output legitimacy. The distribution of power among members assumes there is decision-making power granted to members, which is not the case for all SRDBs included in this chapter. Most have adopted a similar structure to that of the World Bank and RDBs, with boards comprised of representatives from member states.

Comparison to the World Bank

In comparing SRDBs to the World Bank the expectation is that the more an SRDB mimics the World Bank in terms of its membership and governance structure, the more likely it is to reflect emerging development norms of increased transparency, accountability, and evaluation standards. This is likely to occur as a result of existing patterns of norm diffusion from dominant members or primary principals in the World Bank (i.e. the West) to less developed regional members (Simmons, Dobbin, and Garrett 2006) and the process of aid harmonization (Park and Strand, this volume). It should also be noted that variance in policy failures and external shocks (Park and Vetterlein 2010) can be used to explain differences in adherence to these norms; membership and governance structure are not sole predictors.

The exclusivity of SRDB membership is in stark contrast to the inclusiveness of the near-universal World Bank, in which primary principals tend to be donor states while beneficiaries or borrowers have far less decision-making power due to the limitations of weighted voting, executive board voting groups, and other governance features. Furthermore, the Bank's governance structure reflects the post-WWII power structure in terms of weighted voting and arrangement of voting groups, though this has lessened to some degree as the Bank has increasingly allocated additional shares to developing countries in response to repeated demands.

Accountability mechanisms

Accountability of development institutions through the availability of post-ante complaint mechanisms have also been explored at the multilateral and regional level (Levi, Finizio, and Vallinoto 2013; Moss 2007; Park 2010, 2014; Rowden and Irama 2004; Stewart and Wang 2003; Zweifel 2006). Accountability mechanisms were adopted in the 1990s by the following development banks: African, Asian, Inter-American, the European Bank for Reconstruction and Development, and the World Bank (Park 2014). The ideal mechanism includes options for internal review of an organization's actions in accordance with its own policies, rules, standards, and processes and external review through opportunities for outsiders to pursue complaints. The presence of accountability mechanisms can increase both input and output legitimacy. Output legitimacy can be enhanced if an organization learns by making specific changes in response to outside complaints on the ill effects of its policies.

200 Tina M. Zappile

Simultaneously, the mechanism can function as a type of input, though ex-ante, which is open to non-state actors who are often the intended beneficiaries of bank-supported projects.

Table 10.3 presents a summary of SRDBs in this sample, limiting reported results to organizations with available data translatable in English. SRDBs are coded as 'low', 'medium', or 'high level' to reflect the degree to which internal and/or external accountability mechanisms exist and operate. Notes are included to account for the variety of mechanisms, most of which are reserved for internal accountability.

BSTDB primarily addresses internal accountability and while the Internal Audit Department provides contact information for potential complainants, it is unclear whether it has the resources to adequately respond to inquiries and complaints from outside the bank. CAF provides whistleblower protection and has established an Ethics Committee; however, there are no publicly available reports of complaints or official responses. CABEI is designated with a higher level in recognition of their Compliance Office and variety of policies communicating a commitment to external accountability. As previously stated, the presence of internal accountability policies and mechanisms may signal a higher level of autonomy, whereas the lack of an internal accountability mechanism might signal a higher degree of input legitimacy as there is simply no need for one if the SRDB is a direct extension of member states, as is with the case of CAF (Humphrey, this volume).

Table 10.3 Presence of accountability mechanisms in SRDBs

Bank	Level of accountability	Additional details
Central American Bank for Economic Integration (CABEI)	Medium level	Compliance Office is specific to the "prevention of money laundering and terrorism financing in order to prevent CABEI from being used as a vehicle for such ends" (CABEI 2014); An Institutional Responsibility Plan (PRI) and Environmental and Social Policy; Social Responsibility Axis and Program and Eco-efficiency Axis (Green Bank) reflect commitment to civil society and environmental accountability
West African Development Bank (BOAD)	Low-medium level	Only financial audits
Black Sea Trade and Development Bank (BSTDB)	Low-medium level	Internal Audit Department identified as primary contact for all complaints
Development Bank of Latin American (CAF)	Low level	Ethics Committee; includes whistleblower protection

Sources: Unless noted, individual bank websites.

Comparison to the World Bank

The World Bank Inspection Panel was created in 1993 and reports directly to its executive directors, serving as the primary external accountability mechanism. Created in direct response to civil society demands for accountability following numerous project failures in regards to the environment and rights of displaced populations (Clark 2003), it investigates the level of compliance of World Bank projects with operational policies, including whether any harm to either people or the environment resulted from Bank-funded development projects. The World Bank's Inspection Panel is somewhat unique in that personnel in this division act independently from the rest of the Bank and cannot be transferred back to operations or management. At the sub-regional level, there have been few attempts to adopt similar accountability mechanisms.

Inclusion of civil society

Formal opportunities for civil society participation are viewed as a key component for a development institution to enhance their effectiveness in advancing their mandate to reflect civil society interests (Nielsen and Tierney 2003: 250). Civil society organizations represent key stakeholders in development planning, implementation, and evaluation. Their participation in development planning alongside member states supports accountability broadly defined, with the hopes that participation is open to a large number of non-governmental organizations and occurs at critical stages of development planning rather than being a token gesture. Of course, the capacity of NGOs within those states is important in determining the quality of participation. NGOs that are granted access to participate in country-led initiatives connected to SRDB planning may also face problems associated with low levels of access granted by autocratic states. Related to civil society participation in project planning and policy discussions is the concern for environmental sustainability (Duraiappah and Roddy 2005; Gutner 2005; Nielson and Tierney 2003, 2005). Research on civil society and environmental accountability has long recognized that development institutions often neglected the interests of people directly and indirectly affected by development assistance projects, sometimes with disastrous results.

High levels of representative legitimacy characteristic of most SRDBs may lead to unintended consequences regarding demand for increased opportunities for civil society participation. Civil society may be less likely to perceive actions by sub-regional banks as threatening to their interests to the same degree as they do for the World Bank or larger regional banks given that SRDBs are led by what may be perceived as regional partners. Further complicating opportunities for participation may be the regime type of member states themselves, as some regions are heavily populated with autocratic states that will be less inclined to provide them. Inclusion of civil society directly

202 *Tina M. Zappile*

supports input legitimacy by increasing opportunities for the beneficiaries of SRDB projects to directly participate in planning, while output legitimacy can be supported if projects then reflect civil society demands.

SRDBs are often limited in their response to civil society inclusion, due either to a lack of communication regarding processes in place or a disregard to this dimension. Table 10.4 presents the results of analysis along this dimension. SRDBs are coded as 'low', 'medium', and 'high level' the number and quality of participatory opportunities. 'NA' signals that data are not available or there are no opportunities, with strong evidence supporting the lack of opportunities for the banks identified in this table. Table 10.4 also

Table 10.4 Inclusion of civil society and environmental interests in SRDBs

Bank	Opportunities for civil society participation and inclusion of environmental standards	Evidence
Caribbean Development Bank (CariBank or CDB)	High level	Environment and Social Review Guidelines; Capacity Building (under Basic Needs Trust Fund); Participatory Poverty Assessment in country reports
Black Sea Trade and Development Bank (BSTDB)	Medium-high level	Environmental and Social Policy includes: "Sustainability; Assessment; Good practices" at EU and World Bank level (BSTDB 2014a)
Central American Bank for Economic Integration (CABEI)	Low-medium level	Institutional Responsibility Plan (PRI) and Environmental and Social Policy; Social Responsibility Axis and Program and Eco-efficiency Axis (Green Bank) reflect a commitment; specific avenues not cited
East African Development Bank (EADB)	Low level	'CSR Principles' include "Ethical conduct, openness and diversity; Sustainable practices that ensure mutual benefit for EADB and society; Partnership and people participation" (EADB 2014)
Development Bank of Latin American (CAF)	NA	
PTA Bank of COMESA	NA	

Sources: Unless noted, individual bank websites.

presents additional details about the number and quality of participatory opportunities, when applicable and made publicly available.

Comparison to the World Bank

Examples of successful inclusion of civil society at the World Bank are found in the areas of debt relief, environment, and health policy (Zappile 2014). In the Bank, NGOs can apply for consultative status to establish a more formal relationship and select organizations can become accredited by the Bank, the highest level of access granted to a non-member organization. In terms of direct participation, the involvement of civil society stakeholders has been identified as a critical component of the Bank's development planning process that is more country-driven than in the past (Moss 2007) and countries are now expected to include them in the poverty reduction strategy paper (PRSP) process. This change implemented was in the 1990s to complement Country Assistant Strategy (CAS) reports to reflect Bank efforts to increase 'country ownership' and 'civil society participation' in development planning (Marshall 2008).

Transparency

Increased transparency has been demanded by stakeholders in the development community including member and non-member states of MDBs and civil society and is recognized as a best practice for aid agencies (Easterly and Pfutze 2008; Easterly and Williamson 2011). Transparency reflects an organizational commitment to its credibility and can increase output legitimacy (Zweifel 2006). Furthermore, it provides opportunities for greater external accountability, particularly when there is a mechanism in place, by allowing civil society access to internal documents related to decision-making, policies, finances, research, results of internal evaluations, and more. Demands for greater transparency have been asserted for decades, as development institutions traditionally protected data related to lending patterns, project evaluation, country progress reports, and other activities. The World Bank only recently committed to transparency across most of its organs and activities, as pressure to do so mounted as its failures became well publicized. Transparency is a key criterion for any organization interested in maintaining credibility, as it is often seen as a necessary condition for accountability.

Sources for transparency in development include the International Aid Transparency Initiative (IATI), Publish What You Fund, and AidData (Easterly and Williamson 2011). Signatories to the International Aid Transparency Initiative (IATI) include the African Development Bank, reflecting a shift toward greater transparency in conjunction with its recently adopted Disclosure and Access to Information (DAI) policy (IATI 2013). Publish What You Fund issues an annual Aid Transparency Index. Regional development banks such as the African, Asian, and Inter-American banks are evaluated and reported in the index along with major multilateral and sovereign aid agencies and banks. However, none of the SRDBs in this study were included in their recent reports.

Table 10.5 presents results for analysis of SRDBs along this dimension. The coding system starts at a 'low level' of commitment reflecting activities such as issuing data and reports suggesting a commitment to transparency despite the absence of an official policy. A 'high level' of commitment reflects the presence of an official policy regarding commitment to transparency, the identification of internal sources responsible for disseminating information, and public availability of publications deemed adequate to meet the stated standards. A 'medium level' consists a stated policy and one of the two additional criteria required for a 'high level'. Banks with 'no stated policy' are also included and coded as 'none' for their commitment to transparency.

The CDB is the only SRDB to meet the standards for high-level commitment, while all others meet requirements for low level or have no stated policy. This is supported by a previous evaluation of CDB's transparency, identifying it as falling above a threshold for available data (Easterly and Pfutze 2008).

Table 10.5 SRDB commitment to transparency

Bank	Commitment to transparency	Evidence
Caribbean Development Bank (CariBank or CDB)	High level	Information Services Centre (ISC); Official Information Disclosure Policy highlighting a commitment to "Maximize Access to Information" (Cari-Bank 2014)
Latin American Development Bank (CAF)	Low level	Informal practice evident by availability of records
Pacific Islands Development Bank (PIDB)	Low level	Informal practice evident by availability of records
Black Sea Trade and Development Bank (BSTDB)	Low level	Internal transparency is recognized as a component of internal accountability
West African Development Bank (BOAD)	Low level	Some evidence of informal practice evident by availability of records; most available in French only
East African Development Bank (EADB)	Low level	Some evidence of informal practice evident by availability of records as of 2012
Central American Bank for Economic Integration (CABEI)	None	No stated policy
Bank of Common Market for Eastern and Southern Africa (COMESA)	None	No stated policy

Sources: Unless noted, individual bank websites.

Comparison to the World Bank

The same external evaluation of transparency in aid agencies identified the IDA as the highest-ranking multilateral agency, assigning the same value to the IBRD. The IDA has also received high marks for all but one of eight transparency indicators in another independent evaluation by the Center for Global Development (Birdsall et al. 2010). This is one area in which the Bank has responded to demands from civil society, shifting from a closed environment to a knowledge bank publicly disseminating development data, project evaluations, research, and other operational activities and policies.

Performance or project evaluation

Internal evaluation of development projects is a critical component of a successful development institution. Often, evaluations along with individual country reports are a primary focus of annual reports in multilateral and regional banks; this is also observed at the sub-regional level. However while the World Bank and RDBs have teams of researchers working on project or performance evaluation, SRDBs lag behind due to limitations in available capital and expertise. Thus, the existence and effective use of internal mechanisms for performance or project evaluation indicates a higher level of operational legitimacy.

Table 10.6 presents results for the analysis of evaluations. A 'high level' signifies the presence of an independent evaluation unit. However, most SRDBs do not go beyond relying on the annual report as the primary evaluation tool, which is designated as a 'low level'. A 'medium level' signifies the existence of an evaluation policy beyond the annual report but falls short of an independent evaluation unit. Banks that had no stated policy or did not make their policy available were excluded from these results. A normative assumption is that all development institutions should have a mechanism for evaluation; however, in the case of SRDBs, some like the Pacific Islands Development Bank are struggling to expand operations as they strive to increase their presence in the region (PIDB 2009). It is likely that many smaller SRDBs rank lower or are absent along this dimension for the same reason.

The Latin American Development Bank (CAF) conducts ex-post consulting, or evaluations, of their funded projects through an Ex-Post Evaluation Unit (UEE). Evaluators focus on the following dimensions: a) design or "project formulation, its logic, as well as its structure and the consistency of the basic elements that constitute it", b) results that "compare(s) the established objectives and goals with the activities that took place in the execution of the project", and c) impact or "the effect of changes on the beneficiaries and anything that may have been significantly affected by the execution of the project" (CAF 2014). Individual and organizational consultants are hired as part of the evaluation process, expanding the ability for corporate and non-government stakeholders to contribute to the evaluation process and potentially, outcome.

Table 10.6 Evidence of performance or project evaluation

Bank	Degree of Evaluation	Evidence
Development Bank of Latin America (CAF)	High level	Ex-Post Evaluation Unit (UEE)
Black Sea Trade and Development Bank (BSTDB)	High level	Independent Evaluation Office; Post-Evaluation Policy; Operation Performance Evaluation Reports; Annual Evaluation Overviews; Evaluation Studies (BSTDB 2014b)
Caribbean Development Bank (CariBank or CDB)	Low-medium level	Annual and other comprehensive reports
Central American Bank for Economic Integration (CABEI)	Low level	Annual reports
East African Development Bank (EADB)	Low level	Annual reports

Sources: Unless noted, individual bank websites.

Comparing to the World Bank

The Development Bank of Latin America (CAF) and Black Sea Trade and Development Bank (BSTDB) have created evaluation units similar to that found in the World Bank. The World Bank's Independent Evaluation Department (now Group or IEG) was established in 1973 and now evaluates the World Bank, IFC, and MIGA activities including but not limited to lending project assessments, impact evaluations, reviews of portfolios, and interviews with Bank staff, country officials, and civil society. In addition, the Development Impact Evaluation Initiative (DIME) was established in 2005 to enhance knowledge regarding the effectiveness of specific policies. These units were established many years after the Bank was formed, supporting the contention that an assessment of SRDBs along this dimension may not be an appropriate indicator of its overall effectiveness as many are in their nascency and there may be a natural time lapse between initial operations and establishing procedures for evaluating previous output.

Discussion and conclusion

Results from this analysis suggest that while some SRDBs have adopted a structure and policies that mimic the World Bank and RDBs, most have retained features that are distinct. While select SRDBs have organizational and policy features that reflect a medium to high level of democratic governance structure, the existence of accountability mechanisms, and some commitment to transparency, as a group they have not pursued the same strategies to progress along these dimensions to the same degree as the World

Bank or RDBs. Norms of democratization in international organizations have clearly not diffused to this subset of MDBs, in most cases. SRDBs that mimic the World Bank's governance structure do adhere to some norms along other dimensions. For example, the CDB, CAF, BSTDB, PIDB, and EDB have a traditional membership structure yet only the CDB and CAF allow non-regional or institutional members. Following this, the CDB ranks high along the dimensions of inclusion of civil society and commitment to transparency, low-medium for project evaluations while CAF ranks high for project evaluation, low in dimensions of accountability and commitment to transparency, and is unaccountable regarding the inclusion of civil society. This is in contrast to the BSTDB, which is restricted to regional members yet has a traditional structure and ranks high for project evaluation, medium-high for inclusion of civil society, low-medium for accountability, and low for commitment to transparency. The BSTDB performs better across these dimensions than SRDBs without a traditional governance structure. Perhaps a combination of a traditional governance structure and a restricted membership can be combined with a high degree of convergence along the dimensions of accountability, inclusion of civil society, and project evaluation.

Considering these dimensions in terms of how they reflect levels of representative legitimacy and operational legitimacy, the following conclusions can be drawn about this set of SRDBs. The CDB, CAF, BSTDB, and CABEI arguably have greater levels of operational legitimacy stemming from higher levels of accountability, implementing project evaluation, and the inclusion of civil society and environmental interests. A high degree of representative legitimacy is maintained by SRDBs without non-regional or institutional members, such as the PIBD, FONPLATA, EDB, and CASDB. Note the lack of crossover of SRDBs in these two areas of legitimacy. Representative legitimacy and operational legitimacy may not be necessary conditions for SRDBs to effectively achieve their regional mandate(s) as they may not be compatible in the regional context.

Primarily, SRDBs are created to serve regional interests and they remain poised to do so by restricting membership or granting a high degree of decision-making power to regional members while increasing access to technical expertise, focusing limited resources on the primary activity of lending or otherwise supporting development projects for regional members, and providing channels of access for civil society within regional states to ensure they serve that population through their activities. However, as noted in this chapter, SRDBs face a dilemma. For example, by restricting members, the PIDB retains a high degree of representative legitimacy but this could be at the cost of access to additional technical expertise provided by non-regional members from which a bank like the CBD can benefit.

A paradox of this analysis exists: it evaluates the sub-regional organizations according to criteria that may *not* be valued across all regions. In other words, the norms included in this research that have been adopted at the multilateral and regional level due to external pressures from transnational networks of

NGOs and individual experts or internal sources of change from powerful member states or staff may not be of importance to the SRDBs. The availability of resources may also limit organizational changes in these areas as many are limited in funds due to membership being comprised of mostly developing or middle-income countries. The CDB's commitment to transparency and inclusion of civil society in development planning and assessment may have developed in part from its high degree of partnership with regional and multilateral banks, thereby providing opportunities for the CDB to learn and adapt in similar ways, much like the pattern followed by the Asian Development Bank with its adoption of accountability mechanisms (Park 2014). Alternatively, the degree to which norms within the region align with those more broadly identified as 'best practices' for development institutions may be reflected in the institutional features of those regional and sub-regional banks.

Opportunities for future research on SRDBs abound. First, do SRDBs that reflect the current World Bank model, whether a result of external or internal pressure, maintain a greater degree of organizational legitimacy in their region or the development policy community? Do SRDBs face increased pressure to respond to demands from member states regarding the dimensions identified in this chapter if they expand operations or extend membership beyond the region? Furthermore, does the combination of institutional features arguably unique to SRDBs matter in terms of their policies or performance? Scholars interested in SRDBs or regional development should turn their focus to evaluating their performance or effectiveness (Birdsall et al. 2010; Easterly and Pfutze 2008; Easterly and Williamson 2011; Easterly 1999; Gutner and Thompson 2010; Humphrey 2014) as a next step in endorsing or advancing a regional focus.

In conclusion, this mapping exercise to identify the hybrid of institutional features of a variety of SRDBs is an important first step in further exploring the diffusion of norms, adoption of recognized best practices, and explaining reactions to external shocks and pressures at the sub-regional level. Select SRDBs have already realized the potential while others stand poised to become major actors in shaping regional development strategies and enhancing deeper regionalization. Therefore, understanding SRDBs in terms of what we already know about development institutions is critical.

Notes

1 Central American Bank for Economic Integration. 2014. "Approved Operations." Available at: www.bcie.org/?cat=12&title=Approved%20Operations&lang=en.
2 BOAD. 2014. "BOAD in Brief." Available at: www.boad.org/sites/default/files/boad_in_brief_2014.pdf.
3 Eurasian Development Bank. 2014. "Brief results of MDB's investment activities." Available at: http://eabr.org/e/research/publications/MDB_activites/.
4 PTA Bank of COMESA. 2013, "2013 Annual Report." Available at: www.ptabank.org/images/downloads/reports/PTA_Bank_Audited_Financial_Statements-31_December_2013.pdf.

5 Caribbean Development Bank. 2013. "2013 Annual Report: Volume 2." Available at: http://www.caribank.org/uploads/2014/05/2013-CDB-Annual-Report-Vol2.pdf.
6 East African Development Bank. 2014. "2013 Annual Report." Available at: http://eadb.org/eadb-annual-report-2013/.
7 Corporacion Andina de Fomento. 2013. "2013 Annual Report." Available at: www.caf.com/media/2377200/ia-annualReport2013-25jul.pdf.
8 Pacific Islands Development Bank. 2013. "2013 Annual Report." Available at: www.pacificidb.com/wp-content/uploads/2014/05/55351-PIDB-AR-2013_Part2.pdf.
9 Black Sea Trade and Development Bank. 2014. "Project Center." Available at: www.bstdb.org/project-center.
10 See Malesky, Schuler, and Tran (2012) for a review of literature on transparency in democracies and its effect on the behavior of agents.

References

African Development Bank (AfDB). 2014. "Projects and Operations." Available at: www.afdb.org/en/projects-and-operations/ (accessed 1 August 2014).
Barnett, M. and M. Finnemore. 2004. *Rules for the World: International Organizations in Global Politics*. Ithaca, NY: Cornell University Press.
Beattie, A.. 2014. "A BRICS bank: Can it outdo the World Bank?" *Financial Times*, 19 June. Available at: http://blogs.ft.com/beyond-brics/2014/06/19/a-brics-bank-can-it-outdo-the-world-bank/ (accessed 1 August 2014).
Birdsall, N., H. J. Kharas, A. Mahgoub and R. Perakis. 2010. *Quality of Official Development Assistance Assessment*. Washington, DC: Brookings Institute and Center for Global Development.
Birdsall, N. and L. Rojas-Suarez (eds). 2004. *Financing Development: The Power of Regionalism*. Washington, DC: Center for Global Development.
Black Sea Trade and Development Bank (BSTDB). 2013. "Annual Report." Available at: www.bstdb.org/investor-relations/annual-reports/BSTDB_Annual_Report_2013.pdf (accessed 30 October 2014).
Black Sea Trade and Development Bank (BSTDB). 2014a. "Environment and Social Sustainability." Available at: www.bstdb.org/about-us/how-we-operate/environment (accessed 22 February 2014).
Black Sea Trade and Development Bank (BSTDB). 2014b. "Evaluation." Available at: www.bstdb.org/about-us/how-we-operate/evaluation (accessed 22 February 2014).
Buira, Ariel, ed. 2005. *Reforming the Governance of the IMF and the World Bank*. London: Anthem Press.
Central American Bank for Economic Integration (CABEI). 2014. "Organizational Structure: Compliance Office." Available at: www.bcie.org/?cat=1427&title=ComplianceOffice&lang=en (accessed 1 February 2014).
Development Bank of Latin American/Andean Development Corporation (CAF). 2014. "Ex-Post Consulting." Available at: www.caf.com/en/resources/employment/ex-post-consulting (accessed 22 February 2014).
Caribbean Development Bank (Cari-Bank). 2014. "Information Disclosure Policy." Available at: www.caribank.org/about-cdb/cdb-information-disclosure-policy (accessed 22 February 2014).
Clark, D. 2003. "Understanding the World Bank Inspection Panel." In *Demanding Accountability. Civil Society Claims and the World Bank Inspection Panel*, edited by D. Clark, J. Fox and K. Treakle. Lanham, MD: Rowman & Littlefield, pp. 1–24.

Copelovitch, M. S. 2010. "Master or servant? Common agency and the political economy of IMF lending." *International Studies Quarterly* 54(1): 49–77.
Duraiappah, A. K. and P. Roddy. 2005. *Integrating the Environment into the Poverty Reduction Strategy*. Winnipeg, MB: International Institute for Sustainable Development. Available at: www.iisd.org/publications/integrating-environment-poverty-reduction-strategy-papers (accessed 22 February 2014).
East African Development Bank (EADB). 2014. "CSR Principles." Available at: http://eadb.org/eadb-csr-principles/ (accessed 22 February 2014).
Easterly, W. 1999. "The Effect of International Monetary Fund and World Bank Programs on Poverty." World Bank Policy Research Working Paper no. 2517, World Bank Group eLibrary. Available at: http://dx.doi.org/10.1596/1813-9450-25171-31 (accessed 5 June 2015).
Easterly, W. and T. Pfutze. 2008. "Where does the money go? Best and worst practices in foreign aid." *Journal of Economic Perspectives* 22(2): 29–52.
Easterly, W. and C. R. Williamson. 2011. "Rhetoric versus reality: The best and worst of aid agency practices." *World Development* 39(11): 1930–1949.
Gutner, T. 2005. "World Bank environmental reform: Revisiting lessons from agency theory." *International Organization* 59(03): 773–783.
Gutner, T. and A. Thompson. 2010. "The politics of IO performance: A framework." *The Review of International Organizations* 5(3): 227–248.
Hillman, J. 2013. "African Development Bank Publishes to IATI." International Aid Transparency Initiative (IATI), July 1. Available at: www.aidtransparency.net/news/african-development-bank-publishes-to-iati (August 1, 2014).
Humphrey, C. 2014. "The politics of loan pricing in multilateral development banks." *Review of International Political Economy* 21(3): 611–639.
Humphrey, C. and K. Michaelowa. 2013. "Shopping for development: Multilateral lending, shareholder composition and borrower preferences." *World Development* 44(4): 142–155.
Inter-American Development Bank (IADB). 2013. "Annual Report." Available at: http://publications.iadb.org/bitstream/handle/11319/6423/IDB%20Annual%20Report%202013.%20%20Financial%20Statements.pdf?sequence=1 (Accessed 1 August 2014).
Johnson, T. 2011 "Guilt by association: The link between states' influence and the legitimacy of intergovernmental organizations." *Review of International Organizations* 6(1): 57–84.
Levi, L., G. Finizio and N. Vallinoto (eds). 2013. *The Democratization of International Institutions: First International Democracy Report*. London: Routledge.
Marshall, K. 2008. *The World Bank: From Reconstruction to Development to Equity*. New York, NY: Routledge.
Moravcsik, A. 2004. "Is there a 'democratic deficit' in world politics? A framework for analysis." *Government and Opposition* 39(2): 336–363.
Moss, T. 2007. *African Development: Making Sense of the Issues and Actors*. London: Lynne Rienner.
Nielson, D. L. and M. J. Tierney. 2003. "Delegation to international grganizations: Agency theory and World Bank environmental reform." *International Organization* 57(02): 241–276.
Nielson, D. L. and M. J. Tierney. 2005. "Theory, data, and hypothesis testing: World Bank environmental reform redux." *International Organization* 59(03): 785–800.

Pacific Island Development Bank (PIDB). 2009. "Annual Report." Available at: www.pacificidb.com/docs/downloads/annual-report/pidb-2009-annual-report.pdf (accessed 1 August .2014).
Park, S. 2010. "Designing accountability, international economic organisations and the World Bank's inspection panel." *Australian Journal of International Affairs* 64(1): 13–36.
Park, S. 2014. "Institutional isomorphism and the Asian Development Bank's accountability mechanism." *The Pacific Review* 27(2): 217–239.
Park, S. and A. Vetterlein (eds). 2010. *Owning Development: Creating Policy Norms in the IMF and the World Bank*. Cambridge: Cambridge University Press.
Rapkin, D. P. and J. R. Strand. 2006. "Reforming the IMF's weighted voting system." *The World Economy* 29(3): 305–324.
Rowden, R. and J. Ocaya Irama. 2004. *Rethinking Participation: Questions for Civil Society about the Limits of Participation in PRSPs*. Washington, DC: ActionAid.
Scharpf, F. W. 1999. *Governing in Europe: Effective and Democratic?* Oxford: Oxford University Press.
Simmons, B. A., F. Dobbin and G. Garrett. 2006. "Introduction: The international diffusion of liberalism." *International Organization* 60(4): 781–810.
Stewart, F. and M. Wang. 2003. "Do PRSPs Empower Poor Countries and Disempower the World Bank, or Is It the Other Way Round?" QEH (Queen Elizabeth House) Working Paper no. 108, University of Oxford, Oxford.
Strand, J. R. 2014. "The Democratization of the International Monetary Fund." In *The Democratization of International Institutions: First International Democracy Report*, edited by L. Levi, G. Finizio and N. Vallinoto. London: Routledge, pp. 80–93.
Tierney, M. J., D. L. Nielson, D. G. Hawkins, J. Timmons Roberts, M. G. Findley, R. M. Powers, B. Parks, S. E. Wilson and R. L. Hicks. 2011. "More dollars than sense: Refining our knowledge of development finance using AidData." *World Development* 39(11): 1891–1906.
Zappile, T. M. 2014. "World Bank." In *The Democratization of International Institutions: First International Democracy Report*, edited by L. Lucio, G. Finizio and N. Vallinoto. London: Routledge, pp. 80–93.
Zweifel, T. D. 2006. *International Organizations And Democracy: Accountability, Politics, And Power*. Boulder, CO: Lynne Rienner.

11 The RDBs in the Twenty-First Century

Jonathan R. Strand and Susan Park

The practices of the regional development banks (and the sub-regional development banks) are at the heart of debates regarding what constitutes international development and how it should be done. Despite this, the RDBs remain understudied while ample resources have been expended by scholars in examining the IMF and World Bank. This volume therefore provided crucial insights into the workings of these well-established international organizations. Created in the midst and at the conclusion of the Cold War, these IOs have played an important regional role in facilitating development: through attracting additional capital to developing regions, fostering regional integration, and providing a voice for regional member states in their own international development institution. Yet they remain relatively unknown by scholars of international political economy and international organization.

We began this volume by questioning why there was such a glaring oversight of these long-standing IOs. We posited that it may have been because scholars presumed that RDBs are like the World Bank or that because they operate within developing regions they may only be of interest to those regions. The volume dispelled both notions. First, RDBs engage with the same policy issues as the World Bank but they do so at different times, speeds, and depth, which complicates any straightforward assumption of transferring ideas from the World Bank to the RDBs as a constellation of organizations. As discussed below, because RDBs occupy the same policy space as the World Bank they address the same policy concerns as they arise in global economic governance. Second, the RDBs are not just regional but also *global* institutions in at least two important ways: membership and development policy. Scholars of *global* economic governance need to recognize RDBs as the global actors they are and understand how they differ from the World Bank. Some effect change more quickly and more deeply than others and this can be attributed to both regionally specific causes (such as the Asian Financial Crisis for the ADB) and the resource dependence and legitimacy concerns of the institution itself.

An examination of the resource dependency and legitimacy of RDBs offers additional contexts for studying the inter-relationship between material and ideational motivations for institutional behavior and change (Hawkins et al.

2006; Park and Vetterlein 2010; Weaver 2008). What we are presented with are cases from the RDBs that demonstrate that both resource dependence and legitimacy are important in determining policy change and governance arrangements. This conclusion examines 1) the extent to which the banks are driven by resource dependence or legitimacy when determining their policy agenda and operations, and 2) whether and how they differ from the World Bank, while arguing that more needs to be done to ascertain whether current explanations of IO behavior and change – including whether change is driven from inside or outside the organization – help us understand the practices of these longstanding regional institutions in the twenty-first century.

As demonstrated by the contributors to this volume, attention to these 'lesser' multilateral development banks provides valuable evidence on how international organizations behave and how they adapt to change. This includes how and when they differ from the universal international development institution, the World Bank. Indeed, one of the most important contributions of this collection is rethinking the relationship between RDBs and the World Bank, as well as reconsidering how international development practices change, in terms of both policy shifts and multilateral development bank implementation. In the introduction we conceived of this as a question of when and why the RDBs follow or resist the policy approaches of the World Bank (for example, an RDB may espouse the rhetoric but not change in reality with regard to a policy initiative of the World Bank). This thinking needs to be recast. Instead of conceiving global economic governance as a centered on the (IMF and) World Bank surrounded by the RDBs, we need to refashion our conception of global economic governance to recognize multiple sites of change in policy and practice. These multiple sites include the IMF and the World Bank as well as the RDBs and SRDBs. The cause of such change is based, we argue, on concerns regarding both the banks' resource dependence and their legitimacy.

In short, given the vitriolic debates over the impact of the World Bank (and the IMF) it is surprising that little has been done to establish to what extent the RBDs reflect or reject the practices espoused at the global level, especially as the World Bank is considered to be driven by US hegemony while the RDBs were designed to provide more room for regional players (Ascher 1992; Woods 2003; Wade 1996; White 1970). Concepts such as good governance in the RDBs have manifested differently to good governance in the World Bank (Jokinen 2004), but – for instance – although the ADB was the first of the MDBs to have a formal policy on good governance, the literature on the ADB and good governance is noticeable by its absence compared to that written on the World Bank. We began this book asking about the place, role, and significance of RDBs in global economic governance and it is clear throughout the volume that we need to attend to these IOs not as satellites of the World Bank but as important players in their own right with the capacity to pre-empt the World Bank as well as follow it (and modify or reinterpret World Bank policy).

Contributors to this volume have demonstrated that RDBs cannot be assumed to reflect the development practices and governance of the World Bank, although they often espouse neoliberal-style development in their lending. In some instances this means that RDB practices reinforce World Bank doctrine through 'cross-conditionality' (Mingst 1990); in other instances the RDBs provide more wriggle room for borrowers than does the World Bank (see Humphrey, this volume). In some cases both are true, as in the AfDB when the same policies are established as those of the World Bank but with substantially less oversight (Mingst 1990). In other ways still, the RDBs' differing interpretations of the same policy concerns is a means of translating policy issues into regionally specific practices (for example, anti-corruption measures in the case of the ADB and environmental and social safeguards in the case of the IADB). More research is needed to untangle what this means for players – lenders and borrowers alike – in the international political economy.

The role of the RDBs in the international political economy

As articulated throughout the book, RDBs and SRDBs are central players in multilateral development. The RDBs funnel resources from developed countries to projects in middle-income and lower-income countries; they are positioned on the contour lines between regional integration and global cooperation. Overall, the volume shows that RDBs do reflect many of the dominant, mainstream ideas about development policies and practices, including: governance, gender and development, the environment, and poverty alleviation for the AfDB; anti-corruption efforts and engaging with civil society for the ADB; neoliberal constructions of the market for economies in transition for the EBRD; taking on the mantle of the Millennium Development Goals for the IADB; and the adoption of human rights rhetoric by all of the banks. Moreover, many of the more recent governance structures such as accountability mechanisms have been adopted by the RDBs, with many SRDBs also coming on board.

Although the RDBs have their own takes on policies, one of the main findings of the volume is the extent to which RDBs do actually emulate the World Bank. While we argue that RDBs implement policies and ideas differently to the World Bank, we were surprised at the overall degree of coherence amongst the banks. This is because the RDBs reflect the interests of their members as well as bureaucratic responses to ideas and 'policy norms' within the international political economy (Park and Vetterlein 2010). Membership in the RDBs is more complex than membership in the World Bank. Nonetheless, one of the goals of each RDB is to maintain a regional flavour, and to accomplish this regional interests must be taken in consideration and regional members are a regularized part of their operations. For this reason we wanted to probe the extent to which the banks are different – both from the World Bank and from each other. While regional considerations are important in the

RDBs, evidence in this volume shows that they are subject to and respond to global forces.

This point is perhaps most forcefully made in relation to the AfDB, the institution having taken up many of the same polices and development approaches as the World Bank but after a significant time delay. While the donor-driven agenda is evident in being tied to capital increases and soft-financing replenishments, the AfDB is also concerned with maintaining its legitimacy. Once ideas have been adopted and endorsed by the majority of multilateral and bilateral development financiers it becomes increasingly difficult not to endorse global 'best practice'. This is particularly important for an IO that has positioned itself as the premier regional lender for the African continent. As is evident throughout the volume, RDBs and SRDBs face the same policy concerns as the World Bank: non-economic considerations of human rights, gender and development, engagement with civil society, MDGs, anti-corruption, accountability, and governance. These issues have been added to the RDB repertoire by non-state actors and non-regional member states; all MDBs were designed to be apolitical, technocratic institutions with the single aim of furthering economic growth. Although regional members may not have been in favour of incorporating such concerns for resource-dependent reasons (i.e. reliance on Western donors), non-regional members were added to the banks' operations. As the chapters reveal, the legitimacy of incorporating new policies and operational standards operates at two levels: the degree to which the RDBs follow best international practice in terms of adopting the latest iteration of specific policies and the extent to which the policy adopted is endorsed by the majority of regional members and borrowers. In the chapters by Chris Humphrey and Tina Zappile, the tension between traditional (Western) donors of the banks and their borrowers is stark. Trade-offs between continued reliance on capital from these sources and the desires of borrower member states are evident. For Zappile, the benefits of having traditional sources of capital from Western donors in the SRDBs are the resources and the technical knowledge that can aid bank operations and therefore its output legitimacy. This contrasts with being solely responsible to regional members and therefore having representative legitimacy.

As national economies continue to be globalized and the role of states and of social forces evolves, IFIs like the RDBs are likely to remain focal points for discord among states as well as forums within which ideas and norms are debated, defined, and implemented. This is particularly important given the presence of emerging and rising powers in each of the banks: China and India in the ADB; South Africa in the AfDB; Brazil in the IADB; a relatively powerful Russia in the EBRD (although as a borrower, not as an increasingly powerful shareholder). It is therefore crucial to question how these rising powers will affect not only global institutions such as the World Bank but also their regional institutions. Fundamental to that is the voting power and flexing of financial muscle of rising powers within the RDBs. As Jonathan Strand

and Michael Trevathan have pointed out, what is curious about RDBs is actually how little such material gains have altered the composition of shares within the banks. As we continue to see the creation of new multilateral development institutions by China and the BRICs, it is odd that the RDBs for the most part remain donor-driven and dependent on donor resources while still retaining governance structures that have built-in protections for regional members.

Students and scholars of international relations need to move beyond their fixation with the World Bank and IMF and consider RDBs and SRDBs in their analyses to help explain why these institutions are not changing along with their primary beneficiaries. Scholars of IOs expect there to be slow change in international organizations and it seems remarkable that there has been so little change in organizations that uphold the rights of developing countries, considering the rise of emerging powers and other middle-income countries. Quite simply, the current international development arena is substantially different from the Cold War period yet the governance structures of these banks have not altered. This directly translates into the types of policy adopted by the RDBs and SRDBs. Further research is needed to ascertain the extent to which the absence of meaningful change is a result of a lack of interest by rising powers to alter the status quo, an inability to achieve their preferences (if change is their intention), or stalemate within the RDBs over changing the balance of power at the level of members' voting power. Indeed, this lack of institutional accommodation is the most striking and unexpected finding of this volume.

The contributions in this volume also suggest several lessons for international relations and international organization-specific theories. First, it is clear that the RDBs operate within the same policy domain as the World Bank yet they offer observers unique institutional contexts and the opportunity to better understand the role of organizations. Most of the chapters herein examine the extent to which the banks have adopted policies promoted by external forces such as member states (on anti-corruption, poverty alleviation, gender, the environment) and civil society (on human rights, accountability, and engaging with civil society), and it is clear that how the banks do this varies. Theorizing about global economic governance requires consideration of multiple institutional contexts and lessons from the RDBs add valuable details and nuances to our understanding of IFIs. This volume demonstrates that the AfDB has belatedly taken on the same policies as the World Bank as a result of external material and ideational forces, while the ADB adopted the same policy as the World Bank with regard to anti-corruption as a result of external forces (again material and ideational) but significantly altered the meaning of the concept to suits its regional and institutional context. The IADB has incorporated particular MDGs that fit its institutional approach and the concerns of its major borrowers. Meanwhile, the EBRD acts as an 'organic intellectual' in espousing the dominant international economic ideology for development by carving out its own space as a development actor within its region. It seems to speak in chorus with the World Bank and IMF rather than as a backing vocalist. Excepting the EBRD, it seems as though many of the policies taken up by RDBs come from external forces. However, the banks take certain aspects of these policies and make them their own. For this reason, perhaps, there is less opposition to RDBs than there is to the World Bank. The RDBs and their main regional member states carve out their own space within the dominant economic ideology. This allows them to access resources from the traditional industrialized member states while retaining legitimacy within the region. As scholars continue to examine the cause of IO behavior and change, more can perhaps be done to identify when and how material and ideational factors prompt IO (re)actions, whether there is a sequencing at work of material and ideational factors, or whether it remains useful to delineate causal variables in this way.

In future research on RDBs and SRDBs we need to further probe the extent to which internal forces shape how this policy space and legitimacy is created and maintained. Further analysis should investigate whether the banks' managements are able to shape the interests and preferences of member states and whether staff members are able to influence management. This will provide greater insight into the actual workings of the organizations, which is important since they have different national staffing ratios, as Jonathan Strand and Michael Trevathan point out. Moreover, these banks are frequently spoken of in terms of their different organizational cultures (White 1970; Park 2014). For example, the ADB president is always Japanese, and the ADB is often described as having a Japanese managerial culture (Yasutomo 1983: 93; Pascha 2000). In contrast, the chapter in this volume by Chris Humphrey demonstrates that the culture of the IADB means that while the bank formalizes specific policies, they may not be interpreted as rigidly as in the case with the World Bank. This may reflect a different organizational culture, where culture is defined as a "system of meaning that govern staff expectations and behavior" (Chweiroth 2008: 133). That the IADB has similar policies but fewer internal checks and balances may be not just a resource issue but also an organizational cultural one. In other chapters, such as Stuart Shields', it is patently clear that the EBRD acts as what Shields terms an 'organic intellectual' in promoting neoliberal development in Eastern and Central European states on the basis of a strong adherence to this economic ideology. The organization has been imbued with this ideology since its inception (Bronstone 1999). Meanwhile, Anders Uhlin's chapter shows how the ADB has changed quite significantly in opening itself up to engaging with civil society. In this case, there is very real evidence that the ADB is becoming more transparent as well as allowing civil society to influence its policies and create new organizational structures. This is a substantial shift within the ADB toward greater political liberalization and one that needs to be comparatively examined in relation to the behavior of other RDBs. We encourage scholars to not only pursue more comparative analyses but also investigate further when organizational culture is significant in determining how the banks address external pressures and specific global policy concerns.

Empirically, more research is required on the role of smaller IOs in global economic governance. As explored in Chapter 10, there are MDBs beyond the RDBs. Sub-regional development banks and related IFIs remain largely uncharted in the field of global economic governance. A major gap in the study of international organization and global governance is the lack of attention to SRDBs, a gap that has begun to be filled here. Tina Zappile's chapter demonstrates how the further one gets from the size and universality of the World Bank, the greater is the variation in institutional design. While there are similarities between the World Bank and the rest of the RDBs in terms of governance and the addition of non-economic units within each organization, there are significant differences with how the SRDBs operate. In part this reflects the lean institutional structures of smaller organizations, but it also follows from having regional shareholders that are also the SRDBs' recipients or borrowers. Of course, operating below the radar of donors and being more responsive to the 'end user' also raises questions of trade-offs. As mentioned in chapter 10, this means that while the smaller micro-banks do not have the same 'hassle factors' identified by Chris Humphrey in Chapter 8, they may also not have the same level of technical expertise as the larger banks.

Chris Humphrey's chapter is striking for demonstrating how the increase in non-economic policy conditionalities of the World Bank and IADB reflects the governance structures of these IOs, where the greater share size and voice of traditional industrialized country donors dictate the agenda. This compares to the Development Bank for Latin America (CAF) where the shareholders are also the borrowers, which leads to fewer bureaucratic lending procedures, less red tape, and fewer built-in protection measures (particularly in relation to environmental and social standards but also to fiduciary oversight). The sliding scale, from the World Bank's high degree of protection and borrowing 'hassle', to the still bureaucratic but more flexible IADB, to the minimal oversight of the Development Bank for Latin America, perfectly matches the amount of influence of the traditional industrialized donor countries in these banks. Of particular interest for scholars of international political economy is just how quickly the Development Bank for Latin America is becoming a major avenue of development financing within the region, undercutting and rivaling both the IADB and the World Bank. Whether the CAF will come under pressure from traditional donors to adopt similar non-economic protection policies (such as stronger environmental and social safeguards) remains to be seen. In this instance, there may be competing legitimacy demands on the CAF: to be responsive to its shareholders (who are also its beneficiaries) as well as being held up to international development standards promulgated by organizations like the World Bank driven by traditional donors such as the U.S. and states in Europe.

Regarding the legitimacy of IFIs, international relations scholars can also learn from the RDBs – especially when there is substantial change to the external environment such as the emergence of rising powers or major financial crises. Legitimacy for an IFI is a source of authority (Hurd 2007). A number of questions remain to be answered, however, regarding how IFIs develop different strategies to maintain legitimacy. How do the internal bureaucratic dynamics of an RDB respond to changes to its external environment? Does the creation of new, alternative IFIs complement or undermine the legitimacy of existing IFIs? There is variation in membership and 'great power' activity and influence within different RDBs. Thus, institutional adjustments to rising powers, the adoption of new practices and policy norms, and the maintenance of legitimacy will vary from one RDB to another. Just as we find that RDBs do not parrot the World Bank, we should not assume that RDBs respond in the same way to material and ideational change in world politics.

For example, while it is perfectly clear that all IOs support the Millennium Development Goals, the extent to which IOs will walk the talk or go beyond rhetoric is never clear. In the case of the IADB, although there is no dramatic push to identify projects as addressing these goals, it is clear that the bank endorses the MDGs in its own practice. According to Chapter 4 by Kenny Retzl, this is accounted for by the long history of the IADB in social lending policies, many of which directly address various MDG goals, but is also due to a former IADB president – Enrique Iglesias – taking up social concerns as part of shifting the direction of the institution in the 1980s. It was therefore a legitimate concern for the bank to endorse the MDGs, and current efforts to map social lending to the MDG goals bear this out. Legitimacy is also a concern of the AfDB, as outlined in Chapter 5 by Karen Mingst. In that case, differentiating ideational concerns from material concerns – or gauging the extent to which the bank has been forced to adopt new, non-economic policy concerns or done so out of a belief that it was the right thing to do – is nearly impossible. Quite simply, donors in the AfDB and other multilateral and bilateral lenders had already instituted the same non-economic policy conditionalities elsewhere, to the extent that they had become best practice. Not only did the AfDB have donors wanting the same for the African Bank, it had come to be seen as how international development should be done.

Third, multifaceted explanations are needed for us to understand the complex environment and bureaucratic structures of RDBs. One-dimensional explanations of the politics surrounding RDBs are inadequate. Nuanced understanding arises when rationalist accounts and ideational accounts are used to explain change and resistance within and outside of the RDBs. We take this view in our analysis of variation in the practice of RDBs below, and subsequently examine these practices in light of current theorizations of IO behavior and change.

Variation in RDB policies

To reiterate, the RDBs are truly global institutions, considering where they fit in the corpus of international financial institutions. Although they do not have universal membership like the World Bank, RDBs do have large memberships that include most major powers and many rising powers. In addition, they engage in international development practices and are part of the same policy domain as the World Bank and other multilateral, bilateral, and private lenders. To one degree or another, then, the RDBs are expected to react and contribute to policy and ideological debates. The response by RDBs to changing practices is instructive as there is great variation in the adoption of emerging development 'policy norms' across the institutions (Park and Vetterlein 2010). For example, the AfDB adopted new standards and practices related to environmental concerns as well as gender and development, both of which are donor-driven concerns, yet it lagged significantly behind the World Bank (see Chapter 5). Meanwhile, the ADB's adoption of anti-corruption policies was also a response to evolving ideas and authority in its external environment. It has kept pace with the World Bank in this policy area and, despite its unique regional approach to its engagement with borrowers, has grappled with the same implementation problems as the World Bank (see Chapter 2). Further research is needed to establish why there is policy adaptation variation across similar global institutions. In sum, the RDBs do not simply mirror the World Bank but respond in particular ways to the framing of development practices, sometimes immediately after the World Bank, sometimes a long time after. Sometimes this occurs simultaneously, as in the case of the EBRD. The cases also demonstrate the different ways in which RBDs' environments influence their adoption of policy change: the EBRD as a strong adherent to neoliberal ideology embraced further neoliberalisation in Central and Eastern Europe; the ADB has maintained its commitment to both engaging with civil society and anti-corruption measures. The weaker commitment of the AfDB to non-economic concerns may be due to fewer resources. That all the RDBs are as weak as the World Bank with regard to human rights is perhaps unsurprising given their apolitical technical focus on economic growth.

Global institutions addressing development and development-related policies do not speak with one voice. The World Bank has received overwhelmingly the most attention from scholars and policymakers, but this volume has demonstrated that RDBs and SRDBs also matter in development policy. RDBs are much more diverse than many scholars of global economic governance recognize. Going forward, three themes regarding RDBs will continue to matter. First, RDBs remain resource dependent. This does not necessarily mean they will remain dependent on the United States and other traditional multilateral donors. As discussed at the end of Chapter 7, alternative multilateral organizations are being created by rising powers and it remains to be seen whether the resource-dependent RDBs will gain or lose in this new multi-polar, multilateral environment. The RDBs remain dependent on the resources of their members, as well as dependent on borrowers as customers. The United States and other major donors may well continue to use this resource dependence to exact policy accommodation and governance changes from the RDBs. The number of rising powers within the RDBs, however, raises questions about competition for resources, as China, India, Brazil, and others seek opportunities within existing multilateral institutions. It may be that an increased number of potential donors can attenuate RDB dependence on the United States, Japan, and European contributors. Alternatively, the increased number of major donors could mean that the RDBs have to respond to the disparate interests of more donors. And as Chapter 7 in this volume found in regard to institutional accommodation of rising powers, the World Bank and the RDBs have yet to truly reform their governance systems in a manner that would reflect the importance of these new multilateral donors. Failure of extant IFIs to accommodate rising powers may ultimately undermine the legitimacy of these institutions and lead to the creation of additional competing multilateral forums such as the NDB.

A second theme is the continuation of the importance of institutional legitimacy for both the internal governance of the RDBs and the implementation of their policies. In the post-Washington Consensus era, the legitimacy of the Bretton Woods Institutions and the legacy of the RDBs and SRDBs are in flux. For the RDBs it seems clear that part of their legitimacy rests on their regional identities. AfDB has touted its African characteristics. The ADB has highlighted the uniqueness of the development experiences of Asian economies. The legitimacy of IFIs also derives from how they are viewed and how they view themselves as experts and controllers of esoteric information. The RDBs use their regional characteristics to filter, identify, and classify problems in development, as prominently articulated in Stuart Shields' chapter on the EBRD. Regional identity informs how the RDBs do such things as engage with civil society, identify policy areas for projects, and institutionalize policy norms. In other words, regionalism is a symbolic component of their existence and constitutes a source of authority for the RDBs. For RDBs to simply copy the World Bank would undermine their legitimacy. In fact, looking at RDBs as global institutions with a regional flavor we see that their legitimacy is in part a function of their differentiation from the Bretton Woods institutions. There is also a social function for legitimacy in the RDBs when they engage with civil society actors. More needs to be done to distinguish different types of legitimacy, the subject of Tina Zappile's chapter.

A last theme is the continuous policy and ideational changes to the development policy domain. The environment within which each RDB operates is not static. RDBs can be viewed as reflecting unique acculturations of development policy ideas. Adoption of policy norms, such as anti-corruption, is neither universal nor uniform across development organizations, as is made clear by the contributions in this volume. The question becomes: Why do different institutional settings adopt policy norms differently? What explains the variation? To what extent do policies take on a life of their own and result in policy inertia and a status quo bias? The main actors exhibiting authority within the RDBs are often the governments with influence in other global institutions (e.g. G20), as well as the bureaucracies, each with their own incentives. Together, these factors contribute to unique organizational cultures that filter, change, and implement ideas from outside the organization. The RDBs, like other bureaucratic organizations, change gradually and can be insular in the face of shifting global norms and changes in material power relations among actors.

Conclusion

Global economic governance is an emerging area of expertise for scholars and policymakers. Over the next several decades, new influential actors will emerge as key players in the governance of economic relations. Longstanding great powers are likely to resist attempts by emerging powers to alter the status quo within IFIs. Nevertheless, emerging powers will not only add additional resources to development policy endeavors but, more importantly, contribute new ideas and adjustments to existing norms. More work will need to be done on the relationship between RDBs and private actors/civil society organizations. There is also room for more attention to be paid to the relationships between IOs. Going forward, we can identify several areas for future research. First, the bureaucratic cultures of the RDBs and SRDBs need to be more fully examined. Bureaucratic and organizational cultures impact on the ways that IFIs incorporate new policies, engage in the maintenance of legitimacy, and obtain some degree of autonomy from their members. But as the major RDBs differ greatly in their organizational culture, staffing policies and leadership selection, we need to develop a more nuanced understanding of the particular features of each RDB.

A second area for future research focuses on changes to lending practices due to recent interaction with civil society actors. Cross-institutional comparisons of, for example, the adoption of gender and development policies will improve our understanding of how forces outside of the RDBs affect policymaking. Relatedly, the effect upon civil society actors of interacting with IOs needs to be explored if we are to learn how civil society is changing in response to engagement with RDBs and other IOs.

Lastly, we invite future research to continue working with the concept-driven approach that this volume has adopted. Evidence from the chapters indicates that no single theory has a monopoly on explaining the internal and external politics of RDBs. Theoretical and methodological pluralism is essential to understand the position of RDBs and SRDBs in debates about how global economic governance should be organized and which paradigms dominate. This is especially true when considering the establishment of new IOs and continued debates about reforming existing IOs.

References

Ascher, W. 1992. "The World Bank and U.S. Control." In *The United States and Multilateral Institutions: Patterns of Changing Instrumentality and Influence*, edited by M. Karns and K. Mingst. London: Routledge, pp. 115–139.

Bronstone, A. 1999. *The European Bank for Reconstruction and Development: The Building of a Bank for East Central Europe.* Manchester: Manchester University Press.

Chwieroth, J. M. 2008. "Normative Change From Within: The International Monetary Fund's Approach to Capital Account Liberalization." *International Studies Quarterly* 52(1): 129–158.

Hawkins, D., D. Lake, D. Nielson and M. Tierney (eds). 2006. *Delegation and Agency in International Organizations.* Cambridge: Cambridge University Press.

Hurd, I. 2007. *After Anarchy: Legitimacy and Power in the United Nations Security Council.* Princeton, NJ: Princeton University Press.

Jokinen, J. 2004. "Balancing between East and West: The Asian Development Bank's Policy on Good Governance." In *Global Institutions and Development: Framing the World?* edited by M. Bøås. London: Routledge, pp. 137–150.

Mingst, K. 1990. *Politics and the African Development Bank.* Lexington, KY: University Press of Kentucky.

Park, S. 2014. "Institutional Isomorphism and the Asian Development Bank's Accountability Mechanism: Something Old, Something New; Something Borrowed, Something Blue?" *Pacific Review* 27(2): 217–239.

Park, S. and A. Vetterlein. 2010. *Owning Development: Creating Global Policy Norms in the IMF and the World Bank.* Cambridge: Cambridge University Press.

Pascha, W. 2000. "Asian Development Bank in the Context of Rapid Regional Development." In *Economic Globalization, International Organizations and Crisis Management,* edited by R. Tilly and P. J. J. Welfens. Berlin: Springer-Verlag, pp. 155–183.

Wade, R. 1996. "Japan, the World Bank, and the Art of Paradigm Maintenance." *New Left Review* 217 (May/June): 3–36.

Weaver, C. 2008. *The Hypocrisy Trap: The World Bank and the Poverty of Reform.* Princeton, NJ: Princeton University Press.

White, J. 1970. *Regional Development Banks: A Study of Institutional Style.* London: Overseas Development Institute.

Woods, N. 2003. "The United States and the International Financial Institutions." In *U.S. Hegemony and International Organizations,* edited by R. Foot, N. MacFarlane and M. Mastanduno. Oxford: Oxford University Press, pp. 92–114.

Yasutomo, D. T. 1983. *Japan and the Asian Development Bank.* New York: Praeger.

Index

A Better World for All 42
accountability 12, 16–17, 21, 30, 60–2; civil society 64, 75–6; contemporary role 215–16; human rights 112; partnerships 81, 84–6, 89; sub-regions 193, 199–200, 203, 207
accountability mechanism (AM) 61–2, 64–8, 73, 76, 100; contemporary role 214; human rights 107, 112–13; sub-regions 188–9, 193–5, 199–201, 206, 208
accumulation 169–70, 175, 179
Africa 4–5, 15, 80–3, 86, 90–6; Advisory Council 89; *Africa in 50 Years' Time* 93; *African Development Report* 89; *African Statistical Journal* 94; Charter of Human and People's Rights 109; contemporary role 215, 221; Development Facility 16; human rights 106, 108; Information Highway 94; Infrastructure Knowledge Program 94; post-communist transition 167, 171, 179–80; power relations 130, 133; Smart Manifesto 93; Symposium on Statistical Development 94; Water Facility 94
Africa China Growing Together (AFCT) 135
African Development Bank (AfDB) 3–5, 8, 13, 15–16, 80–98; contemporary role 214–16, 219–21; human rights 99, 101, 104–5, 107, 109, 111, 113; power relations 126, 129–31, 133–6; sub-regions 190–1, 199, 203
African Development Fund (AfDF) 9, 81
African Guarantee Fund (AGF) 95
African Union 92–4
Africanicity 80–3

agenda-setting 23, 25, 62, 87, 89; contemporary role 218; human rights 104; post-communist transition 176; power relations 124; role comparison 91–3; sub-regions 188
Agreement Establishing the African Development Bank 89
Aid Transparency Index 203
AidData 203
Algeria 81
Amazon 83
ambivalent engagement 99–118
Andean Development Corporation (CAF) 17, 144, 149–50, 152, 154; borrower demand 156–61; contemporary role 218; sub-regions 187–8, 191, 194–5, 198, 200, 205, 207
Anticorruption Unit 31
Arab Spring 167
Argentina 40, 132, 159
Armenia 130
Article 19, 69
Asia 4–5, 11, 16, 21–2, 25–31; borrower demand 158; civil society 60, 64, 73; corruption 33–4; financial crisis 121, 212; Monetary Fund 121–2; power relations 138
Asian Development Bank (ADB) 3–4, 13–16, 21 38, 84, 99; civil society 60–79; contemporary role 212–13, 215–17, 220–1; human rights 101, 105–6, 109–13; power relations 126, 130–1, 134–5, 138; sub-regions 190, 199, 203, 208
Asian Development Facility (ADF) 8, 23–4
Asian Development Fund (ADF) 22
Asian Infrastructure Investment Bank (AIIB) 11, 14, 138–9

Index 225

Asian NGO Coalition (ANGOC) 63
Association of Southeast Asian Nations (ASEAN) 123
attributed influence 63, 66, 75
audits 31, 200
Aureos Capital 95
austerity 172
Australia 64, 134, 138
Austria 40
autonomy 91–6, 193–4, 198, 200, 222

Babb, S. 81
balance of payments 3
Bangladesh 73
Bank Information Center (BIC) 66, 69, 108
Bank of Japan 135
Bank of Latin America (CAF) 17, 144, 149–50, 152, 154; borrower demand 156–61; contemporary role 218; sub-regions 187–8, 191, 194–5, 198, 200, 205–7
base-superstructure model 170
BASIC countries 123
Belgium 40
Berglof, E. 177
Berlin Wall 174
Beschel, R.P. 30–1
best practice 15, 95, 124, 189, 198, 203, 208, 215
bilateral assistance 9, 12–13, 94, 121, 144, 159, 215, 219–20
Black Sea Trade and Development Bank (BSTDB) 188–9, 191, 200, 206–7
boards 15, 24–5, 30, 32, 66–70; borrower demand 147–9, 153, 156–7; civil society 73, 75; human rights 106–7, 112–13; post-communist transition 167; power relations 121–2, 126–7, 133–7; role comparison 84; sub-regions 195
Bøås, A. 90
Bolivia 40, 48
bonds 8
borrower demand 143–66, 194, 215, 218
Botswana 130
bourgeoisie 172, 178
Braaten, D. 16, 99–118
Brazil 7, 11, 14, 40, 48; borrower demand 144, 148, 159; contemporary role 215, 221; power relations 122–3, 125, 129, 131–7; role comparison 91, 95

Bretton Woods Institutions 3, 121–2, 125, 127, 137, 221
bribery 26
BRICS countries 11, 13–14, 16, 122–4, 126; borrower demand 161; contemporary role 216; power relations 130, 133–9
BRICSAM countries 123
broadband technology 93
brokers 80–98
Bronstone, A. 173
Brown, L.D. 62
Brunei 130
bureaucracy 6, 12–13, 24, 26, 61; borrower demand 144–5, 148–9, 158, 160; contemporary role 214, 218–19, 221–2; post-communist transition 178; power relations 134; role comparison 83–4, 87, 90
Burma 73

Cambodia 73
Campos, J.E. 27
Canada 40, 95, 132–3
capacity building 21, 26, 30, 88, 90; human rights 105; post-communist transition 175; power relations 135; role comparison 92–6
capital flight 11
capital-to-lending ratio 8
capitalism 76, 169–70, 172, 180
Caribbean 4, 14, 106, 158
Caribbean Development Bank (CDB) 3, 187–91, 195, 204, 207–8
Carroll, T. 176, 179
Carter, J. 41
CCE Bankwatch Network 102
Center for Global Development (CDB) 187, 205
Central African States Development Bank (CASB) 188, 207
Central African States Development Bank of the Central Africa Economic and Monetary Community (CEMAC) 191
Central American Bank for Economic Integration (CABEI) 188, 195, 207
Central and Eastern Europe *see* Eastern and Central Europe
Chad-Cameroon Petroleum and Pipeline Project 112
Chakrabarti, S. 138, 167
Chasma Right Bank Irrigation Project 66
Chile 40, 149

226 *Index*

China 7, 9, 11, 14, 25; borrower demand 144; civil society 69; contemporary role 215–16, 221; corruption 28, 33; poverty 40; power relations 121–5, 127, 129–39; role comparison 91, 95; sub-regions 198
China-IIC SME Equity Investment Trust Fund 135
CIVETS countries 123
civil rights 100–2, 112
civil society 6–7, 11–13, 15–16, 27, 29; borrower demand 156; contemporary role 214–17, 220–2; partnerships 80, 83, 85–6, 88, 95–6; policy reforms 60–79; post-communist transition 170, 172, 175; poverty 48; power relations 135; sub-regions 188–9, 192–5, 201–3, 205, 207–8
Civil Society Coalition on the African Development Bank 86
Civil Society Engagement Framework 86
civil society organizations (CSOs) 60–80, 84–6, 89–90, 95, 110, 112
class structure 168–72, 176, 180
climate change 10, 85
ClimDev-Africa Programme Special Fund 9
coercion 170
Cold War 4, 27, 40, 80, 102, 121, 126–7, 172, 212, 216
Colombia 40, 55, 123, 135
colonialism 81
Comité de Negocios Corporatives 149
Comité de Préstamos e Inversiones 149
Committee on Environmental and Social Impact (CESI) 151, 153
Common Market for Eastern and Southern Africa 92
common sense 17, 167–86
Commonwealth Human Rights Initiative 69
communism 5, 167–86
comparative advantage 25, 49, 189, 193, 195
compensation 101, 109, 152–4
competitiveness 168, 173, 175–7, 179–80
complex principal concept 144–5, 168
Compliance Advisors 68
Compliance Review Function 113
Compliance Review Panel (CRP) 67, 113
conditionalities 9, 16, 81–2, 89, 146, 171, 214, 218–19
Congress 40, 84, 128, 154, 156–7
Congress for Cultural Freedom 172

Connect Africa Summit 93
Connecting Africa 93
consensus 17, 25, 33, 76, 90, 107, 148, 160, 171
consent 10, 74, 169–70, 172, 175
constructivism 6, 22–4, 61, 144, 168
Contingent Reserve Arrangement (CRA) 137
Contract Watch 90
Convention on the Rights of the Child 100
Copelovitch, M. 144
Corporate Scorecard 147
corruption 16, 21–38, 89–90, 198, 214–16, 220–1
Cost of Doing Business Task Force 158–9
Costa Rica 40
Council of Europe 102
Country Assistance Strategy (CAS) 203
country partnership strategies (CS) 24
Country Safeguard Systems 74
Country Strategy Papers 85
Cox, R.W. 44, 168, 171
Credit Guarantee and Investment Facility 135
Croatia 40
cronyism 29
Cuban Revolution 41
Culpeper, R. 49
currency devaluation 11

debt 8, 42, 44, 82, 104, 143, 203
Decade for Women 87
Declaration on the Rights of Indigenous Peoples 74
deforestation 83
democracy 17, 27, 30, 49, 60–1; civil society 63–4, 68; human rights 101–2; post-communist transition 167, 174, 177–8; role comparison 89; sub-regions 188, 191, 198, 206–7
Denmark 40, 95
Department Impact Evaluation Initiative (DIME) 206
developing countries 3, 7–9, 11, 13–14, 44; borrower demand 143; civil society 67; contemporary role 212; human rights 107; power relations 122, 124–5, 135; sub-regions 199, 208
developing member countries (DMCs) 21, 25, 28, 30, 32, 34
development aid 83–91, 187–211
Development Assistance Committee (DAC) 42

Index 227

Development Bank for Latin America *see* Bank of Latin America
Development Bank of Southern Africa (DBSA) 191
Development Effectiveness Review 90, 92–3
development practices 3–20
Disclosure and Access to Information Policy 86, 203
dispute resolution mechanisms 153
Division of Social Protection and Health 45
Doing Business 171
Dominican Republic 40
donor leverage 23, 28–30, 33–4, 68, 72; borrower demand 149, 155, 158, 160–1; contemporary role 215–16, 218–21; partnerships 82–3, 89–91, 95–6; sub-regions 198–9

East African Community 92
East African Development Bank (EADB) 188, 190, 194–5
East Asia 158
East Asian Paradox 27
Eastern and Central Europe (ECE) 17, 102, 167–9, 171, 173–80, 217, 220
Eastern and Southern African Trade and Development Bank 188
Economic Commission for Africa 94
Economic Commission for Latin America and the Caribbean (ECLAC) 54
Economic Community of West African States (ECOWAS) 91–2
Economic Development Institute 31
Economic and Monetary Community of Central African States 92
economism 170
Ecuador 40
Egypt 81, 123
El Salvador 40
elites 7, 168, 171
English, F.P. 83
English language 67, 200
entrepreneurship 93, 102, 167, 172, 175–6
environment 8, 12, 16, 29, 48; borrower demand 145–6, 148–54, 156, 158–61; civil society 61, 64, 72, 74, 80; contemporary role 214, 216, 218, 220; human rights 104–7, 109–13; post-communist transition 173; poverty 42–4; power relations 128; role comparison 83; sub-regions 188, 192, 201, 203, 207

Environment and Sustainable Development Unit 84
Environmental Policy Institute 63
Epstein, R.A. 168
ethics 21, 200
ethnicity 45–6, 101
Eurasian Development Bank (EDB) 188, 207
Europe 15, 17, 40, 64, 73; borrower demand 148, 154–7; contemporary role 218, 220–1; human rights 102; post-communist transition 17, 167–9, 171–80, 217; power relations 122, 127, 132–3; role comparison 86
European Bank for Reconstruction and Development (EBRD) 3–4, 7, 13, 15, 17; contemporary role 214–17, 220; human rights 99, 101–3, 106, 110, 113; post-communist transition 167–86; power relations 126, 138; sub-regions 190, 199
European Commission 167
European Convention on Human Rights 102
European Investment Bank (EIB) 167, 178, 190
European Stability Mechanism (ESM) 122
European Union (EU) 125, 175
evaluation 205–7
Ex-Post Evaluation Unity (UEE) 205
explicit political orientation 167

Feinberg, R.E. 56
feminism 87
financial crises 3, 8, 11, 16, 22; contemporary role 212, 219; corruption 26, 28–30, 33–4; post-communist transition 168, 172, 177–80; power relations 121–4, 137
Financial Fund for the Development of the River Plate Basin (FONPLATA) 188, 207
Financial Stability Board 3
Fine, B. 176
Finland 40, 133
Finnemore, M. 23, 44
Focus on the Global South 69
followers 80–98
Fordwor, K.D. 81
foreign policy 6
Forest People's Program (FPP) 109
Fox, J.A. 62
Fragile State Facility (FSF) 104–5, 107

Fragile States Initiatives 85–6, 88, 104
France 40, 134, 138, 147, 154
fraud 31–2
Friedman, E.J. 62
Friends of the Earth 63
Fukudu-Parr, S. 39, 44
Fund for Special Operations (FSO) 8–9
future research 180, 188, 208, 214, 216–20, 222

G7 144–5, 148, 156–7
G20 3, 122, 221
G77 124
Gates Foundation 95
gender 8, 10–12, 16, 29, 42–6; civil society 64, 75; contemporary role 214–16, 220, 222; human rights 101, 104–6, 108, 110–11; partnerships 86–8; poverty 48; role comparison 80, 90, 96
gender and development (GAD) 87
Gender and Development Group 87
Gender and Diversity Fund 106
Gender Mainstreaming Strategy 87
The Gender Policy 88
Gender and Social Development Monitoring Division 88
General Assembly 123
general capital increases (GCIs) 8, 23–4
Georgia 130
Germany 40, 85, 95, 138, 154, 198
global economic governance 3–20
Global Environment Facility 85
Global Program on Forced Displacement and Regional Centers of Excellence in Social Development 104
globalization 13, 104, 215
governance 45, 49, 60–2, 64, 80; borrower demand 144–6, 148, 154, 156, 159–61; civil society 68, 72, 76; contemporary role 212–16, 218, 220–2; human rights 105, 111; partnerships 88–91, 96; post-communist transition 168, 171, 175; power relations 122, 124–6, 128, 133–9; subregions 188–9, 191–3, 195–9, 206–7
Governance Action Plan 31
Governance and Anticorruption Action Plan (GACAP) 32
Gramsci, A. 7, 9, 61, 167–72, 175–6, 178
Green Growth Knowledge Platform 94
gross domestic product (GDP) 94, 143
Guatemala 40, 48
Gutner, T. 144
Guyana 48

Haiti 40
Harmonized Consumer Price Index 94
Harrison, B. 40
hassle factors 143–66, 218
Health in Africa Fund 95
hegemony 7, 61, 167–72, 180, 213
Helping Countries Combat Corruption 27–8
Herrera, F. 54
HIV/AIDS 10, 43, 82
Honduras 40, 46, 48
House of Representatives 40
HSBC 123
Hulme, D. 39, 44
Human Development Report 42
human rights 11, 16, 30, 89, 99–118, 215–16, 220
Humphrey, C. 16–17, 136, 143–66, 194, 200, 214–15, 217–18
hunger 43, 45

identity 6, 23, 88, 111, 126, 221
ideology 10, 23, 25, 137, 168–74, 178–80, 216–17, 220
Iglesias, E. 16, 49, 54–6, 219
Independent Evaluation Group (IEG) 206
Independent Inspection Panel 84
Independent Review Mechanism 86
India 7, 11, 14, 25, 33; civil society 69, 73; contemporary role 215, 221; power relations 122–3, 125, 129–30, 133–8; role comparison 91, 95
Indigenous populations 46, 48, 61, 72, 74; borrower demand 154; human rights 101, 106–11, 114
Indonesia 11, 28–9, 33, 123, 144
Indonesian language 73
Information Policy and Strategy 69
infrastructure 5, 25, 34, 41, 49; borrower demand 152, 159, 161; civil society 76; human rights 101, 103–4, 107, 111; post-communist transition 173; poverty 54; power relations 137–8; role comparison 85, 92
Infrastructure Consortium for Africa 92
Infrastructure Project Preparation Facility 92
innovation 80, 91, 93–4, 172
Inspection Committees 67
Inspection Functions 66
Inspection Panels 66–8, 85–6
Institutional Capacity Strengthening Thematic Fund (ICSF) 135

Index   229

institutional change 87, 121–2, 126–33, 136, 138; contemporary role 212, 216, 219; post-communist transition 168–9, 171, 173–7, 179–80; sub-regions 187
institutional culture *see* organizational culture
Integrated Safeguards System (ISS) 109
Integrity Principles and Guidelines (IPG) 31
Inter-American Development Bank (IADB) 3–5, 8–9, 13–16, 24–5, 39–59; borrower demand 144, 148–61; contemporary role 214–19; human rights 99, 101, 106, 110–11, 113; power relations 126–7, 131–5; role comparison 84; sub-regions 190–1, 195, 199, 203
Interdepartmental MDG Group 45
interest rates 8, 161
intergovernmental organizations (IGOs) 80
Internal Evaluation Group (IEG) 154, 158
International Aid Transparency Initiative (IATI) 203
International Bank for Reconstruction and Development (IBRD) 104, 159, 205
international community 10–11, 23, 39, 46, 80, 83, 176
International Comparison Program for Africa 94
International Convention on the Elimination of Discrimination Against Women 100
International Covenant on Civil and Political Rights (ICPSR) 99
International Covenant on Economic, Social and Cultural Rights (ICESCR) 99–100, 106
International Development Association (IDA) 8, 23, 84, 104, 205
International Development Goals (IDGs) 42
International Finance Corporation 68, 95, 110, 206
international financial institutions (IFIs) 3, 7–9, 11, 66, 68; contemporary role 215–16, 218–19, 221–2; human rights 111; post-communist transition 176–8; role comparison 82; sub-regions 193
international law 99
International Monetary Fund (IMF) 3, 6–7, 10–11, 13, 27; borrower demand 143; contemporary role 212–13, 216–17; post-communist transition 171, 173; poverty 42; power relations 121–2, 124–8, 134, 137; role comparison 85, 88; sub-regions 189
international organizations (IOs) 3, 6, 8, 11–12, 14–15; borrower demand 144; civil society 60–79; contemporary role 212–13, 215–19, 222; corruption 22, 24, 26–7, 33–4; partnerships 80; poverty 42, 56; power relations 121–4, 126–33, 138–9; sub-regions 188–9, 194
international relations 216, 218
International Rivers Network 66
Involuntary Resettlement Policy 72, 74, 99, 106–12, 114, 150, 152–4
Ireland 130
Islamic Development Bank 190
Israel 40
Italy 40

Japan 9, 15, 24–5, 40, 64; borrower demand 147, 157; contemporary role 217, 221; power relations 121–2, 125, 127, 129–30, 132, 134–5; sub-regions 198
Japan Special Fund 9

Keck, M.E. 62
key officers 24–6, 126–7, 134–5
Kim, J.Y. 109
knowledge hubs 93–4
Knox Report 82
Komori, Y. 16, 21–38
Kuroda, H. 134

Laos 73
Latin America 4–5, 13–15, 39–41, 46, 54, 56–7, 106, 143–66
legitimacy 5–12, 17, 21–3, 33–4, 44–5; civil society 60, 76; contemporary role 212–13, 215, 217–19, 221–2; post-communist transition 169–70, 172; power relations 121–2, 124, 128, 138; role comparison 80, 82–3, 91, 96; sub-regions 187–90, 193–5, 198–203, 205, 207–8
liberalization 21
Liberia 82
Libya 81
Loan Committee 153
loan pricing 146
loan-processing time 145–9, 159
Lyne, M.M. 103–4, 107, 144–5

McKeon, N. 62
macroeconomics 90, 143, 176
Malaysia 11, 28
Marshall Plan 173
Masinloc power plant 63–4
Mauro, P. 27
media 67, 73
Medium-Term Strategy Framework (MTSF) 30
membership structure 195–9, 207–8, 219–20
Mexico 40, 48, 54, 72, 123, 132, 144, 157
Michaelowa, K. 145
Middle East and North Africa (MENA) 167, 171, 179–80
middle-income countries (MICs) 14, 144, 155, 161, 208, 214, 216
military 60, 173
Millennium Development Goals (MDGs) 11, 16, 39–59, 92, 105, 214–16, 219
Millennium Summit 41
Mingst, K. 16, 80–98, 105, 219
MINT countries 123
Moreno, L.A. 54, 135
Moving Transition Forward 176
Mule, H.M. 83
Multi-donor Partnership Program 95
multilateral development banks (MDBs) 3–20, 22–5, 33, 61, 203–4; civil society 66, 68–9, 76; contemporary role 213, 218; hassle factor 143–66; human rights 99–118; partnerships 81, 86, 92; power relations 127–8, 133; sub-regions 187, 190, 194, 203, 207–8
Multilateral Investment Guarantee Agency 68, 206
Multilateral Organisation Performance Assessment Network (MOPAN) 187
Murphy, C. 168

Nakao, T. 134
nationalism 5
neo-Gramscianism *see* Gramsci
neoliberalism 13, 17, 26, 29, 42; civil society 61, 76; contemporary role 214, 217, 220; post-communist transition 167–86; power relations 136
Nepal 134
Netherlands 40, 95, 147
New Development Bank (NDB) 11, 14, 91, 137–9, 221
New International Economic Order (NIEO) 124
New Partnership for Africa's Development (NEPAD) 92, 94, 104
New Vision 88, 91
Nicaragua 40, 46
Nigeria 81, 123, 129
non-governmental organizations (NGOs) 27, 30, 62–4, 66, 69; borrower demand 151, 153–4, 156, 160; human rights 102, 107–11; NGO Forum on ADB 64, 66, 69, 72–5; NGO Working Group on ADB 63–4; partnerships 85; role comparison 84; sub-regions 201, 208
Nordic Fund 190
Nordics *see* Scandinavia
norm diffusion 23, 27, 34, 39, 44; contemporary role 214, 219–22; post-communist transition 174; power relations 121, 124, 127; sub-regions 199, 207–8
North Africa 167, 171, 179–80
North America 73, 157
North American Development Bank 188, 190–1
North American Free Trade Agreement (NAFTA) 190–1
Northwestern University 29
Norway 40

Office of Anticorruption and Integrity (OAI) 31
Office of the Auditor General (OAG) 31
official development assistance (ODA) 4, 44
oligarchy 174
Ombudsmen 68
Open Society Foundation 86
Operational Directives 84
Operational Manual Statement (OMS) 86
Operations Policy Division 157
organic intellectuals 167–86, 216–17
Organization of American States (OAS) 27, 56, 133
Organization of Economic Cooperation and Development (OECD) 27, 42, 122, 136, 138, 143
organizational culture 6–7, 13, 22–6, 33–4, 76; autonomy 91–6; borrower demand 143, 156; contemporary role 217–18, 221–2; human rights 113; partnerships 81, 83–4, 87; post-communist transition 172; power relations 126

Index   231

Ortíz Mena, A. 54
Oxfam 66, 86

Pacific 14, 21, 25, 31, 158
Pacific Islands Development Bank (PIDB) 187–91, 205, 207
Pakistan 33, 66, 73
Pan-African University 93
Pan-American Conference 40
Panama 40
Paraguay 40, 46
Park, S. 3–20, 76, 83, 188, 193, 212–23
partnerships 80–98
Pelosi Amendment 128
pension funds 95
performance evaluation 205–6, 208
Peru 40
petit bourgeoisie 178
petrodollars 121
Philippines 33, 63–4, 134
pluralism 7, 89, 102, 167, 222
Policy on Confidentiality and Disclosure of Information 69
policy variation 24–6, 31–3, 60–79, 219–22
political economy 4, 7, 10–12, 15–16, 27; contemporary role 212, 214–19; political mandates 102, 167, 173–4, 179; post-communist transition 171–2, 174, 180; power relations 133
Portugal 40
post-communist transition 167–86
Post-Washington Consensus 3, 12–13, 17, 179, 221
poverty 8, 11–12, 25, 34, 64; alleviation 39–59; civil society 70; contemporary role 214, 216; human rights 100, 103–6
Poverty Reduction 49
Poverty Reduction Strategy Papers (PRSP) 85, 203
power relations 7–9, 11–13, 15–16, 60, 121–42; borrower demand 143–4, 160; contemporary role 216, 222; post-communist transition 168–70, 179–80; sub-regions 199, 208
Pradhan, S. 27
preference attainment 63, 66, 73, 75
presidents 15–16, 25, 27, 30, 39–40; borrower demand 149; civil society 72–3; contemporary role 217, 219; human rights 109–10; post-communist transition 167; poverty 49, 54, 56–7; power relations 127–8, 134–5, 137; role comparison 81–2, 89, 93; sub-regions 195

Principal-Agent (P-A) model 6, 10, 144, 194, 198
private sector 9–10, 13, 28, 31, 44; civil society 67–8, 70, 72–3; human rights 105; partnerships 80–1, 90–1, 93, 95; post-communist transition 167, 173, 175, 178–80; poverty 54; power relations 138
privatization 167, 173, 175, 178
Problem Solving Function 112–13
process-tracing 63, 66, 69, 73, 75
procurement rules 145–7, 157–8, 160–1
profit 179
project evaluation 205–7
property rights 88, 105
PTA Bank of Common Market for Eastern and Southern Africa (COMESA) 188, 191, 195
public communication policy (PCP) 61–2, 68–73, 76
Public Disclosure Advisory Committee (PDAC) 72
public sector 21, 28, 31–2, 54, 89, 93, 167, 179
public-private partnerships 92, 95
Publish What You Fund 203

race 46
rationalism 6, 10, 144, 174, 194, 219
realism 143–4
recessions 122, 173
Regional Bureau for Africa 94
Regional Cooperation and Poverty Reduction Fund 135
regional development banks (RDBs) 3–12, 23–4, 26, 34, 39–41; borrower demand 159; civil society 61–2, 68–9; contemporary role 212–23; human rights 99, 101, 103, 112–13; partnerships 80, 84, 93–4; political economy 214–19; post-communist transition 167–8, 171–2; power relations 121–42; project lending 14–15; shifting role 12–14; sub-regions 187–91, 193, 198–9, 201, 203, 205–8
Regional Integration Strategy 92
Regional Safeguards Advisor (RSA) 151
regionalism 14, 49, 91–3, 96, 126, 187–211, 213–14, 221
remittances 94–5
rent-seeking 174

Report of the Task Force on Improving Project Quality 30
repression 100, 102
Resettlement Committees 153
Resident Missions (RMs) 32
resource dependence 5–12, 17, 22–4, 33, 91; contemporary role 212–13, 215–17, 220; power relations 121–2, 136; sub-regions 187, 190, 194, 198
Retzl, K. 16, 39–59, 219
Review Paper of Safeguard Policy Statement 73
Rich, B. 84
rising powers 121–42, 215–16, 219–21
Russia 11, 14, 122–3, 125–7, 136–7, 191, 215
Russian language 73
Rwanda 82, 93

safeguard policy 61–2, 72–6, 84–6, 99–100, 103; borrower demand 145–60; contemporary role 214, 218; human rights 106–14
Safeguard Policy Statement (SPS) 73, 109–10
Samut Prakarn Wastewater Management Project 66–7
Sarfaty, G. 113–14
Sato, M. 30
Saudi Arabia 121
scandals 29
Scandinavia 133, 147, 154, 156
Schlemmer-Schulte, S. 112
Secretary General 44
Security Council 121
Senate 40
shareholders 10, 15, 23–5, 28, 128–9; borrower demand 144–5, 148–50, 154–7, 159–60; contemporary role 215, 218
Sherk, D. 83
Shields, S. 17, 126, 167–86, 217, 221
shock therapy 173–5
Sikkink, K. 44, 62
Simmons, B.A. 44
Slovenia 40
small and medium-sized enterprises (SMEs) 95, 173, 178–9
social development 39, 41–2, 46, 49, 54; borrower demand 145–6, 148–54, 158–9, 161; contemporary role 214, 218–19; human rights 99–100, 103–7, 114; post-communist transition 169, 173; poverty 56

Social Protection Index 105
Socio-Economic Division 84
sociology 144
Somalia 82
South 69, 123–4, 135
South Africa 7, 11, 14, 72, 122–3; contemporary role 215; power relations 125, 130, 133–4, 136–7; sub-regions 191
South Asia 158
South Korea 11, 29, 40, 125, 130–2, 135, 138
Southeast Asia 135
Southern African Development Community 92
sovereign development banks (SDBs) 191
sovereign wealth funds 95, 191
Soviet Union 40, 127, 167, 178
Spain 40, 95
Spanish language 149
special funds 9, 127–8, 133, 135
Special Project Facilitator (SPF) 67–8, 113
Sri Lanka 66
state-owned enterprises (SOEs) 178
Statistical Business Registration 94
Stiglitz, J. 176
Strand, J.R. 3–20, 81, 121–42, 188, 193, 212–23
Structural Adjustment Programs (SAPs) 5, 42, 89, 99, 178
sub-regional development banks (SRDBs) 3, 5, 11, 15, 187–212; contemporary role 213–16, 218, 220–2; governance 17; role comparison 80
sub-Saharan Africa 94
Sub-Saharan Africa: From Crisis to Sustainable Growth 89
super-norms 44, 46, 56
surveillance 82, 177
sustainability 43–4, 64, 80, 83–5, 88; human rights 104–6, 110; role comparison 96; sub-regions 201
Sweden 40
Switzerland 40

Taiwan 121, 127, 134
Task Force on Project Quality 82
taxes 90, 95
Taylor, I. 168, 171
technocracy 176, 179, 215
Thailand 11, 29, 66, 73
theoretical framework 22–4
there is no alternative (TINA) 9

Index 233

Transforming Africa Conference 93
Transition Report 171, 174, 177
transitology 169, 174–9
transparency 17, 21, 30, 60–1, 67–8; civil society 68–70, 72–3, 75–6; contemporary role 217; partnerships 84–6, 89; post-communist transition 178; sub-regions 188, 192–4, 199, 203–8
Transparency International 27
trench system 168
Trevathan, M. 11, 16, 121–42, 216–17
Turkey 123, 125, 144
Tussie, D. 49, 54, 56

Uhlin, A. 16, 60–79, 217
United Kingdom (UK) 40, 69, 154, 173
United Nations Development Programme (UNDP) 42, 87, 94
United Nations (UN) 8, 27, 41–4, 56, 74; civil society 62; human rights 109; power relations 121, 123–4, 134; role comparison 85, 87–8, 94; sub-regions 187
United States (US) 5–6, 23–4, 28, 40, 56; borrower demand 144–5, 147–8, 154–7, 160; civil society 63–4, 69; contemporary role 213, 218, 220–1; human rights 111; partnerships 90; post-communist transition 173; power relations 122–3, 125–6, 128–38; role comparison 81, 83–4, 86; sub-regions 198; Treasury 84, 156
Uruguay 40, 54

Venezuela 40, 46, 48, 133
Vestergard, J. 126
veto power 126–7, 157, 160
Vetterlein, A. 83
vice-presidents 127, 134–5, 148–9
video conferencing 148
Vienna Initiative 178
Vietnam 73, 123
voluntary sector 13
voting shares 25, 40, 121–2, 125–30, 132–3; contemporary role 215–16; power relations 135–6; sub-regions 198–9

Wade, R.H. 126

Wapenhans Report 30
Washington Consensus 17, 89
Weaver, C. 84, 87
Weber, M. 170
Wei, S.-J. 27
West 5, 22, 28, 33, 66; borrower demand 161; civil society 68–9, 75; contemporary role 215; human rights 107; post-communist transition 173–4; role comparison 81, 94
West African Development Bank (BOAD) 188, 191, 194–5
West African Economic and Monetary Union 91–2
West African Monetary Union (WAMU) 191
West African Monetary Zone 92
Western Europe 86
whistleblowers 200
Winters, J. 29
Wolfensohn, J. 27
Wolfowitz, P. 89
Women in Development (WiD) 86–8
World Bank 3–17, 21, 23–7, 80–96, 99; borrower demand 144–61; civil society 62, 66, 68–9, 72; contemporary role 212–21; corruption 28–31, 33–4; human rights 101, 103–4, 107–10, 112–14; post-communist transition 168, 171, 173, 176, 178; poverty 41–2, 44, 56; power relations 121–2, 124–8, 133–4, 136–7, 139; sub-regions 187–9, 191, 193, 195, 198–9, 201, 203, 205–8
The World Bank and Aid Effectiveness 95
World Bank Group 68, 94, 108, 110, 188, 190
World Bank Independent Inspection Panel (WBIP) 112–13, 201
World Conference on Women 87
World Development Report 42, 171
world polity 7
World War II 199

Yang, L.T. 28

Zaire 82
Zappile, T. 17, 91, 145, 187–211, 215, 218, 221